HOUSES, HISTORY & HUMO
Agent In France)

By L. Phil

Synopsi

An amusing real life account of the journey of a British Estate Agent in France, showing the true side of what actually happens to sellers and buyers alike, and the hurdles along the way. Filled with hope, humour, and a little bit of history, this is mostly FUN!

Not always polite, sometimes quite the opposite, it does however redeem itself with the Writer's integration as the only 'anglais' amongst a team of eleven, managing to rise above the very different humour of les français!

It covers the beauty of **Poitou Charentes**, the houses instructed to sell, and the colourful history behind closed doors. The Reader travels through bravery and sadness, when not laughing in other chapters. To homes where Refugees are hidden from Germans; to local young women cavorting with the enemy; to Collaborateurs paid with solid marble and mahogany. The book is dotted with snippets of French (and British) history, but perhaps the most evocative story is that of the former Maquis speaking of what's really down the well ....

From the bare bones of meals so disgusting it's hard not to gag, to the mouth watering enjoyment of haute cuisine, this account is a realtor's satirical romp through facts and frustrations.

From scepticism to eventual arrival, appreciation and acceptance, it's a tough road taken!

Chapters

1	From Taunton to Poitou
2	The Old Smithy
3	Italian Cat Guards Cash
4	Job Offer In Cognac
5	Feral Cats & Hunting Dogs
6	"You Are Not Mother Theresa"
7	Legal In Saintes, Dutchman In Segonzac
8	Oradour
9	Sales Conference Limoges
10	Enemy Down The Well
11	WW2 Refugees In Beauvais
12	Collaborateur In Matha, Owls & Toads
13	Enemy Liaison In Varaize
14	Offally Awful Lunch, Divine Chocolate Shop
15	Cahors, The Lot, Rocamadour
16	Rouillac Market, Kennels & Fleas
17	Team Tuesdays & Foul Formules
18	Americans In Weobley
19	French Humour, Missing Blighty
20	Ships, Slaves & 'Shit'
21	Yoga & Apple Eating Rat
22	Cultural Differences
23	Snakes To 'Civilisation'
24	Wild Boar Hunt In Chizé Forest
25	Stalactites & Stalagmites
26	Slave Or Leave
27	Job Move To Saint Jean d'Angely
28	Initiation Day In Saintes
29	Catherine de Medici & La Belle Hélène

30	The Tin Man
31	The Latin Mass
32	Food, Fashion & Fame
33	Tea In Bohemian's Barn
34	Army & Quiz In Beauvais
35	Stilettos In Mill At Brie
36	The Rise Of British Cafés
37	Christmas In Expatria
38	Old Folks' Homes & Fosses
39	Irish Invasion, Trip To Brittany
40	Twelth Century Monks In Anville
41	Angelica In Marais Poitevin
42	Brits Do Moonlit Flit
43	Expat Moans & Groans
44	Motor Bikes & George Clooney
45	Dell Boy & Barbezieux
46	Cultural Differences Encore
47	Lingo, Ladders & Lamplight
48	Biryani, Books & Baked Beans
49	Grabbed In A Kiss
50	Matha, Israel & Palestine
51	Time Wasting Stealth In Gibourne
52	Au'revoir et à bientôt

With thanks to David Gilman for cover photography and to Marion Chorley for her Pilgrims at Pons, this book is dedicated to my daughter Lizzie.

1 From Taunton to Poitou

I've been told to write a book

And now I have a reason! The trouble is, where to start?

It's 2002, sometime around Easter at Taunton Race Course. I've recently lost two sales. I'm an estate agent in Hereford, and deal with holiday lettings and the occasional sale in Tuscany. I send two singles, they never meet, but they both let me down. I send them to my 'oppo' in the hills of Lunigiana. One stays three weeks. She takes her boyfriend with her, actually her one time lover, now back with his wife. They stay in an agri-turismo and savour the tastes of caprese, penne arrabbiata, garlic and olive oil, and the good old pick-me-up (that's what it means) tiramisu. It doesn't work. She can't afford to buy anything, and he doesn't offer! She rings me from her converted chapel in the wilds of Herefordshire: "Sorry, can't afford Italy, but I'm buying a house in .... (She says the words very quickly, too quickly for me to understand what she's talking about) ... Poitou Charentes."

It's a tough one when French is from the distant past of school desks on Merseyside, the Wirral to be precise, a peninsula bordered by the Rivers Dee and Mersey, taken away from Cheshire and given to Merseyside. The natives protested and managed to win it back!

The second one rings from his mansion in the Cotswolds, where he's an antique dealer not far down the road from 'The Royals.' He's also had a great time with my 'oppo' in la bell'Italia, and he has money, lots of it. The commission is already counted, half of it spent: "Sorry, I'm not buying in Italy but ... I wait for him to stutter out the blasted 'Poitou Charentes' but he doesn't. Oh no, not the beautiful but low priced, Brit enticing hillbilly land of sunflowers and vineyards, lovely though they be ... in Aquitaine," its decidedly more upmarket neighbour. Pau, Bordeaux, Medoc, Saint Emilion. Dream on!

I lose two sales, and the home market's not brilliant. I want to know where my competition lies, not in Hereford (my main bread and butter) but with my side line in Italy. The advert for Taunton looms forever large in 'Living France.' I HAVE to be at the Exhibition and Taunton's a quick nip over the River Severn.

I've not been to a Race Course since Aintree, aged about eight and not for the Grand National, thank goodness. I don't approve of steeple chasing! Masses of hopeful agents pout their Francophile jargon to the vast numbers of escapist dreamers. But I become one of them, armed with carrier bags full of literature. I'm no longer just identifying the competition, but I'm part of it.

My spouse of thirty two volatile years, we dated eleven weeks before the nuptials, is getting hungry. He likes his food, and is a great chef. Hamburger stands and chip stalls around the turf where horses tread do not appeal to him. I've dragged him along for the ride, so now it's his turn. We head into Taunton. We've not been here before and haven't a clue where to eat. We don't even see any restaurants. There must be some. But, ah, there's a sign: 'The Castle,' with a teeny inkling that it may also be an eatery of great temptation. It is! We drive up, in our weekend tattiness, pin stripe for him and tailored suit for me, ok sometimes just a skirt and blazer, but always with a crisply ironed shirt, in our weekday lives. This is embarrassing. It's exceedingly posh, and it's Sunday. Families out of Church and into 'The Castle.' But everyone is very polite, very welcoming. We relax. He always melts when good food and wine's on offer, years of experience in Hong Kong, Italy, Switzerland, Denmark, Morocco ... he's already worked in 16 countries. Me? Just Beirut and Hong Kong, oh and I'm forgetting Wales, and Como. How could I? Does the Isle of Man count, too?

The restaurant is beautifully calm and welcoming, no carrier bag carrying crowds here (I've left mine in the car) and we're led to a spacious table, elegantly dressed, unlike us, and with sinking into comfortable chairs, needed after umpteen gallops around the Race Course. The food is excellent, the wine delicious, not that we have very much as there's the drive back ahead of us. With a perfect ambience to carry us away to even more of 'the good life,' we decide that our next great meal will be in that gourmet paradise over the Channel (we have a lot to learn!)

Back in Hereford, I arrange ferry passages to France, and check out maps to take us down to that region fated to haunt me, Poitou Charentes, never having heard of it before my last two clients let me down. They have done me a favour, I decide, not realising what is to come next.

The Easter holidays are upon us, I'm granted an extended leave of absence by the Big Boss, and Megan, our Colliedor (that's a Collie crossed with a Labrador) and Gemima, our

Italian feral cat (she followed me home from work one day in Como) are in their respective doggeries and catteries. I've even booked a gîte, and we've never had the joy of one of those before, either!

We set off for Portsmouth, to join even more heaving masses of mankind than we were mingling with at the Race Course, as we board the ferry. There are very few French registered cars, lots of Spanish lorry drivers, and a few coaches of school children, no doubt on tours of the Normandy Beaches of the Second World War. We wonder if we should have booked a hotel in Caen, explored the Cemeteries and Beaches ourselves, spent a day at the Bayeux Tapestry, but oh no, off we have to go for, yes, that blastedly named Poitou Charentes. It is, after all, where my competition lies so I have to fulfil the object of the exercise.

It's pretty much a straight road from Caen to Tours, a main road, not a motorway but a main road, so we reckon we can find a coffee stop after an hour or so, but this is France, not known for its pitstops! We get all the way down to Falaise before we strike lucky, but do we? Of course not, it's Monday! Trying to find anything at all open on Mondays in France is like trying to find a lost hair clip in the Dune de Pilat. (That's a sand dune, the biggest in Europe, and it's way down on the Atlantic Coast, a couple of hours west of Bordeaux. We plan to visit it one day.) The villages get sparser and sparser, and those we see get drabber and drabber. We daren't acknowledge this to each other. Eventually, we find an open Bar and the lady very kindly serves us our first ever coffee together in France. The room is straight out of the 1950s, and the toilet facilities out of the 1850s. Thomas Crapper has yet to visit parts of this Gallic Nation, but they mostly don't give a ....!

Back into the car, by this time it's almost mid-day and we have a lot of empty road ahead of us. Most of the traffic has left us behind not far from Caen, so this is a pleasant experience after the M25, even the A49! We skirt Alençon, which is a pity as I always like to detour into towns and cities, but the Driver is an A to B man. This also applies to Le Mans, a mediaeval masterpiece of a city, as well as home to ear splitting motor racing. Not to worry, I've been to Monza so I guess I shouldn't be greedy. Ah, but hunger strikes (him, not me, I just get stiff legs) so we slow down as we approach a little town just into the Loire Valley. We don't, however, slow down enough for me to read the signpost telling us which little town, and it's Monday so I can't ask anybody.

The streets are deserted, but there really is a restaurant with an 'ouvert' (that means 'open') sign outside. In we go, fearlessly brave enough to tread where many Anglo-Saxons would never dare, and that's just the place, never mind the food. He who is hungry says he'll have 'le formule' (set menu) but his courage turns almost to culinary panic when he's presented with une langue de boeuf (cow's tongue, and not like his mother used to serve up, out of a tin, in the 1950s). He nearly pukes and I want to gag as soon as I smell it. I'm lucky, I've ordered an omelette, the reliable stand-by for non offal eaters in France. Spouse of thirty two volatile years leaves his blood curdling strip of leather on the plate and says "let's crack on, we've got a lot of miles to cover yet, Chuck" (since when was I a hen, and did I ever visit Australia? No, never!)

We can't find the car. We've left it pretty darned near the restaurant of the leathery tongue and sloppy omelette, and the unhygienic 'loo' of course, but we absolutely cannot find it. Well, it's navy-black, pretty run of the mill in colour, but it's a VW (Passat, to be precise) and this is France, so nationalistic that if it's not a Citroên, a Renault, or a Peugeot, forget it, you'll wait months for spare parts. So then, ours must be the only German car in the Loire, apart from wrecks in barns and garages, left by their fleeing owners in 1944. I don't mind, we need a walk, and it's the first French country town I've ever visited, be it only of the one horse variety. We trundle and strutt the pavements and non pavements (they don't seem to do those in France very much, a bit like the States of America I've visited) and eventually, lo and behold, it comes into vision. Another row averted, and we're only on day one!

The Loire is all around us, but we can't see it. What I do home in on, too closely to ever be able to forget it as we pass by on one of the tree lined avenues Napoleon marched his men along, is a woman with a motionless calf in front of her on a wooden table. It's black and white, and I prefer not to think of its fate, try and persuade myself that it's having an after lunch kip, that it somehow managed to get itself up on the table, perhaps to sunbathe, rather than about to be prepared for the next day's 'formule' in the little town we've just left, where time stands still, but there is a café open on Mondays.

We're impressed with Napoleon's trees. He had them planted along the main highways his troops would march, to give them shelter. Very sensible fellow! He must also have bought 'quality' for so many of them to survive to this day. They are everywhere, and the drive is glorious. I'm beginning to appreciate why so many harassed Brits escape to France, shunning memories of M4 traffic jams, police sirens, and service stations filled with screaming children and stressed out parents. Here, is total silence as we drive along. Deserted landscapes have that effect, almost worth the leathery tongue and sloppy omelette as opposed to what? Greasy chips and soggy white bread! At least the chopped baguette in a basket was appetising, in the little town we know not what is called!

South of Tours we enter, oh yes, we're arriving, we enter Poitou Charentes. The scenery doesn't change, not yet, but it will. The further south we head the fields will be ablaze with golden sunflowers sprouting up amidst a wide landscape stretching as far as the eyes can see, a land of far horizons, with fields of newly seeded maize replacing the winter wheat. Suddenly, though, we find ourselves with more trees, as we drive alongside the outer stretches of the Forests of La Guerche and La Groie. We're glad we've come off the main highway and on to the N10. Our elation soon fades as we approach Poitiers and we forget that we are in Rural France. It's horrid! Industrial and commercial estates glare at us with misplaced pride in their ugliness. Traffic builds up to an aggressive crescendo, and we still have a couple of hours left before reaching our destination. Poitiers is a place I shan't be in a rush to see, even though it does have an excellent university, TGV station, and an airport used by Ryanair. How could I forget? It's also home to Futuroscope (google it!)

We dither no longer, and speed as fast as we are legally allowed to. We could be on any road, in any country, now. At least we've left behind the billboards of Poitiers' periphery. Not tempted to stop at Vivonne, nor at Couhé, although we are both gagging for a cup of tea, we continue. After all, it's still Monday and afternoon tea cafés will be surely closed. Afternoon tea cafés! We are novices in France, and only just beginning to climb one of our biggest learning curves.

I see the sign for Ruffec and want to stop. I want to stop right now! Oh no, on we go, another day perhaps to explore the town where the two survivors from the 'Cockleshell Heroes' rested before the Résistance got them to safety via the Pyrenées and Spain. It took a full year for them to eventually arrive in England. Theirs was one of the most daring actions of the Second World War, officially named 'Operation Frankton,' and immortalised in the film starring Trevor Howard. 12 Royal Marine Commandos canoed down the Gironde Estuary to launch an attack on the German Fleet, only two canoes actually reaching their destination in Bordeaux. Of those four, only two managed to escape with their lives, Major 'Blondie' Hasler and Corporal Bill Sparks. They miraculously got themselves to Ruffec, more than a hundred miles inland, in the Charente. (Yes, in Poitou Charentes!) I make a mental note to come back for a meal in what was their interim hiding place. Called the Café de France back in 1942 when the Raid took place, it is now the Hôtel de La Toque Blanche. My mind sidetracks to that wonderful television series, 'Allo, 'Allo' with greatest respect, as well as picturing René flirting with young Michèle! The bravery of every one of the original twelve will long continue to be remembered, not just that of the two who survived to be lucky enough to find the safety and selfless hospitality of La Résistance.

We're less than half an hour from the gîte we've rented, and are not prepared for the shock of that 'iffy' type holiday home much loved and sought after by countless Brits. Used to comfort (Spouse has been spoilt by too many business trips, and I never did like camping) we arrive in the little Charentaise village of Charmé. Upon first sight it does indeed look charming, but where is the gîte? We follow the owners' directions and the car just about fits up the little chemin (lane, more like an alleyway) passing hissing geese, roaming hens, and inquisitive 'natives.' We arrive at a pair of substantial metal gates, suitably ornate in their time, and drive round to the main house, thinking how nice it all is. It is. It is delightful! The owners are as charmant as we expect them to be. I found them in The Sunday Times, so one expects no less. Of course not!

Ah, but here lies the rub! The gîte is through a gate in the wall and is probably an old cow shed, perhaps a converted stable block. It's big, prettily and substantially furnished, and looks out over a courtyard with washing lines and, la pièce de résistance, a little corner splash pool. It gets hot in Poitou Charentes, but it's only April so we'll not be using it. Not that it has any water in it yet. The living room is énorme and one wall still has the old cow, or horse, feeding troughs, all very rustic and all very chic, if you like that sort of thing. It's very different from where we live in the City of Hereford, opposite the Cathedral, in a restored Edwardian town house, splendidly refurbished with all singing and dancing 'mod cons.' I don't do 'shabby chic,' with its soggy sofas and falling to pieces old dressers! I imagine the gîte being loved by folk from Notting Hill, and other parts of London many escape from, swapping hectic lives for the serenity of Chiantishire, Dordogneshire, and Poitou Charentes!

We seem to be expected to be hosting a dinner party, it's obviously what the Notting Hill crowd do, given the size of the table and the number of chairs, but it's not on our agenda. We're a bit short of people to invite. The kitchen forms just a little area at the end of the old cow shed, or horse stables, and is very typically française rustique, with its low level sink (we are both tall, 6'3" and 5'7" at the last count, no doubt about to start shrinking, especially he who is about to approach his seventh decade) and height challenging shelving. This is all hidden behind jolly, cotton gingham curtains, far cheaper to install than doors and oh how the anglais adore them, except this one! There's very little work surface and much of it is trendily cluttered with the obligatory paraphernalia tirelessly searched for at the Sunday brocantes (think car boot sales) which the whole of France is famous for. There's at least one a week throughout July and August, if you're desparately short of tatt!

Then we rather nervously check out upstairs. A treat awaits us. Both double bedrooms have rickety old iron framed beds the likes of which René's mother-in-law lives and communicates from with her ear trumpet in 'Allo, 'Allo.' The mattresses slope into the middle with great abandon, no doubt jumped on and humped in by generations of rural folk for whom 'bed' was the only thing worth staying up for. I'm not even sure that television has reached the darkest depths of Poitou Charentes yet. Broadband certainly hasn't, and mobile 'phones, forget it. To make calls we'll have to walk down to the village 'phone box. At least there is one, so we must count our blessings.

Used to decent sized beds at home, and wondering how on earth two grown people are supposed to be restricted to a mere 2'3" of bed per person, which a standard double declares to provide sufficient space, we take a bedroom each.

It doesn't last! The bedroom I choose is so darned damp that I can stand it no longer so, not wanting to end up in a sanatorium, move in with he who is not only height challenged, but width challenged into the bargain, and would win the hardest of snoring competitions. It's a bad mistake for both of us, and with: "Right mess you've got us into this time Ollie," I agree that a week will be too long. We survive two more nights, helped by a small bottle of rather superb cognac we find at the little patisserie in the village, nectar with every sip. We have done precisely no house hunting, no competition hunting at all.

Charmé may be charmant, but it's not for us, too far inland and too backward culturally to even consider. I guess that we're in for a shock in much of Rural France, only just beginning to realise why it is so darned cheap to buy property amongst its villages where time has stood still, and won't learn to walk again for many a decade yet. But why am I thinking this way? This is a business exercise, so why am I getting psyched up about buying property? We're not here to do that, not at all! Besides which, we can't even find an estate agency in Ruffec, although there must surely be some. It's 2002 and they do exist, although the notaires (property conveyancing solicitors amongst other things) seem to do a lot of the selling transactions, so perhaps that's why.

So with no property search afoot, I study the map and find a town about the same distance west of Charmé as Ruffec is east. Aigre turns out to be absolutely delightful (as is Ruffec in many ways) and one of the first things we spot is the market square. Fortunately, there's no marché today so parking's facile (easy) and then what do we see, right there on one side of the market place, and what time is it? Oh yes, it's mid-day and there in all its splendour is a restaurant. Not expecting the earth, we find ourselves treated to a fair sample of it. It's good, it's welcoming, the food's great, and we breathe joint sighs of relief and launch into the menu, full of truly mouth watering dishes to order. We are not disappointed, especially when the dessert trolley is wheeled to our table, after a splendid selection of cheese. Oh how civilised it is all becoming. And surprise, surprise, we spot an estate agent's shop after our cure-all lunch.

"We're looking to spend around 150 000 euros (a random figure created on the spot). What have you got?" We're shown a little terraced house in the town itself, ideal for anyone seriously looking, and then, and then, a stunningly beautiful converted old water mill. "It's a bit over budget (it's 250 000 euros). Do you think they'll take an offer?" 'Other Half's' shooting daggers in my direction, so I look the other way, at the glorious millstream and enticing woodland, at the stylish layout of the interior, the best of old and modern combined. I'm love struck, with a water mill in the depths of Poitou Charentes. At last, I'm appreciating why I've lost two potential sales in Italy to France.

"But we're not buying, remember! Let's get the hell out of here," he mutters back in the Immobilier's (estate agent's) office in Aigre.

I could live here, I really and truly could, but our life is back in Hereford. I have a job; he has a business; we are settled! The nest has emptied, but the County of Herefordshire is still 'home' and also one of the loveliest in the United Kingdom, lovelier than much of France, much of Italy even. The car is already packed. We've told the lovely people who own the gîte that we're heading west for the coast and pay them the full week's rental anyway, so we leave with handshakes rather than hisses. All is well, all is calm, for now!

A taste of what's to come ...

2 The Old Smithy

I've decided that St Jean d'Angély has a nice ring to it, not knowing it's home to a prestigious school of music, nor that the head of Saint John the Baptist was reputedly left there and survived in place until the Huguenots torched the abbey and chucked it, irreverently, on the fire. However, I don't know which town notes to believe, as Amiens, up in the Somme Région of Picardie, also claims to have part of his head. I find both versions particulary 'yuch.' But then I was convent educated, forced to listen to the dramatic accounts of martyrs being systematically tortured whilst trying to eat an already revolting lunch in the refectory. The nuns took it in turns to brainwash us into terrified subservience to a deity few of us would ever fully accept, and never fully understand.

But they did us proud in 1963. We got a television! Why? It was the year of Pope John XXIII's death and Paul VI's succession to the Papacy, shortly after his predecessor started the Second Vatican Council. Theories persist to this day regarding Pope John's death. Some say he was murdered, but we've heard that before throughout history. Media hype had arrived at Upton Hall Convent, and with it eventually came curriculum modernisation and language laboratories (I could have done with one of those whilst I was there), and even, shock horror, well equipped science and computer labs. I wonder if the rose garden survived, my escape pod from the horror stories about the Blesseds, Edward Campion, Margaret Clitherow, John Bosco, John Kemble, John Houghton (lots of Johns). I shall never forget them. How could I, how could such prolific imagery escape a child's brain?

And here we are, approaching St Jean d'Angély. I've arranged a meeting with an estate agent in the town centre, a British lady working in France. We are on time, we're English (the French are rarely punctual) and have a few minutes to spare. The car park is full. It's a good sign. This town may be little, but it has life. What's more, it's delightful. I'm falling in love with it and swan into the Agent's office with enthusiasm and expectation, unlike 'Signficant Other' who's wondering what mess I'm getting him into this time. "Ah" says Receptionist, "Madame has other clients to see, you will have to wait." Madame's "other clients" walk into the agency after us, obviously looking more serious, if a bit scruffy, beach shorts and flabby white women's skin oozing out of cropped tops, tatooes on the men. I secretly think they'd do better in Spain! O.k. then, she's obviously done her homework and decided she's more likely to get a sale from them than she is from us, but how darned rude, and how unprofessional not to warn us in advance!

I stand my ground, and insist they find us another agent tout de suite, making a mental note NOT to do business with Madame, not now, nor at any time in the future. I don't, and she loses a sale. Hah! WE are told the only one they might have available works in Matha, a little town about twenty minutes' drive away. SHE, the receptionist, is told that, no, we won't drive there ourselves. We have an appointment and one way or another, it will be honoured. Not able to make such a difficult decision herself, she calls the Owner of the Agence to the scene, not the most friendly of men I've come across, and I certainly wouldn't fear competition from him if he worked in Hereford.

We agree to return to the Agence in half an hour, giving their Man from Matha ample time to get himself to St Jean d'Angély. Meanwhile, we explore the little streets and sip iced tea under a sun shade in one of the delightful, tree lined, squares. It's a joy after the desolate towns and villages of the inner Charente. We are now just over the Border into Charente Maritime, still almost an hour's drive from the coast but it feels closer, the air is purer, the sky lighter, all heralding a world of difference after the last few days incarcerated in the back of beyonds. A new life is upon us, in more ways than one!

After ordering even more iced tea (it's a hot day and the weather seems better the further west we've come) and lots of 'oohs' and 'ahhs' at the pleasantness of St Jean d'Angély, we head back down to the next little square to meet our Man from Matha. Eric is charming, tall, slim, elegantly dressed, beautifully spoken, everything the men in our profession do well when they 'do' it at all. (Not all do, as we all know!) After handshakes and "venez avec moi" (come with me) we decline the offer (shucks) to share his car, and follow behind him to the first property he shows us, in a deadly little hamlet somewhere near Varaize, nearer to St Jean than it is to Matha, and probably one of the houses Madame introduced to the market. Is there a conspiracy going on between them? I hope not! We are saved from any potential awkwardness of the situation when a motor bike screams past, firing on all deafening cylinders. Motor bikes are complete anathema to Spouse, so it's a verbally insistent 'non merci' and on we go. But why are we even worrying about motor bikes and conspiracies? It's not as if we're going to buy anything!

Our Man from Matha leads us through country lanes barely wide enough for tractors, and we follow one at snail's pace for some distance. It gives us time to study the scenery, mile upon mile of open fields turning yellow with deliberately planted rapeseed, and red with poppies which have planted themselves. Every so often we pass a little chapel in the middle of nowhere, a statue to Mary, the mother of Jesus, with an offering of artificial flowers at her feet, a grand old stone house, a humble smallholding within a cluster of similarly crumbling down cottages, and then more open spaces and wide horizons of agricultural splendour until we reach the small, but thriving, market town of Matha. We seem to be heading inland again, which was not our intention, but signs indicate that we are not far from the larger town of Cognac, and Matha itself is within the classified area of its grape production.

We follow Eric into his office. His charm has already won us over and we find ourselves asking if he has any other properties he thinks may be of interest to us. (We're not buying, you understand!) Back into the cars, back into the country lanes, back towards St Jean d'Angély, carefully avoiding the main road linking the two towns, lest we're put off by the traffic. In this part of France, I don't think so! The countryside is glorious, and we pass through vineyards both sides of the narrow little road and down a steep slope into the village of Esset, part of the Commune of La Brousse. We've yet to find out that une brousse in French is a bush, a stick, a thick stick; it's a language where one word covers many options. There are lots of villages and hamlets in France called La Brousse and most of them are, indeed, in 'the sticks.'

It's still mid week, we've left the gîte an hour or so east away, and have yet to book into the hôtel we're eventually heading for before evening meal time, but it'll be daylight for another couple of hours. We have our own wheels, we don't want to disappoint our lovely young estate agent, so we follow him through the wide opening wooden gates and into an enormous garden.

Standing before us is the Old Village Smithy. It's as wide as the whole of our terrace of four houses in Hereford put together. Two sets of double opening doors give access to magnificently undulating views across the vineyards we've just left behind, and immediately opposite the roadside elevation is a field planted with sunflowers, hundreds of thousands of them. From early summer to late autumn the horizon will yield an artist's paradise of colossal yellow sunflower heads giving way to light green, and deep purple, grapes. The property comes with over half an acre of grass, two enormous stone built barns, and one small one, all of them in excellent condition. The parking space alone would be let out for commercial purposes in Hereford. It even has its own swimming pool, taking up more space than our paved yard back home. The whole of the property is gloriously secluded from its neighbours by a 6' high stone wall, all of it in perfect condition. I stand on the inner dwarf stone wall dividing the near garden from its field, complete with cherry and fig trees, and declare that we just have to buy it, before we've even gone inside! Whatever we find indoors, we'll accept and take the consequences. An on the spot decision!

We make an appointment to revisit in two days' time and head back to St Jean d'Angély, to the hôtel and its restaurant. It's time to have our second mega property related meal, and it's promising to be every bit as exciting as the first, that day in Taunton when we had not a clue how different our lives were destined to become!

I remind myself that as soon as we get back to Hereford, I must cancel the flights we've booked to Pisa the following month. We have an appointment to view a property near Lucca, a lakeside villa, in Italia. It's always been our intention to move back to the Italy we loved, lived and worked in back in the mid 'nineties. The big Six 'O' is happening to Spouse this year, and the time is right to start looking for our retirement pad in Tuscany, so just what, precisely, are we playing at?

That's a question several of my students ask me. I've been teaching Italian at Herefordshire College of Technology for the last 7 years. My night job! And for the last year, a full Thursday morning every week has been added in to my ever increasing workload. The Big Boss is happy to let me escape from my normal house selling duties, hoping for another business avenue to open, another load of properties to bring into the market place. It isn't! People aren't selling up in their droves to buy in Italy, not just yet, the occasional one, that's all. Those who buy in Italy usually have more money at their disposal, keeping their homes in England. The mass exodus at the beginning of our twenty first century comprises mostly people selling up lock, stock and barrel, just like we are about to do, aka the ones who buy in France and Spain. Italy is for the rich and the brave! But all contacts, all networking, are good in sales and marketing and that's precisely what estate agency is all about in the final analysis. That and being an 'agony aunt,' especially on Friday afternoons when conveyancing solicitors have a tendency to leave well trained secretaries to field our 'phone calls. Completions fail to meet deadlines, and clients collapse into tears as I face them across my desk, tissues at the ready! Of course, it's always us estate agents who get the blame, we who do the bulk of the work. Many a removal van waits idly on the kerbside, unloading at dusk instead of dawn. Why? Because the solicitor hasn't given permission for us to release the keys before disappearing for a long pub lunch.

One of my students is totally gobsmacked when I break the news to the class that I'll not be returning in September.

"But why FRANCE?"

"Why not, what's wrong with France?"

She has a holiday home in Tuscany, as do several of my students. They are not Francophiles, and make no bones about saying so. She's not alone. Many of them look down on les français, with their reputation for 48 hour deodorants, and costly restaurants with filthy 'loos' and no wash hand basins. They mock the salads topped with throat innards, and bread that goes stale by lunch time.

"The FRENCH!"

3 Italian Cat Guards Cash

"This will suit me just fine," says our buyer, a lady already turned 80. I don't for one minute believe it'll run to completion, no-one of that age, living on her own, wants a 5 bedroomed Edwardian terraced house. But the sale goes through, she's delighted, and we panic. We host a 'farewell party' amongst the vast piles of packing boxes. Gemima is in pussy cat heaven with her ever growing climbing frame, just like the one she had when we moved from Lake Como down to Tuscany, not realising it'll soon all be put in a removal van, and she in her travelling cage. Megan spends more and more time in the little courtyard garden I've turned into a floral haven. The business moves premises. It's been in the top two rooms of our family home since the nest emptied, and has now relocated to Whitecross Road, just round the corner from Bulmer's Cider Museum. It's promised to deliver financial returns to us for the next few years, sadly only to be short lived, but these things happen!

It's not the only thing to go pear shaped, there's an immediate one. The stress is too much for he who doesn't like moving at the best of times. We've moved many times, but it's always been me who's done every darned thing. This time he's around to be part of it, to see the cupboards emptied and the boxes filled. He's always managed to avoid being present for relocations so far. My generation of corporate wives do such things solo, uncomplainingly and efficiently. The husbands (that's what my age group have usually had; 'partners' used to be business equals) have gone on in advance, oh how convenient.

I seek refuge on a friend's farm for a few days, it's necessary, believe me! I nearly, very nearly, don't move to France, but I do! The deal is signed, we are committed to buying the country pile in the wilds of La Brousse, and what's one more 'tiff' in 32 years! A feather blowing in the wind. If it's not, it's a hole forever sinking further into the ground.

The day comes! Neighbours arrive to say 'goodbye' and we sit and have coffee together amongst the garden furniture 80 year old lady has asked us to leave for her. It all looks very normal, very lovely, as if we're going nowhere. But the removal men are busy loading those of our cherished chattels not already donated to charity shops and church bazaars, youth groups, local children, antique centres, anywhere that'll take our carelessly collected clutter.

Gemima legs it into next door's garden shed. It's impossible to retrieve her. It's a haven of security, full of sharp tools, work benches, shelving roof high, a cat's paradise. She glares at me from behind an old bed frame, her eyes telling me she's not part of our plan, glowering at me, hissing when I try and reach her. This is fun! I should have put her in the travelling cage hours ago, but wanted to minimise the amount of time she'd spend in it. The journey ahead is a long one. I wait, and wait, and wait. She eventually leaves the shed, neighbour and I try and catch her, and fail! Spouse is totally unworried, utterly detached from the job in hand, wondering if he'll get his Telegraph crossword in France. The removal van is now heading southerly for La Brousse and we have a hotel booked in Poole, and a boat to catch the next morning, to Cherbourg.

She dashes through the house, all doors open, and hopefully not on to the ledge the other side of the riverbank's iron railings. She's done that before, knowing fully well we can't reach her at that point. I breathe a sigh of relief as I see her jump over the into the front garden, out of the gate little walls between the other houses in our Terrace. It turns into a game of 'you can't catch me,' but I finally, after falling over dramatically en route as I hurdle the barriers, and with arms scratched to blazes, grab her. I look, and feel, a wreck. She's fine!

We have an emotional moment or two saying au'revoir (see you again, to the next time, not 'goodbye') to our elderly neighbour the other side of the house which is now officially no longer ours, and whose shed would have been much easier to catch Gemima in. Sadly, we don't see Doug again, not properly, just from a distance when I return a couple of years later, see him asleep in his chair through the window, and decide not to wake him. I should have done!

Onwards and downwards (not upwards; we're heading south, and that's down) direction the English Channel, la Manche as we'll soon be calling it. Gemima miaows incessantly until she finally gives up and goes to sleep. Megan, calm and patiently sitting beside her, lets out a sigh of relief and drifts into doggy dreamland. We've told her she's to have un jardin énorme (an enormous garden) and lots of neighbouring hens and ducks to chase, of trips to sandy beaches, and her very own paddling pool. It gets hot in Poitou Charentes!

As it happens, we make good progress through Ledbury, Herefordshire's last market town travelling east, beautifully adorned with the splendid architecture of numerous black and white buildings. The County is famous for its other timbered towns and villages, Eardisley, Eardisland, Pembridge, and Leominster, all of them superb reminders of a once glorious past (for some!) It is one of the most beautiful areas in the whole of the British Isles, and we are leaving it all for Rural France, not really knowing what we are going to find, how much adjustment we'll need to do, even if we'll like it there, or not.

The winding country lanes of Gloucestershire meet us next, and the houses change from timber to stone, mellow, almost yellow, Cotswold stone. We skirt Cirencester, knowing it well and loving it every time we visit, especially remembering lunch one day in its ancient hotel right in the middle of town, 'The Fleece,' with my American Aunt Sheila. Raised in the Liverpool suburb of Crosby (the Seat Dame Shirley Williams took for the Liberals from the long ruling Tories), and leaving on a troop ship bound for New York City back in 1944, aged 19, still a slip of a girl and one of the last of the G.I. Brides, I totally understood why Cirencester so impressed her. I guess they don't have hotels dating back to the 17th century Stateside!

And France? Well, bien sûr (of course) they have their chateaux, but one poses the question: why, then, has Raymond Blanc moved his culinary expertise to le Manoir de Quatre Saisons, in neighbouring Oxfordshire? I doubt that we shall ever find out. The days of fine wining and dining are over for us. The new budget will be geared to buying plasterboard, a staircase to allow us to change the hayloft into bedrooms, gravel to extend the car parking, varnish for the tired looking shutters, kitchen units to replace the revoltingly dark and dismal old country French ones, demolition tools, roof rafters, and no doubt stacks of unseen purchases we'll have to make for our ancient stone pile in La Brousse. And we are actually buying an old stone pile in relatively newly modernised condition, but to French standards, and they are exceedingly different. We have a lot to learn, and the first will be how to tackle a bath which is new but has never been plumbed in. C'est très français. At least there's an inside 'loo,' not something to be taken for granted in the little hamlet of Esset where I'm told 7 out of a total of about 50 homes still have no indoor sanitation, save for a cold tap in the kitchen, a sink if they're lucky. That's quite a high percentage.

My thoughts turn back to the English countryside we're driving away from, and we pass through the twisting lanes of Wiltshire at its best, down the hill which is Marlborough's main street, reminiscing of staying there with my parents and one time fiancé (we cancelled the wedding two weeks before it was scheduled to happen) before I flew off to a new job in Beirut, just months after Yom Kippur. The three of them must have been seriously worried as the 'plane took off from R.A.F. Lyneham, at least my parents would have been, but all I felt was sheer excitement. It was my first ever flight, and the first memory of anything is usually the strongest.

Salisbury looms on the horizon, its spire splendid as ever from the ring road. We don't go into the city, we know it reasonably well already. It's lovely, but dog and cat are peaceful and we still have an hour or so ahead of us before we reach Poole. What a disappointment! The commercial estates are hideously ugly, there are road blocks everywhere, and when we finally reach the hotel it's an uninteresting looking collection of houses knocked into one building. The people are welcoming, the room is fine, and that's the main thing, enough space for Megan's bed and Gemima's travelling cage. We open the door and offer her the freedom of the room and the bathroom, but she stays in the security of her cage, now accepting of the situation and snug as a bug in a rug.

A good little Italian cat, already moved from Como to Tuscany to Hereford, she eventually emerges to use her litter tray (travelling with cats is almost as cumbersome as travelling with babies) and we humans take it in turns to catsit, not leaving her alone in the room for one minute, lest a member of staff inadvertently lets her out. We've already eaten, in a yacht club of all places, somewhere on the coast, not long after driving through a tatty housing estate. Not bad food, pleasant people (sailors usually are, and we've met plenty in our time) and perfect for walking Megan. I take her out for an evening stroll before a desperately needed night's sleep, along Poole's horrendously busy roads, not in the least bit attractive. I see a grotty looking shopping mall in the distance, run down houses everywhere, rubbish in the streets. Where's 'Sandbanks' then? Where's the pretty harbour we've read about? Poole? Forget it! Onwards to France we go, Cherbourg must surely be more inviting.

Up at the crack of dawn, breakfast on board the ferry, dog and cat safely guarding the car, hopefully not too frightened in the process. They are fine when we get ready to disembark, absolutely non plussed, both of them, but lots of tail wagging and miaowing. Aren't we rotten!

The drive down to St Jean d'Angely comes with mega stress. It's not every day we carry so much cash and certainly not in a black brief case. We may have lived in

29

Italy, but we are not Mafiosi. Selling in Hereford and buying in Esset have not coordinated as easily as we'd've liked. There's to be gap of three days between both completions, and the bank in Hereford refuses to make life easy for us. Since when did bankers do that? They take our money, use it and lose it as they wish, and play God into the bargain. The only option they leave us with, is to pay for the house in France in euro notes. "Bank transfers take time, Sir." The lawyers aren't any more helpful, either, but to give them their due, it's not their problem. The firm we've used have been very good, very kind in more ways than they've needed to be, carefully chosen by me from the many most provincial towns, even cities, seem to unnecessarily have. They are not from the 'Friday afternoon in the pub' brigade, although many of their competitors are. Husband is anything but happy, in fact he's a nervous wreck. We can't stop for lunch, oh no, it might get 'nicked.' To be fair, it was a close run thing in the hotel when we paid the bill. It burst open, to reveal wads and wads of deliciously tempting notes. Good job there was no-one else up early!

We stop at our first motorway service station the French side of the Channel and husband opens the boot. Bad mistake! Huge mistake! The brief case is there for all to see, and he's convinced people (what people) will know what's inside. So 'muggins' (that's me) sprints into the self service area, buys some pathetic looking sandwiches and a couple of bottles of water, chocolate bars, and mints for the onward journey. I suggest he puts the brief case underneath Gemima. Nobody would take on our little Italian feral cat! Not even get close, not even incarcerated in her travelling cage as she is. And Megan? Lovely, calm, Megan, until she's guarding her car. With the deep bark of the Labrador, and the speed and intelligence of the Collie, she's a great guard dog when needs be. But it's no more stops, just get to the Agency in Matha as quickly as we darned well can, and it's a good few hours away yet. France is a big country and Poitou Charentes is a long, long, way down. 6 or 7 hours from the Port.

The Old Smithy

4 Job Offer In Cognac

Our Man in Matha is ready to hand over the keys to us, even though we're not completing until Friday and it's now only Tuesday. This has its advantages, in the shape of our feral feline from Lago di Como, Gemima, spelt with a 'g' because the letter 'j' doesn't exist in the Italian language, except where it's borrowed; think Jessolo, although that's hardly Italiano, more Benidormo! She can move in to the Old Smithy before the rest of us, pas problemo. But first, there's a bank account to open and tout de suite (as soon as possible). Man in Matha escorts us to Caisse d'Epargne and introduces us to the hugely delighted to meet us manager. It's not every day he's handed a brief case full of euro notes, this is France not Italy. Even Megan is welcome in his office. I'm liking France already. Lots of handshakes (pawshakes may have been pushing it a bit too far) promises to stick with his bank through thick and thin, back to the Agence, take keys, back into the car and into the wilds of La Brousse.

But hang on a minute, where IS La Brousse? It's three months since we've set eyes on it and we'll never, ever, find it again, be it only 8 kilometres from Matha, direction St Jean d'Angely. That much we know, and there our knowledge and memory stop! If we take a wrong turning, we'll end up in Aulnay, or Cognac, Saintes or even La Rochelle. Matha is to be centre of our universe from this day forth. We've burnt all our bridges, and there's no turning back. We'd better eat humble pie and plead ignorance, and ask if we can play 'follow my leader!'

Man from Matha duly escorts us and we wonder where on earth have we committed ourselves to, what on earth are we buying on Friday, and where the blazes is it! The vineyards are all in grape and the sunflowers are a sea of bright yellow, all very lovely but they make it extremely difficult to see where Eric is leading us to. Nothing is familiar, and not many houses and hamlets are visible. The sunflowers are sky high, and the roads are mere tracks between the fields where they grow like this every summer. We had no idea just how tall they'd become, when we saw them back in April. Their beauty, though, is utterly outstanding. It's as if every single one of them is smiling, welcoming us to their domain. It's not only people who can direct emotions, but places and even plants. They dissolve any previous worries I may have had, fears I may have harboured, stupidity I may have accredited myself with. It's all coming good!

The oldest part of the house, a recently partitioned part of the old stables and now a rear corridor, forms almost a separate annexe complete with its own glass panelled door from the spacious and elegant hall. Few houses in France have halls, so we've struck lucky, except that we wouldn't be buying a house without one, even if push came to shove, which it didn't. It locks, alleluja! Off I trundle with travelling case in hand, Gemima miaowing with frustration and probably needing a pee by now. I deposit her kit on the amply wide windowsill, open the door to her cage, put a rug beside it so she can look out of the window and get used to her new neighbourhood (before the rest of us can), litter tray on the floor, make sure she has ample food and water, give her the run of the inner hall and the bathroom as well, and then scarper! Lock the door from the hall, pocket the key, she's safe, she'll be fine until morning, she WILL be fine!

Enfin (at last)! We're back at the Hôtel de la Paix, at the crossroads in the ancient town of St Jean d'Angely, the one which claims to have had the head of St John The Baptist before the nasty Huguenots threw it on a bonfire, but I prefer not to think of that. It's something pretty normal I'm looking forward to having put before me on a plate! I've negotiated the same room we had back in April, when we escaped from the perishing freezing and damp at night gîte in Charmé. There's plenty of room for Megan, and almost opposite the hotel is plenty of lawn for her to pee on before bedtime (it's o.k. I always carry little black bags for the purpose of anything else). She's happy, we're happy, well I am. Spouse is just hungry, a real foodie, nurtured by too many corporate meals on expenses and a sea faring father with sophisticated tastes. I have few! Why does French food come doused in so much sauce? To hide the naff offering underneath? Why do they eat so much offal? Because they can, they actually like the stuff, especially when fried in masses of garlic. Why don't they use side plates? Because they've not long had kitchens with sinks to wash them in. Why do they use the same cutlery for course upon course? See previous answer! Do I like French food? Ask me in a few years time!

We awake refreshed. It's a pleasant hotel to stay in, very clean, no carpets on the walls (often the French idea of wallpaper, and always dirty brown or pewky green) adequately sized rooms (many in French hotels are the size of broom cupboards) excellent staff, great location, private car park, well cared for flower beds, and even the food's acceptable, some of it actually rather good. Not a patch on The Castle in Taunton, though! But I must stop thinking like this. That was then, and this is now, and we're here to stay.

We get a call from Ledbury Removals to say they're delivering all our stuff on Thursday morning, but the house won't be ours until Friday! No worries, the Man from Matha says that's fine, and Gemima will be pleased to have us back a day early, not that she's counting them. She's happy on her windowsill, and we visit her daily, but it's not quite the same.

Of course the van can't find us, of course not, so off Spouse sets to guide them from the main road to the house. They'll be lucky. He'll be lucky. He hasn't even got a mobile 'phone on him, and every little road looks identical, narrow and lined with maize, sunflowers, or vines. A local villager recognises the foreign car, German, with English number plates, bought in Italy, now in France. Oh what fun awaits us legalising it! I have no idea how the conversation goes, but imagine it's something to do with a lot of arm waving and "merci beaucoups." Success, they arrive, one huge removal van following one VW Passat. I'm impressed! I'm even more impressed, gobsmacked actually, as the enormous vehicle glides easily through our wooden gates and parks right in front of the house, INSIDE our very own walled garden, well, what will be our very own garden tomorrow.

And tomorrow comes, and we now own The Old Smithy of Esset, within the Commune of La Brousse. We've done it. We've bought a pile of old stones in France, stones probably worth more than the whole of the 'estate' put together. Just like our house in Hereford, where the famous old Lugwardine tiles covered the whole of the ground floor, and we were told were worth more than the value of the house itself. One of the last trips I made was to the Hereford Museum and Library, with boxes of spares, hopefully still on display in their glass cabinets. I see no reason why they shouldn't be. My collection of milk bottles went that way, too. Not just any old milk bottles, but a splendid selection of everyday glass adorned with adverts for everyday products. Not really worth the haulage rates to France, nor my packaging collection, either!

The summer's taken up with designing layouts for the larger of the two barns, and the grenier (attic, former hay loft). The barn has a splendid well in one corner and I have visions of it being the focal point of the kitchen. A living room and three bedrooms, at least one bathroom, will all fit in comfortably, and the front will have arched windows, naturally with stone lintels. The grenier will provide two extra bedrooms for the family and a large bathroom in one part, and the rest will be converted into a 4 bedroomed apartment, independently accessed from the outside wall at the end of the house, next to the garage, which started its life as a cow shed. We appoint a structural engineer to do a feasibility study, and all's good. We're on course to being gîte owners, but ours will be superbly equipped and certainly not damp! The other large barn will function as an al fresco dining area, big enough to sit the whole of the village in, should we so wish. It already has a brick and stone built barbecue at one end, perfect for summer entertaining.

We plant trees to give shelter to one of its open walls, and passion flower plants to ramble up the timbers on the side facing the house. I expound mega energy as summer progresses hurrying between the two, laden with plates of food and bottles of vino. It's hard work but a great novelty, and we love it. So do our guests, who find us in their droves, even though most of them go round in ever increasing circles until we receive an S.O.S. and I cycle round the lanes to find them and escort them to Esset. We still get lost ourselves, Spouse frequently, as every sunflower field and vineyard has the habit of looking the same as the next one.

And then it happens! It's 'adieu' (farewell forever, stronger than 'au revoir') to the gîte idea. I've been offered a job! Word has reached Poitou Charentes ahead of me. Or perhaps I've told someone I'm an ex estate agent from Blighty, highly likely as we've been to the Anglican Church in Cognac a few times, Expatria at prayer, and I guess a fair few of them are Tories, too!

But there are bound to be enough Socialists to address the balance, as half the congregation seem to be retired teachers, health service workers, and social workers, many of them harbouring grievances against Maggie Thatcher's days in power. It's the same wherever the Church of England congregates 'abroad,' but it does a great job nonetheless, bucking the trend of falling numbers by actually increasing them. It becomes a life line for many, and there's not much wrong with that, until they start organising social functions, coffee rotas, flower arranging and everything else associated with Middle England. Then there can be dissention in the ranks, 'trubble at mill, aye lass,' it happens! The few do the work of many, 'twas always thus.

"Can you stay back a few minutes after the service?" asks one particular lady, obviously from the hierarchy.

"Of course, no problem."

So instead of concentrating on the sermon (or joining those who use it to doze, more often than not the only way of surviving the boredom) wonder what I'm about to be asked to do, guessing it'll be the coffee rota for starters, graduating to flowers or (heaven forbid) cleaning.

"I've heard you're an estate agent. We're opening up in Cognac and wondering if you'd like to be our English speaking person there."

Blimey, a job! That was quick!

I'm over the moon, far too young to retire, and what an opportunity. Of course I accept, on the spot. I've worked in the Isle of Man, Beirut, Hong Kong, Italy, and now I'm going to be working in France, in Poitou Charentes. Oh what a favour those two lost clients shot my way, better even than the commission they deprived me of. I'm deliriously happy, far too young to be retired. I'm in my early fifties for goodness sake. Lots of energy left in the not so old girl yet. And then it all goes pear shaped.

Christmas is my most dreaded time of the year. I hate it, with a passion normally associated with Easter. Something always go wrong, and for many women it carries a history of scrimping and saving for children's presents, shopped solo, whilst husbands prop up bars at office parties and flirt with secretaries, fall in the door paralytic and then expect to be king of the home on Christmas Day. It sucks! I leave him three days before we're supposed to be all jolly and dance around the Christmas tree, and kiss under the (non existent) mistletoe. As it happens, I have my best Christmas ever, in The Swan in Hay-On-Wye, eating cheese and onion crisps and drinking Guinness. The restaurant is all booked up, but it doesn't matter, not one jot. The freedom of not having THE meal is very heaven. And then a walk with Megan, just down from the town, by a little natural beach formed at the riverside years ago. If it weren't so far inland, I could settle in 'Way On High,' as its beauty and surrounding countryside sends me. Gemima has stayed in France, a fair swap, and cats hate travelling. Megan loves car journeys, even packed between cases in a little blue Peugeot. Paris is challenging and we nearly end up in Boulogne, but not the one on the Channel, rather a little suburb of the capital of France. We see the Eiffel Tower twice, though!

I assume I've given up all chances of taking the job in Cognac, and I've not decided how long I'm staying in Hereford for, although I have a family house to stay in for as long as needed. I'm lucky, but I come in useful. There's a new kitchen to be fitted and I'll make sure the job's done properly. The whole place is lovely but would fit in the living room of The Old Smithy, but I feel at ease, the worries and stresses of the relocation to France fading into insignificance.

Interviews start. I'm offered the chance of managing a new estate agency opening up in Hereford in March. I get called to a leading girls' public school for the position of housemistress, much to my surprise and incredulity. It comes with a flat, which I'll be able to use all year round, wow, anything's possible. They'll obviously take anyone, even me and my dog. I enjoy walks along the River Wye with Megan, visiting friends I thought I'd left behind for good, and slipping back into my old life as though it had never been disrupted.

But 32 years are a lot to give up. We speak again for the first time in six weeks. He arrives by train, a mammoth journey. We have a fabulous lunch back in Hay-On-Wye, at The Kilvert, and set off for France the following morning.

Eurostar speeds us through the Channel Tunnel, and we make the long drive from Calais to Dinan, in Brittany. We stay at the first hotel we come across, by the rail station, and it's awful. From the rickety staircase up to the bedrooms, the walls are all covered with, oh yes, with yuchy green carpet. But it's a cold and blistery February evening, about to go dark, and the snow is falling thick and fast. Its saving grace is that it's part of the Logis Group, so we get a decent meal. The Hotel group is renowned for its restaurants, but Dinan is perishing freezing when I walk Megan through the Castle grounds at night. Brrrr ....

La Rochelle, Charente Maritime

5 Feral Cats & Hunting Dogs

The job's still mine for the taking, so let the fun begin! I start on the first Tuesday in March, 2003. It's the weekly Caravane, an excellent idea and one we should have adopted in all the years I worked in England. It's a big office, with lots of agents putting houses on the market for sale, eleven of us as and when the market dictates. Every Tuesday, we pile into two or three cars and head off to inspect all the properties introduced to the Agence in the previous week, stopping for lunch together en route. There's to be no "'sorry, I haven't actually seen the property" here, and what an excellent way of doing things.

We start with the regular town houses in Cognac, move on through the maisons de maître (grand town and country properties) and end up in the riverside town of Châteauneuf sur Charente, where we stop for our mandatory team lunch. The owner of the franchise I'm contracted to is with us, and he's a bit of a flirteur (flirt), naturally very charming with it. His wife, the office manager, is not amused when he playfully swishes the derrière (backside) of one of the équips (agents). She responds as flirtatiously as she's played with. They are French!

Châteuneuf is a typical sleepy little town en route to the city of Angoulême, one of Eleanor of Aquitaine's last French staging posts. Unfortunately for her, the TGV took a while longer to reach her 'Queendom,' or she may well have been one of its first customers. She can't have had much fun with old Louis VII, or the marriage wouldn't have been annulled. No sex was the only excuse in those days (we're talking twelfth century here)! As it was, she had to wait 'till Henry

II swept her off her French royal feet and carried her away to England, where they had such fun that they produced none other than our very own Richard The Lionheart, and his brother John.

Le déjeuner (lunch) gives me a chance to meet my new colleagues. They treat me with absolute Gallic politeness, hiding their intrigue behind the smoothness of "enchantés" and "bienvenus" (pleased to meet you, welcome). I hide my dislike of all things to do with offal and ask for an omelette, the staple meal for all of us born north of Calais. The sight of pimpled brown tripe being eaten in front of me makes we want to gag, but I know if I make a hasty run for the 'loo,' I'll be greeted with the disgustingness of seeing men pee. I suffer in silence.

Heading back towards Cognac, we pass by St Amant de Graves, where I wonder at the beauty of this region I'm so honoured to be working in. We are now right in the heart of the main cognac producing area, not far from Segonzac, the capital of the premier cru (top quality) grape production. The land between St Amant and our next stop, Juac, is stunning. Spring is filling the fields beside the vineyards with bright red coquelicots (poppies) not that I can pronounce that word yet. It takes me years to get it right. It takes me years to get the pronunciation of many French words right, and I still don't always manage to.

Back in the office, late in the afternoon, I'm called into the manager's office. She lights a cigarette (yuch) and proceeds to blow the smoke into the room with ceremonious aplomb. I withhold the sensation to gag for the third time in less than three hours, and retain my British nerve, and dignity! She's not an unattractive woman, dressed a bit too young for her age, but they all love doing that. The mode (fashion) seems to be a quest to look as tarty as possible. Being French, like the Italians, they mostly get away with it. We Brits just look stupid whenever we try, in my case never. There's mystery behind the veil!

She reminds me of my friend in Italy who's slap bang in the middle of an affair with a chap who's actually bought a flat on the shores of Lago di Como, just so they can conduct their liaisons dangereux when her husband thinks she's out shopping. I think back to my Fridays in Milan, and how I used to look enviably at the dapper guys in their handmade suits and pure silk ties (from Como). An Italian colleague told me I didn't stand a chance, never would do.

"Why?"

"Because you inglese women don't know how to give off the right vibes."

O.k. then, might as well give up now. The lot of us. All of us not quite so still young English roses. How sweet that sounds, almost as sweet as Swiss women being compared to edelweiss. That's our problem. I am not alone, but then George Clooney does have a house on Lago di Como.

Ummm, "I'll have a voluto please, George!"

Don't you just love her for not asking for an espresso!

I'm given my secteur, the territory only I'm allowed to put properties for sale in, but my colleagues can sell them if they beat me to it. No worries, I can sell their listings just the same. We have une autre guerre (another war) upon us! My secteur is énorme, all the way from the northern fringes of Cognac up to Matha and beyond, taking in the delightful little towns and villages of Cherves-Richmont, Migron, Brizambourg, St Hilaire de Villefranche, even St Jean d'Angely and St Savinien if I so wish. I'm also given the towns where time has stood still, and will continue to do so unless I find an influx of anglais to buy there (I do).

Within no time at all I'm heading north for the tiny market town of Aulnay, not far from La Brousse as it happens. Aulnay is a pleasant little place, with a friendly market square and a couple of restaurants, on the pilgrimage route to St James de Compostelle in Spain. It's in lots of guide books, famous for its magnificent Romanesque church bedecked with splendid stone gargoyles. Even the Four Horsemen of the Apocalypse can be found here. But go beyond Aulnay, and it's another world. Paysan (peasant) is not a rude word in French, and this is the land of many of them. A secretive, shutters closed in winter to keep the cold out, and in summer to keep the heat out, way of living. The villages, and worse still the hamlets, are ghostly and unwelcoming, devoid of people, or so it would seem. Those I do happen to see, stare at me as if I'm a foreign invader. I guess I am! But they'll be glad to let me sell their hovels; in time they will.

Feral cats give birth, only to have their kittens drowned, or worse. Many cats are deliberately poisoned. Many roam the countryside looking like death has already taken them, stray dogs the same! I'm told it's worse in India! I'm also told, by one of my French colleagues, that people here often have two dogs, one to kick and one to cuddle. I see houses where beautiful chasse (hunting) dogs live in dreadful outside conditions, their excrement never cleaned, locked up for all but weekly outings when Monsieur takes them hunting, and then Madame emerges from her occasionally, but not often, pristine but old fashioned house with a silly little yappy dog in her arms. What I'm told is absolutely right, and it appals me. I long to free the chasse dogs from their wretched existence, but am powerless to intervene.

The Country French won't pay for sterilisations, and dogs and cats breed freely, for the cycle of neglect to continue. Many of the owners are not in a position financially to afford to. One has to ask the reason before lodging the inevitable criticism, but it beggars belief to the invading anglais, of whom of course I am one. At times, I find this side of my job hard and on the Caravane repeatedly put my size 7 feet in where the manager wishes I'd stop treading. Tough! I'll say anything to help the cause, bring some education where it's badly needed.

It's not just in Poitou Charentes, but all over France. When people become silent, the World collapses. Fortunately, animal rescue centres are now becoming the norm. but it will take time. Television will help the new generation of French to learn to love and care for animals better. Often all it takes is a film, I'm thinking 'Beethoven,' or a school haversack with cartoon puppies, an advert for Catsan, for Sheba, cats being cuddled not chucked out. It seems to be less of a problem in the towns I work in, again down to perhaps that most important word in any language, 'education.' However, fortunately it's not all bad, far from it. Many French people I meet, from both town and country, do love and treat their animals well. It's not as if the U.K. is always perfect in this respect, either!

The area north of Matha is also a land of great beauty, of rolling hills and as far as the eye can see horizons, of driving home at night with the sun setting on one side of the road, to the moon slowly rising on the other. I often park the car and stand between the two, transfixed by the sky just before dusk. By summer, I'm in our very own pool, in our very own garden, floating on my back with nothing between me and the stars, for the first time in my life not even a swimming costume. Shock horror! I can see every constellation in the sky, just can't identify them yet! I can almost touch them. Where's Patrick Moore gone?

The little town itself has all we could ask for, our bank (one of three in Matha), a post office (which is in great need of decommissioning and moving to new premises), several pâtisseries (they eat a lot of baguettes in France), a chocolatier's mouth watering shop, doctors and dentists (we choose a more modern one in St Jean d'Angely) insurance offices, the notaire's practice, two supermarkets, lots of individual shops including a marvellous old fashioned haberdashery, a weekly market, two parks (one has tennis courts and the other, a château and a stream, great for Megan on a hot day) a cinema, a sports' hall (I enrol for yoga) and best of all, a couple of restaurants. I make a mental note to introduce the Caravane to the delights of Pinocchio's, especially in summer, eating al fresco on their delightful terrace, but first I have to get cracking finding those houses to sell, tout de suite (straight away). No sitting in the garden for me yet!

Who's going to mow the lawn ? Perhaps these Poitou Donkeys

6 "You are not Mother Theresa"

I have my first clients, but I'm not yet legal! A golfing friend of the office manager comes to my aid and she puts me instantly at ease. She looks happy, very approachable, sitting in the reception area chewing gum and smiling warmly in my direction. We set off on foot for the Chamber of Commerce, where I try to register as an Agente Commerciale. It's cheaper for the Agence for me to remain self employed, as most of my colleagues are, but frighteningly expensive for yours truly. At this stage, I have the pits and troughs of that to find out. We've come to the wrong place. Of course, c'est la France. I'm told to go to the Hôtel des Impôts (the tax office) but that they'll be closed for lunch. The two of us have already bonded and are having fun. She's French but married to a Brit. I'm disappointed when she tells me she has to go home.

Returning to the office on my own, I realise I've left my car keys on my desk and have yet to be given a front door key to the hallowed Agence. It's pouring with rain now, and we're a little bit out of town, direction Angoulême. I steel myself and walk to the nearest eatery, a McDonald's! I've only ever been in one before, in Hereford back when my children were all still at home. I wasn't impressed, in fact I was appalled at the concept of eating food, all food, with fingers and from cardboard paper boxes. I ate later, but they seemed to enjoy the experience at the time. We'd been to Malvern, to see a friend's new house. I admired the staircase:

 "Yes, but I shall have to get a new knob!"

Oh how McDo's has changed, at least in France. I can't comment on anywhere else. I'm not a fan of fast food and the mountains of rubbish its users create on the streets, on motorways, and even otherwise picturesque country lanes. But the one in Cognac is immaculately clean, almost in town, so most of its clients eat on the premises and use the rubbish bins provided. Perhaps it's the 'drive throughs' which cause the greatest problem to the environment. I'd still like them eradicated! 'Fast Food Nation' should be obligatory reading in schools.

But it serves a purpose. My prawn salad is actually very acceptable, as is the apple turnover, and the coffee is excellent. The 'loos' are immaculate, and the serving staff have been well trained. I lessen my hostility towards old Ronald.

It's not all work, and we have lots of visitors. I make a house rule, not for family of course, but for everyone who suddenly decides a holiday in France would be a great idea. They can stay 3 nights. We'll feed them the first and third, and they can take us out on the second. It's only fair. Visitors rarely realise that sightseeing is not something we'd ordinarily do, nor are copious amounts of lunches out, or posho lunches for those taken at home, not just the usual sandwich. And then there's the extra breakfast food (cereals are costly and hard to track down in French supermarkets), extra wine provided, extra electricity, extra hot water (it's metered in France) copious amounts of fuel for airport and ferry funs, and of course the sightseeing (they'd better appreciate the views).

Houseguests are expensive luxuries! Be warned if you're thinking of moving to anywhere holiday fanciable. Remind them of that old Hebrew saying:

'Visitors are like fish, they go off after three days.'

Hence our time limit!

It was worse in Italy. The first year there cost us a flipping fortune, and guess what, we couldn't afford a holiday ourselves, of course not. That's what happens when you move abroad. I took so many to La Scala's museum in Milan that the man at the desk told me I was so good for business that I (just me, not them) could go in free next time. There wasn't a next time. I prepared a travel schedule for our visitors, dropped them off at Como Station as early as I could get them out of bed, and said we'd see them in time for dinner at night. Things steadily improved, and then we moved to Tuscany, first round over, let the second round begin, and resist the temptation to chuck them from the Leaning Tower of Pisa, or leave them to the mercies of Il Palio (famous horse race) through the streets of Siena. It was our own fault, the enjoyment usually justified the hit on the bank balance, and most were, to give them credit, very generous. But few spoke the lingo, so 'muggins' was left buying tickets, always a problem, especially when it came to trips on the Lake. A fair few had short arms and long pockets, and they were the ones we could have done without.

We're still in round one here in Poitou Charentes. To cap it all, not only do we have people coming to stay, but we all of a sudden become the best thing since sliced bread, but I'm trying to earn a crust. France has so much peace and tranquillity that its Expat residents go through long periods of insufferable boredom. We have a big garden, Spouse is obviously lonely (although he'd never admit to it) so he turns ours into an open bar whilst I'm on the road slaving away in vastly over hot temperatures, and all I want to do when I get home is sit in blissful peace. I do not want to talk, and I do not want to end up having to include the 'vinos' in whatever's on the menu that night. He's too hospitable, always has been, and he's only too happy to oblige this new breed of pensioners wandering around aimlessly almost every evening just before the sun goes down, anticipating it going over the 'yard arm' by the time the first bottle of Rosé's opened (it's what they all seem to get sozzled on). I find it hard not to be rude at times, not to tell them to get lost. Instead I end up feeding them, then shouting at Spouse! C'est normale, c'est la vie en France, glamourised in the Expat Press, made out to be fun. It's not! Not when you're working, although I guess I'm as bad. I wouldn't be an estate agent otherwise!

I can't let such things get to me, always having to be 'en forme' although I doubt that I shall ever be très soignée (that means ooh laa laa dressed) but I discover there's no need to be that, not here in France. Gone are my Hereford working days of serious suits, tailored skirts and blazers, elegant shirts. Quel dommage (what a pity). It was one of the best things about getting up in the morning, dressing to look nice, to look and feel professional. I can wear what I like now, anything goes. In fact, I walk round Cognac and see sexy young things showing off their spindly legs or fat thighs in jeans too tight to move almost, balancing on heels too high to walk straight in (great business for orthopaedic surgeons in years to come) and fat and frumpy older women shamelessly exposing flabby guts in need of gastric bands.

It's a shame. French women also seem to be under the illusion that short, back and sides' haircuts make them look attractive. They do not, especially when they have fat necks. Even more so when what little hair they've asked the hairdressers to leave them with, is dyed bright orange. It's not even as if they've been shaved for collaborating with the Enemy. Times have changed and clothes have lost all sense of beauty and style. They have become a joke, an ugly one at that, just like the latest fashion in home décor. Think French, think chic? Naaah, think French, think naff! Christine Lagarde and Penelope Fillon, you are exceptions. You are both so beautiful with your timeless elegant classicism, but of course Penelope's British; Welsh, actually!

Saturday morning comes, and I opt for smart casual, and sensible shoes. I arrange to meet my clients in Matha, where they're staying in a Parisian run Châmbre d'Hôte (Bed n'Breakfast) a few kilometres down the road. I wish they weren't! We set off into the countryside and lady client gets increasingly more worried about what her husband has in store for her, as the day progresses. She's a city type, and he's obviously the opposite. She asks, in all earnestness, when she'll be able to wear her nice clothes if they move here. Worse still, and despite my instructions, she's in seriously silly shoes, absolutely no good for house hunting in Rural France. I then get a complete run down of their recent trips to Mexico and Spain, and sense she'd rather be house hunting in Malaga. They're a delightful couple, but it's clearly his idea to move to France, and most definitely not hers. But we soldier on, and I manage to show them enough properties to fill the whole day, finishing with a great not so little, but modern, house in Migron. I think it would suit them perfectly. They, however, don't like anything I show them enough to buy, but are worth sticking with, unlike the majority of those who appear on the television's relocation programmes. These will buy, of that I'm certain.

Migron is set to taunt me. I take other clients there, two ladies, a very fit ex county tennis player and her good friend, a lady who introduces herself to me as:

"Just past my Biblical sell by date."

These two are good fun, and delightful company with it. They settle for a beautiful large bungalow with a perfectly landscaped garden, opposite the tennis courts. It'd be ideal, perfect in every way. Migron has everyday shops and is just a short hop away from Cognac.

The deal is set in Charentaise stone, or so I think, so the three of us think, so the Agence thinks. It's my first sale. On average only one sale every three years collapses in French property dealings, and my very first one just happens to be for the block. The legal beavers have been instructed, the sellers are obliged to complete the deal, or face huge compensation costs to the buyers, as well as fees to the Agence and the Notaire (lawyer). Vice versa if it's the buyers who pull out of any deal. These legalities come into place once the initial paperwork has been signed, and received back, by all parties and they are out of their allowed period of reflection. Many British buyers think of this as the '7 Day Period,' but this is a flexible number of days and rarely applies within as little time as one calendar week. On average it takes two or three weeks, in some cases even longer. But people panic! It's also against French Law to demand a deposit, but many agents aren't honest, and insist upon one being paid. I don't. There's no need to. If either side pulls out after this period of reflection, they have to fully compensate the other side with 10% of the agreed selling price of the property, hence negating money being paid up front. However, a deposit is usually given as a token of trust, but it must not be made a condition of purchase. My office manager is a bit of a shark and successfully terrifies buyers into paying one at every opportunity. I try and keep her away from my clients, but don't always succeed. Her eyes follow me like a hawk.

"Who do you think you are, Mother Theresa?" (yells her

Owner-husband.)

The Migron sale has collapsed, the lady of the house deciding she's not going to move to Toulon to be near her grandchildren after all. Her husband is mortified, plays heavily on his wife's stress, says she's had a stroke. It's neither verified nor denied, but I have my own thoughts on the matter and am proved right. She's decided that two ladies living together just have to be lesbians, and she's "not having anything like that" going on in her beloved house. She's quite wrong, they're not, they are just retired teaching colleagues. But there's nothing I can do to dissuade Madame. There's nothing my young colleague I've dragged into the scenario to help me, has been able to do. We fail miserably, and my very first French sale collapses big time, spectacularly so.

My conscience (catholic guilt) won't let me accept my commission, and I do my best to get it wavered in total, feeling sorry for the old lady from Migron, even if she is a prejudiced lost cause. Most people of her generation are still terrified when they think of 'gay' issues.

"If you don't take it, I will. I will have your share as well as mine."

The Biggest Boss is bellowing with all his Gallic might. No charm now, then. The office is nearly exploding and his wife comes into the room, blowing her cigarette smoke in my face with as much gusto as she can manage. I give in. I have no choice. I'm also told, in no uncertain terms, not to try and give any of the money to the sellers, or I'll have my own legal case tout de suite. I bank my cheque, my two lovely ladies receive their ten per cent, and we return to the drawing board, rather the sales' particulars I've translated for every property the Agence is dealing with. It's never been done before, and takes up a considerable amount of my time, but I enjoy it. They have more spending power to their tennis elbows now, and they intend to put it to good use. I can't blame them. But they don't like anything else we have on offer and buy through another agence. You win some, you lose some, but in this case I've won regardless. Twice would have been nice, though. Twice! New York City, so nice I did it twice. (Three times, actually!) Iced lollies on a hot summer's day: "What could be nicer than a 'Pendleton's Twicer,' ice cream with a lolly each end?" Let's not move on to Aurora not forgetting the 'Kiora!'

I'm back with the clients I think would do better buying in Spain, she most certainly. But he's set on France and so we continue. We spend several days ensemble (together) and become good friends. Estate agency's a great way of making them, a bit like dog walking, and standing at the school gate. YES! They have found their perfect home in the sun, with

55

outstanding views over truly spectacular vineyards, totally uninterrupted until the distance reveals an almost Tuscan landscape. This is Segonzac, perhaps the best little town in Poitou Charentes, certainly surrounded by arguably the best countryside. Had we discovered it when we were looking, we'd be living here ourselves now. Tony Blair himself has possibly been here with Chérie. He certainly knows his 'premier cru,' buying copious amounts of cognac from the House of Frapin, based right here in Segonzac. (Or so the lady at the desk takes great delight in telling me). At £150 per bottle, we decline the opportunity to buy any. What's acceptable for the Lord Mayor's Banquet is not acceptable, or possible, for us. But, hey, isn't that what all good Socialists do, send their children to private schools, buy properties for them when they go to university, drink the best claret, and take holidays in Mustique, so what's a mere £150 times however many bottles of cognac are needed for the Lord Mayor and his 'mates!'

The new lady-to-be of the house measures up for curtains, her husband imagines himself on the enormous terrace, surrounded by grapes, and then checks out the sous-sol (basement) where he'll keep his vast collection of D.I.Y. tools and gardening implements. He'll need them. This house has a lot of land. I arrange for them to come into the Agence tomorrow, to sign the necessary paperwork, in the afternoon. Silly me! How can I be so darned stupid, giving them time, that precious commodity linked to all potential sales.

I drive them back to their Châmbre d'Hôte and wish they'd never set eyes on the place. The owner is an officious, overweight, over unfriendly woman from Paris. Some of my best friends in France are Parisians, but this one completely falls into the arrogance bracket they are reputed to belong to, just like we Brits, then! They tell her what a good day they've had, how they love the house they're buying, and then she turns to me, asking: "what did you take them there for?" I suspect a problem, and one emerges. She manages to dig up a house she thinks might be for sale in a village not far from Matha, a run down, ghastly, ghostly place, no facilities, just several houses in danger of falling down before the demolition experts manage to do the job. It's not a patch on Segonzac, in fact it's awful. Ah, but:

"The house is a Maison de Maître"

and they couldn't afford one of those back in Lancashire so easily!

What really upsets me about this, is that Bed n'Breakfast woman obviously had it up her sleeve all along. AND, and here's the crunch, nobody tells my clients that the field in front is rumoured to belong to one of the local dignatories, and is destined to become an estate of bungalows which, in true Charentaise style, will look like storage containers with lids on. I'm furious, my clients deserve better treatment than this, but they fall totally, head over heels, in love with the property. No doubt about it, this is a house of earlier grandeur but it needs a lot of work to restore it to its former glory, and glorious it will become with these two. And then they'll sell it and perhaps move to Spain, as I have a hunch would have been the lady's preference all along! With a ton of luck, and no bungalow building happening before they do, they may get back what it will have cost them, although there's always a huge risk factor to take into consideration in that respect. But for now, I'm totally powerless. It's a truism in my business that people rarely buy what they set out to, and I'm right in the middle of a classic example.

They sheepishly come into my office, as planned, and reveal all. There's to be no signature for Segonzac, but I do get a very lovely bouquet of flowers, given to me with a: "you will still talk to us, won't you?" Better still, I invite them for dinner on Saturday and we cement our friendship over a couple of bottles of Bordeaux and a few little sips of cognac, but not from the House of Frapin! As the many legalities of their purchase progress, they do feel tempted to throw in the towel, not least when the subject of the field of bungalows hits the fan. But they stick with it, restore it to a by-gone beauty, landscape the garden, and provide me with a great stopping off point for cups of tea between my rural appointments, when I'm on my own of course, looking for houses to SELL!

This situation leaves me in a quandary vis à vis avoiding the use of Bed n' Breakfast establishments, and also whether or not to put any transactions in the hands of the notaire whose family is rumoured to have their eyes set on building in the field which may spoil these nice people's view. It's a tricky one, as it tends to be the sellers who decide which legal practice to use, although it's the buyers who pay the fees.

My only solution is to push all conveyancing matters from now on through the charming English speaking notaires in Ruffec, and I try my best to make sure this is what happens. It's not always possible, but I usually swing it on the grounds of the buyers being held legally responsible for whatever they sign, and if the notaire doesn't, or chooses not to, speak English, then they're scuppered before they even begin. Ditto the sellers, for whom any linguistic errors may result in problems for them, too. For the time being, I get away with it, but can see it becoming less and less of an option. It's a long drive to Ruffec and she who manages the Agence does not approve!

Harbour Entrance, La Rochelle

7 Legal in Saintes, Dutchman in Segonzac

I'm still not legal, and go to the Hôtel des Impôts in Cognac. They tell me to go to the Chamber of Commerce. I tell them I've already been there and they've told me to come to the Tax Office, who suggest I go to the Prefecture. They tell me I'm in the wrong place, in the wrong Département of France! "Why?" "Because you live in Charente Maritime, Madame, and Cognac is in Charente." I have to start all over again. I drive to St Jean d'Angely, to their Tax Office, a minor branch and totally useless. Frustrated, I'm sent to their Chamber of Commerce, who send me to their Prefecture. It's the wrong Prefecture. I have to go to the main one and St Jean d'Angely's is just a small satellite office. I assume they mean La Rochelle, but have the sense to ask: "No, not La Rochelle, but Saintes will be able to handle this matter for you, Madame." O.k. then, off we go again, this is fun!

After seven visits to various totally unhelpful establishments, and all but six of them on my own, I finally get an appointment to present myself officially at the Prefecture in Saintes. If it doesn't work this time, I'm retiring! I take Spouse with me for moral support, convinced I'm going to be out of a job before it's really started. He opts to stay in the car, not up for a bout of French confrontation. It's a beautiful building in a splendid Roman town, and I'm finally given my Practising Certificate and a Siret Number. This has its down side. It means I'll be paying French social charges and taxes from now on, regardless of whether I sell any houses or not, and all this not only costs the earth, but

60

much of it has to be paid up front. No wonder the Agence prefers to 'hire' self employed mugs like me.

Better get cracking! I'm getting a fair few instructions, the lingo's coming on in leaps and bounds (it has to) and I'm loving driving round the countryside. Ah, another problem presents itself. Monsieur le Flirteur's wife asks to see my permission to take clients' out Driving Certificate from whoever my car's insured with. I don't have one! Nobody's thought of telling me, of course not. Doubly illegal! Fortunately, our insurance office is just in Matha and they couldn't be more helpful. It's a pleasure to visit them, not least to say bonjour to Réglisse (liquorice) their adorable soppy black Labrador, always there with them. Monsieur Assurance is an exceedingly good looking Frenchman from Madagascar, and has that je ne sais quoi (I don't know what) of European male elegance. He is always très charmant (very charming), and his lovely wife is his perfect match. I decide to give them all my British clients on the spot. They serve them well, and even share their commission with me, not a lot, but every little helps and it comes unexpectedly, without asking.

I've had enough of bureaucracy to last me a couple of days, so I take a break from the one hundred and fifty property specifications I've translated to date, and from scouring my secteur for private à vendre (for sale) boards, which are beginning to lead to a nice little collection of selling clients. I treat myself to lunch at Le Chevalier de la Croix Maron (the Knight of the Brown Cross) inside Segonzac's town centre hotel. The food is always excellent, the ambience superb and it's comfortable. Many are not! We've been here on the Caravane a couple of times now, so I'm happy to fly solo today. Even happier when I'm led to a table next to a Dutchman reading The Herald Tribune, which he passes to me when his starter arrives. A novel chat up line, I accept graciously. We make small talk between courses and I discover that he's a cognac dealer from Hong Kong. Having lived there for four years back in the 1970s, this turns into a fun conversation. Better still, he owns property in St Georges de Didonne, a very fashionable outpost of Royan, on the Atlantic Coast, just down from La Rochelle. I'm tempted to ask:

"Do you come here often?" but resist!

I'm glad I came, but all good things have to end and I never see him again. Is it really my thirst for sightseeing, my inbred curiosity for all things historical, or is it catholic guilt (for flirting with the Dutchman) that leads me inside the little twelfth century church at Gensac le Pallue? I'm en route back to Cognac and just can't resist stopping to take a look. It's beautiful, just like the little square it proudly sits in, taking centre stage as they do. I light a candle, even though I gave up this branch of religion in 1970, when I swapped Rome for Canterbury. The first lot of terrorist nuns (which they truly were) had me 'till I was 7 (8 actually, but you know the saying, the one which the Jesuits coined)! Back to the office, back to the ever increasing pile of French estate agency's non existent, and utterly pathetic, marketing attempts which await my translation into English.

I park my now legally correct car in the little road behind the office, and return to the grindstone, my mind full of Hong Kong, the Netherlands, and cognac. We drank Rémy Martin back in those days, before the Dutchman introduced the Chinese to the House of Frapin.

It's going full swing, the year's turning out to be a good one with virtually every sale achieving the asking price, and I'm confident at last to set out into the back of French beyonds and tout my trade. The Brits are coming in their hundreds, or so it seems. Every agency in Cognac is full of them, and the heat is on. We don't have a mid town location, but we do stay open at lunchtime when clients are around, well I do, and our information is now in English. I seal my first sales, one after the other, attending completions as agent responsible. She who runs the office insists on accompanying me, but she soon grows tired of that. I've been recommending the firm of notaires in Ruffec, not so that I can lunch at Le Toque Blanche, but because their main players speak excellent English, and most of our buyers are currently British. The sellers, of course, are exclusively French at this stage of the game, but that soon changes, as many Brits fail to settle here and return to Blighty, or try their luck in Spain.

Monsieur le Notaire (the conveyancing lawyer and senior partner in the practice) would be more suited to life in cosmopolitan Milan than in very rurally situated Ruffec. He's tall, slim, good looking, and has exquisitely tailored clothes. His English is impeccable and his manners are perfect. His handshake is strong, not limp. French men have a tendency to shake a woman's hand as if they're handling a wet lettuce, although heaven forbid the extreme alternative of a British man filled with testosterone. I invariably drive my buying clients to put their signatures on the vast amount of legal documentation required, every page initialled and the last one with a written attestation in French. This helps put them at ease, and is all part of the service.

The very last appointment in the afternoon is always a good one to request, sometimes ending with a bottle of delicious champagne shared between the sellers, buyers, notaire, and agente (me!) Everyone is present, usually very polite, and bewilderingly happy. Most completions run as smoothly as clockwork. If it's a morning rendezvous, no worries, I'm usually treated to lunch afterwards. I seldom cease to be grateful for the job which evolved from the simple act of attending 'Carols in Cognac' and to the lady who made it possible. Thank you!

Christmas snow between Aulnay and Matha

8 Oradour

The French love their réunions (meetings) and the more boring, the more tedious, the better. This morning's is no exception to the rule. I have a thirty three kilometre drive from Esset to Cognac and I get trapped behind a lorry it's impossible to overtake. I've already risked a few minutes of precious time putting fuel into the car, so this is no joke. In-house meetings are the only time when any French person born outside Paris is punctual, especially those who are salaried employees, fearful they may end up in the gutter. "Il faut manger" (one has to eat) is a regular bleat one hears.

Being on time is not something they are gifted with, and it annoys the hell out of me. Normally arriving at the Agence well before anyone else, I'm late, not much, but enough for the secretary to wield her power and lock the front door, leaving the keys in. She's probably been told to do so. I can just imagine she who manages the office, an expression of pure sarcastic joy all over her face, giving her ever controlling instructions. I'm not the only one who'll be late, but the other is always forgiven no matter what time he turns up. He's an educated type, a real smoothie, knows all the right people, grew up knowing the Mitterands no less, and oh how she sucks up to him. I happen to really like the guy, so this is just a statement of fact, not of jealousy. He'll 'phone after I've been let in and receive the mandatory three kisses on each cheek, from everyone!

I take my mobile out of my bag and do likewise, receiving grunts of disapproval of course, but I'm let in. The secretary's delightful, a bit moody at times, but aren't we all! I'm hugely relieved that I'm excused the farce of the bises (kisses) due to my lateness. Two totally boring young insurance nerds beg us all to transfer our home and health assurance to them. No chance! The réunion lasts until eleven o'clock, goodness only knows why, but they've all been lovin' it. I love the freebies, a very good calculator, and a set of two pens in some designer box or other. I don't do labels. Everything is designed by someone. They think they've won us over, and leave. Alleluja, and thank God they've not been invited to Team Tuesday Lunch!

We return to our desks and pretend to be busy, clogging all the 'phone lines to our sellers, asking them to reduce their asking prices; and to our buyers, asking them to increase their paying power. It's what we do, all part of the job. A very trying part of the job, but it sometimes brings results amongst the "naff off" responses we mostly get, especially from the sellers.

The French set a price and stick with it, accepting that it may take their property four or five years to sell. It's not only the English man who thinks his home is a castle, but the French man and woman not only thinks theirs it, but positively believes it, even when it's a country hovel with no mains drainage or inside 'loo' that they're hoping to sell at some exorbitant price to some foolish acheteur anglais (English buyer) keen to have une maison secondaire (a holiday home) in Poitou Charentes. Even camping cars come with their own facilities, and we've had inside plumbing throughout the U.K. for pretty much a whole century now.

Few realise the cost of installing a bathroom, a kitchen, a staircase, a fosse, as country properties rarely come with mains drainage, often not even connected to relatively large villages and small towns. But there's a buyer for every house and someone will fall in love with the dusty shelves of ancient dining room dressers laden with jars of bottled haricôts vert et blanc (French beans, green and white varieties) and mirabelles (small yellow plums). To see alcoves complete with romantic (in their dreams) sleeping quarters from times gone by, when country women were slaves and their cognac swilling men ruled the chicken roost, at least they thought they did.

Splendidly sewn, and proudly worn, women's bonnets still appear on rusty hooks in rear corridors leading to more shelves full of haricôts. The French leave things as they were, as if they're still expecting Marie-Louise to put her bonnet on and feed the hens again, even though she's gone to join les anges dans le ciel (the angels in the sky). Gardens edged with neat lines of beautiful flowers, still attended to by Cousin Maude, give way to skyscraper rabbit hutches. But these old rusty things are not nice, the rabbits have been for the pot, not to call Flopsy, Mopsy, Cottontail or Peter. Barns house all manner of ancient agricultural tools and paraphernalia. In one, I see the most incredible Victorian (at least) carriage. In another, I see what must be a 1920s Morris going to ruin, in another I see a dog sleigh, never even thinking such things would have been used in France, and not that long ago. One of my colleagues remembers the family dog pulling a sleigh full of grapes at harvest time, and he's younger than I am. It's hard to appreciate how much of a peasant society France has been until very recently. (It's still politically correct to use the word 'paysan' here.)

Like many of the country properties I dealt with in Italy, the French ones seldom have hallways. The exceptions are the maisons de maître, which may only have two bedrooms upstairs, but will have an impressive and elegant hall. Our own house has one because it was once a walk way between the living quarters and the smithy, and wide enough for a horse or two to pass before and after being shod. In most other French houses, the front door leads directly into the kitchen, as always the main hub of the house. The living room, often superseded by the kitchen itself, is nearly always given over to as large a table as will fit into the space, always rectangular and nowadays covered with a gaudy plastic tablecloth. A television stands proudly in one corner, but there are rarely comfy chairs, and hardly ever comfy sofas. Generations of occupants have obviously been conditioned into working in the fields from dawn to dusk, gathering à table twice daily à manger (to eat) and then going to bed whilst it's still light enough to see what they are doing, those who need some light on the situation of course! They still give certificates, signed by the President, for having large families here. There'll nearly always be a bedroom downstairs, and this mode of living carries on to this day, even with the newly built homes.

Creaky and unsteady stairs, often not much more than ladders, lead to the hayloft and to extra bedrooms if the children have been lucky enough to have their own space. Not all have been. These are the houses the Brits love and flock to in their droves, thinking a little bit of TLC will transform them into country mansions. It rarely does, and many end up bankrupt in the process, but there's always someone out there harbouring the dream, and I'm here to help them. I'll still be here when they run out of money and ask me to sell it again, when the children hate school so much that they play truant every day, or when the wives go stir crazy missing 'mum.'

People don't leave the problems they're escaping from behind. They bring them with them to France, to Italy, to Spain, wherever the Brits abroad congregate. I see it all. I wear 'agony aunt' on my forehead, just like I used to do in Hereford, especially on Friday afternoons. Not today, though. The réunion's thrown everybody's schedule into complete turmoil, so we adjourn to a supermarket café for lunch. It's actually not at all bad, much to my surprise, and it's not even self service. I'm impressed with thefood on offer, and with the cleanliness of the sanitary facilities afterwards. Monsieur Leclerc's empire has expanded from his home Département of Finistere, Brittany, pretty much throughout the whole of France. Good on'im!

I have to get used to this team eating lark pretty quickly, have to practise for the sales conference I'm summonsed to in Limoges, two days of hell no doubt. I'm going to be the only mother tongue anglais amongst the sixty two delegates. It's to be pretty action packed, and we're to wear fancy dress at the evening dinner dance. Some of our team are to be provided with outfits, in fact all of us are, but I prefer not to take the risk. This turns out to be a sensible decision. I'm not alone in doubting the costume distribution, and the men decide to hire theirs.

Spouse drives me to Jarnac, and with absolute trepidation I glide into the rear seat of he who had a dog sleigh at home's car. There are four of us insitu and off we go. Car owner is an ex policeman, helluva nice guy, toujours très charmant, but oh how quickly he drives, obviously used to chasing criminals in his past life up in the North of France. We don't have many of those in Poitou Charentes.

We whizz past a sign to Oradour sur Glane. I know I shall never be able to go there. It was here, during the Second World War, that the German SS stormed the village and massacred 642 civilians, including 200 children. It was on June 10th, 1944, not long before the Liberation of France. The men were herded into barns and machine gunned. The women and children were forced into the church, the doors were closed, and grenades took over the job of killing them, all but 5 of the villagers murdered on that day. The entire village was set on fire, all the buildings destroyed, together with those who may have escaped the initial barbarity. To this day, stark reminders of man's inhumanity to man are everywhere in Oradour. Cars continue to rust alongside bicycles and babies' prams. Shops and houses remain burnt out ruins.

It's become a tourist attraction, and appears in a good many guide books, but is one I haven't the courage to visit. The Nazi who gave the orders, Heinz Barth, was finally charged with war crimes but allowed out of prison in 1997, on health grounds, making a mockery of justice, which should have no time line's escape. It seems he's to be allowed to die a free man, winning a war he revelled in half a century earlier.

9 Sales Conference Limoges

Oh, the Sales Conference! Limoges, regional capital of the Limousin, is surrounded by prettily undulating countryside, all very green. The vines disappear as we leave the Charente, east of Angoulême, and the scenery turns into vast areas of forest, and wide fields. What I find especially interesting is the huge number of sheep we're seeing, masses of them everywhere. There's no maize growing, no sunflowers, and none of the cattle the Limousin is famous for. I make a note to research where they are bred. Surprisingly, there are lots of free range pigs, all of them black, pigs not 'wild' boar. Pigs here obviously have a happier life than I'm told most of them do in Brittany, the major pork producing area in France, industrially reared and only seeing the light of day from the trucks taking them to slaughter. The French are all but addicted to le cochon (the pig) and the multitudinous products it gives them. But I'm sidetracking, this is about a conference shortly to begin, and not a vegetarian's hobby horse!

The beauty of the Limousin is outstanding, and also very popular with the buying Brits. This is to cause financial griefas my career in France develops, and competition from these less expensive areas kicks in. Ryanair aren't exactly helping, either, with their flights to Limoges from the low priced property areas in the North of England.

The City of Limoges is very large and in keeping with most French towns and cities, has an unimaginably ugly periphery. We circle the ring road until we find the golf club somewhere in the suburbs where we are to stay. There's to be no chance of a round of golf, not that I play the game, but some of my colleagues do and would have liked to have brought their clubs. We have no time to check into our rooms as everyone is set to head off, by car again, for our first Conference lunch. Enthusiastically, we let out great shouts of approval as we arrive in the centre of Limoges itself. It's very lovely, but there our joy comes to nothing, at least mine does. The restaurant is delightful to look at, splendidly timbered, but the food it serves is absolutely dégoûtant (really disgusting).

The first course is rolls of processed ham. I don't eat factory produced pig, which this very obviously is, revoltingly pink and swimming in brine. Every roll of ham is filled with sandwich spread, oh yes, sandwich spread, just like we used to eat in England circa 1955, my earliest memory of it. Then comes the main course. It's a totally unrecognisable piece of white fish, swimming in an innocuously over salted sauce. The French love their sauces. As my late father often said:

"Used to disguise the inedible food beneath."

He would have been oh so right on this occasion! At this point, I have to admit to having had a half French mother. He teased her endlessly about her eating habits and never ate tripe, but she did. The fish is served with over cooked, tasteless, pommes vapeur (boiled potatoes) instead of the way the French usually eat fish, with balls of over microwaved white rice, hard enough to turn into bombs which stick to the plate when turned upside downand presented to the chef. I actually witness that experience on another occasion, in the fashionable Breton seaside resort of Dinard of all places! I still can't make up my mind which is the most unappetising, rock hard rice or mushy spuds.

Three pieces of cheese are served. From a country which produces more cheeses than there are days in the year, these three all taste, and look, the same. This is nothing new. They may have many, but they group into few!

The puddings arrive, one tiny piece each of tart au chocolat and tarte au rhubarbe. I get quite excited at the joy of eating these, as they look relatively acceptable. But how am I to actually achieve this? Of course, with my fingers! Cutlery has been deemed unnecessary to use for the tarts, and of course they are not served with cream, or ice cream, or even that revolting crème anglaise (cold custard) the français love so much, under the illusion that we whom they name it after, eat it precisely like that, cold. I struggle, determined to eat something! I have a busy schedule ahead. And probably another inedible meal tonight. But one lives in hope and golf clubs usually do things well, except Cognac's on Sunday lunchtimes, where French (?) lamb is served sliced with Indian curry sauce, next to a large dollop of Italian tagliatelle, to expectant Brits thinking they're about to have a traditional Sunday Roast, as the menu's reference to roast lamb indeed infers! (Spouse and son-in-law live on that one for years!)

Back to Limoges, for this meal we have been given, as ever in France, except for in the poshest of restaurants, one plate, one fork, one knife, and one glass. This is très, très normale and I never, ever, get used to this peasant way of eating. The whole meal, all four courses, must be eaten from this one plate. Actually, in this instance I'm taking their name in vain a tad. We're given a new plate when they serve us our three manky portions of cheese, and we're then doled out our puddings on to it. But to have one plate throughout a meal is considered perfectly acceptable. I guess even restaurants didn't have kitchen sinks in days gone by. The only good thing about it, is the cost. 8.50 euros including a glass of undrinkable red wine. Coffee extra, of course.

The 'loos?' Ooop laaa (as they say, and they do). Communal, and of course, filthy. I'm forced to walk past a man in full flow of peeing. I don't even watch my husband when he pees. Shameless Frenchman turns to smile at me, obviously expecting me to be impressed by his tackle. I escape, pretty darned quickly. Get me back to Blighty!

Evening arrives and in troop all sixty two delegates, in various forms and levels of fancy dress. It having been already decreed that our team will all appear full of Middle Eastern Promise, ex policeman takes central stage in his cardinal's robes, a character from the Inquisition perhaps, complete with hat. It suits him, and he's obviously adopted some lateral thinking and extended the theme over the Mediterranean to Moorish Spain. She who manages the office, and her side-kick obviously looking for promotion, walk in wearing extravagant Moroccan gowns, complete with headgear. They look splendid. The translator who has now become a member of staff, and a personal friend, and I are comfortable, and that's about all I can say, the pair of us definitely looking like poor relations and certainly not promising anything! We're predictably disappointed that we haven't been adequately provided for, but my own ever faithful black and gold djellabah fits perfectly adequately, not at all out of place, and she looks lovely, despite what she's been allocated. Mine also fits me just fine, to expand into with all the lovely food we're about to receive. In my dreams!

The lukewarm mushroom vol-au-vent arrives, completely saturated in parsley sauce, making it somewhat difficult to find the food beneath. Next the duck is distributed, roughly chopped into chunks and obviously served on to the plates we've used for our soggily soaked mushroom, and its blood is flowing freely, curdling with the left over parsley sauce. I want to gag! Instead, I ask just to be served the vegetables which will surely be coming soon, and on a new plate. They oblige. I get a bowl that I can't decide would be better used for cereal or morning coffee French style, but at least it's clean. I sit in shock while they ceremoniously deign to put into it a mixture of lukewarm, obviously tinned and very soggy, green beans (those blasted haricôts vert again) and some exceedingly over salted sautéed potatoes. It is all absolutely revolting! My colleagues eat with great gusto, needless to say.

Once more disillusioned, I feel more and more out of place, but hey this is an experience to relish, and to write about! And I'm a survivor for goodness sake, English into the bargain.

Next course, cheese. Alleluja! Not much can go wrong with the cheese course, but I shall have to negotiate a plate. Nope, we're given new ones. Luck lurks round every corner. A plate of several varieties is positioned in the centre of the table, already round, and it's very heaven. I stay in place and nibble away like a satisfied Cheshire cat. Most of my colleagues (the majority of us are here) are on the dance floor. It's an eye-opener to see the various levels of bad behaviour. My mind is particularly alert, as I've not had one single glass of wine and it's getting on for midnight. Meals in France are long drawn out.

I know I have to be en forme this evening, that all eyes will be upon me, that the only other delegate who speaks English refuses to do so. He's already made that clear when I introduced myself to him (not counting my friend who plays golf and helped me at the Chamber of Commerce) earlier in the evening. Of course not, although he's working in France, guess where he's from? Quebec! More French than those who chose to stay in the Hexagon, perhaps too poor to afford the boat fare at the time.

Everyone returns to the table. The lights go out, and several men appear beneath the stage, doing the Desert Dance we Brits used to watch in the '60s, in that hilarious TV series 'It Ain't 'alf 'ot, Mum.' Ohmondieu, non, ce n'est pas vraiment possible (oh good grief, no, it's not really going to happen), but it does.

She who manages the office (her husband is safely away in North Africa) gets up, rushes across to the stage, and actually joins them, tagging on behind and looking completely stupid, but that's nothing to what she's going to look like as the evening progresses. Dirge music fills the function room, the pudding is carried in with great pomp and pride. It's a giant sized Baked Alaska, flaming as it's presented to us all from afar. Everyone seated gets up and sways to the music, clinking glasses as bodies move from side to side. The drama is impressive. The lights go on, the pudding is sliced and distributed. It's actually totally tasteless, all froth and no substance, no flavour at all. But it was well worth watching the ceremony. And now, oh lovely, oh very heaven, and I'm going to have a glass!

A bottle of champagne is put on every table in the room. Rather than open it, though, almost everyone goes back on to the dance floor. Ummm. It's a quarter to one in the morning, I've been sipping water delicately all night, and I happen to love the bubbly stuff. But nobody is opening any of it. It remains corked on every single table. Not one to be scared of taking instant decisions, I pop the cork! Shock horror, it seems I've committed a cardinal sin, surely to land me in the depths of corporate hell. Colleague left at the table with me (one of only two others) asks:

"Why did you do that?"

"Do What?

"Open the bottle, for goodness sake. That is très méchant (very bad) of you."

"What's all the fuss about, nobody else seems to be prepared to open it?"

Oh dear, in the merde (shit) again! The rest of the team returns to the table, horrified that our bottle has indeed been opened. I pose the same question, to be told in no uncertain terms that one has to wait until 'le Directeur' gives permission to do so. But he's nowhere to be seen, possibly even in bed for all I know, possibly knocking off some young floosie. We have one to spare amongst ourselves, not afraid of receiving favours, and there must be many more amongst the sixty two. I'm losing my English reserve and ask, all guns firing:

"What if he doesn't give permission?"

"Then you must wait until he does."

"What if he forgets to?"

"Then you must do without."

"Even if it's still there at breakfast?"

"Of course! It is not your right (here we go again) to take such a decision."

I pour myself a glass, definitely egged on to complete rebellion by this stage. It's delicious and I savour every sip. Gradually, one by one, my colleagues join me. Thank God for that, I was beginning to lose all hope in them. She who manages the office doesn't reappear at the table, obviously making it easier for them to break such stupid rules of misplaced etiquette.

And where is she exactly, and what is she doing, and where is her side-kick? Our office manager is on her knees, throwing herself at a man from another branch, gyrating around his mid-drift until, until she actually starts to tease him, pretending (I hope that's all she's doing) to unzip his fly to give him some oral satisfaction. I am totally, utterly, repulsed.

What makes it even worse, is that young side-kick, still fine tuning her own prowess in the art of seduction, decides to dance suggestively around the pair of them. I've had it! I finish my one glass of champagne and retire to my room, resisting the temptation to take the bottle with me. I'm shortly joined by my room-mate. Thank goodness it's she who speaks English, even if she did shout at me for opening the bottle earlier on! At least some relief has shone upon me. We talk until nearly 3 in the morning, and it cements our friendship.

But oh how lonely I'm feeling. It's been my first sales conference in France, and I'm determined to make it my last. Jamais encore (never again!)

10 Enemy Down The Well

I've built up a considerable portfolio of properties to sell within my secteur, from gracious town houses in Cognac (I'm allowed a small portion of the town itself) to veritable vineyards and equestrian estates, village cottages and country hovels, maisons de maître in need of drastic updating, a few of them already renovated and priced out of the market place, and some properties which come complete not with mains drainage, but with World War 2 history. Of course most of my selling clients are French, and lots of those are elderly, hence they are only too happy to have a captive audience, me!

I also take on the responsibility for translating and writing up my colleagues' properties into English, selectively choosing those which I feel will be of interest to British buyers, and also to the Dutch and Norwegians who are beginning to flock to Poitou Charentes, often with more money to spend than most, and almost all of them speaking excellent English. This is an ongoing job, and takes up a considerable amount of time, but allows me to drive through glorious countryside, treat myself to lunch in those restaurants I learn to trust (there are several) and do courtesy visits to clients I've already sold to. Most of them appreciate these visits for a good while after they've made the big move to France, and of course the better the service provided, the more clients myself and the Agence will get. That, of course, will mean more money for she who manages the office and the 'flirteur,' her husband. They being French, not often given to lateral thinking in the work place, we often come to blows:

"If you do that, we will all have to. It is not your responsibility. Just SELL!"

I lose the battle trying to convince her that after sales service equates to more sales, but I carry on regardless, enjoying the cups of real English tea as I pursue my travels. I also make some very good friends from amongst them, Spouse even picking up a golfing partner or two. Moreover, they say 'hello' in supermarkets and I don't have to hide, unlike many of the agents amongst my competitors, honesty not often a trait associated with estate agency, after all!

One particular morning, I decide to drive down to one of the delightful rural villages between Cognac and Saintes, where the River Charente meanders amongst the vineyards. This is Rémy Martin country. The village itself is pretty deserted, as many of them are most of the time, clients known to ask if there's been nuclear fallout! Remnants of a bygone age are around every corner, not least when I spot a 'Singer Sewing Machine' sign high up on a wall. Further along, 'Dubonnet' is written in large, fading, letters on the side of what could have been the village bar. For comfort, Madame sewed and Monsieur drank!

The imposingly elegant three storey house appears before me and is a lovely shade of pink, with a two storey extension. I assume this part is fairly modern, judging by the mock Georgian window panes and the porthole half way along the upper wall. I've come to write it up for the internet, for the clients who are going to walk into the Agence, having seen it in all its glory in the window. It dates back to the 1850s and the elderly owner now lives in a Maison de Retraite in another part of the village. His son comes to answer any questions I might have for him, as the

British owners are sailing the Seven Seas, well one of them. The land is extensive, with lots of areas previously given over to vegetable crops, which would have been the staple diet for the occupants during the War. I ask if there's any water down the well, seemingly in good condition:

"No, but there are many Germans."

"Excusez-moi, what are you saying Monsieur?"

His father was in la Résistance throughout the War and if what I'm being told is right, the local Maquis heroically disposed of any of the Enemy they managed to bump off, down the well! I decide I'd rather not look, certainly not ask him to raise the bucket which is blocking my view down into its depths. Somewhat unsure as to how I feel about this, our conversation continues nevertheless. There's no holding back on the graphic details which have been passed down through the generations, and village folklore. I pose my question:

"How do you know? Do you believe your father? Perhaps it's like Chinese Whispers (he's not heard of those) and has been blown up, or drowned down, out of all proportion."

"Oui, Madame, I overheard him telling somebody at the last meal the Maire hosted for the Old Folk, and then others joined in the banter, adding more and more to the tale of the German soldiers down the well. It is not the only one!"

"So there must be other Members of the Maquis still living locally!"

"Oui, Madame, certainement. My father comes back here to till the land. The new owners let him. If you are here at the right moment, ask him yourself."

I wonder if they realise, perhaps, that elderly Résistant also comes back to check that nobody has interfered with the human 'souvenirs' lurking below.

"Will it be alright to drink the water, Monsieur?"

"Mais bien sûr Madame, (but of course) ça ne fait pas rien de différence (it makes no difference)."

I'm not so sure about this, and wonder how many wells in Rural France are harbouring the dead corpses of German soldiers, many of them unwilling fighters, just young men relieved to be posted to Poitou Charentes rather than the Russian Front. I picture their ghosts rising to the surface under moonlight and floating amongst the vines and sunflowers they saw all those years ago. Then I do a reality check, and given what their boss did to millions of others, I decide to let the matter drop, not quite with as much ease as dropping centimes into the Trevi Fountain, but deciding that discretion is indeed sometimes the better form of valour.

I bid Monsieur au'revoir, assure him I will keep away from the well, and crack on with describing the interior of this lovely property, but what I have just been told has my imagination running wild. We have two wells of our own. I shall not venture beneath the lids! Spouse uses one to fill the pool, but the purification process is a good one! This all leaves me feeling very uneasy, nonetheless, but I'm so lucky to be working in this land of huge quantities of primary source information, and can't wait to move on to the next property.

Lunch time looms, and in an hour or so I'll have clients knocking on the door. No-one else will be in the Agence to welcome them at a mere 13:30. Heaven forbid, interfere with lunch en France! If their budget is 300 000 euros, I may even bring them here. I cross my fingers and toes and head back through the vineyards, past the French Air Force Base on the southern outskirts of Cognac, past the garage with the enormous plastic blue elephant in its forecourt, and to Leclerc to pick up a sandwich. It won't be as nice as Marks & Sparks, but it'll have to do.

Dog sleigh used in Charentaise vineyard years ago

11 WW2 Refugées in Beauvais

I get a call to put a house on the market near Beauvais sur Matha, not one of my favourite places. Another town where time has stood still, and full of dilapidated houses in desperate need of care and attention, the ghostly atmosphere actually spooks me out, and has been the scene of various crimes of passion and racism lately. Not between the different colours humanity presents itself in, but between tribal elements of the townsfolk versus travelling communities from further East in Europe. This is not restricted to the town itself, either. In one of the little villages not far away, a man goes crazy with a gun, killing his wife and then turning it on their children before trying to finish himself off, which he fails to do. My conscience begins to play havoc with me. I have to market houses here, Beauvais is in my secteur, but how much do I tell my buying clients? I can't lie (catholic guilt) and usually leave them to make their own judgement, the best I can do in the circumstances!

It's not long since we had our Tuesday team lunch in the restaurant in the Square, a pleasant enough place given its location, with caring young owners whom I feel sorry for. They face an uphill struggle. They may do well on Market Day, the only day of the week this little town comes to life. We'd just finished our 'formule.' That's French terminology for three courses of often 'naff' food, starting with a help yourself buffet of pickled grated carrots, pickled grated celery, a sloppy mixture of chopped tinned vegetables in tasteless cold sauce, halves of hard boiled eggs, vast quantities of factory produced cold meat, and prawns if you strike lucky, most of it covered with flies when it's hot

87

weather, regardless of how clean the restaurant presents itself. Perhaps there are some regions in France where the 'formule' is good, great even, but I've rarely found that to be the case here in Poitou Charentes. That said, its 'haute cuisine' is usually excellent, and I do believe that also applies throughout the Hexagon.

The main course in a formule is likely to be a slab of meat served with a mound of either chips or glutinous tagliatelle, or a piece of fish swimming in salty sauce, with a ball of over microwaved rice. I usually ask for an omelette, it's safer! The only vegetable likely to be offered, if served at all, will be les haricôts (tinned into the bargain), or occasionally half a tomato sprinkled with breadcrumbs. I wonder why the French have such splendid potagers (vegetable gardens) but rarely does one accompany a restaurant meal. I've already posed the question, to be told by le Big Boss, le Flirteur, when he was over from Morocco recently:

"If you ask for vegetables, you are telling everyone that you cannot afford to eat meat."

Sometimes cheese will be offered as an alternative to pudding, but we're not talking Camembert or Roquefort here. Most likely it will be some pretty boring offering of whatever's cheap in the local supermarket. The agony continues with a piece of gelatinous fruit tart, with considerably more pastry than fruit, and served on its own (you'll pay extra for a scoop of ice cream, if they have any on the premises), or maybe a pot of yoghurt, or a pot of factory produced crème caramel, nothing tantalising to the taste buds. The only good thing about this experience is that it usually costs anything from a mere eleven, to fifteen, euros. The higher end sometimes provides the more sophisticated dessert choices of crème brulée (cold egg and cream, semi firm and covered with copious amounts of sugar and set on fire before serving), île flottant (a meringue floating on cold custard) or mousse au chocolat. Baskets of chopped up baguettes will be served throughout the meal, and eaten with great gusto. Wine will sometimes be included in the price, but it's not usually palatable. Coffee is nearly always extra, and milk adds a few more cents.

Although in theory ridiculously cheap, I grow to resent all these fifteen euro rubbish meals I'm forced to take. As it's a rule that we all attend, and given that most of us are self employed and paying huge taxes and social charges for the privilege of working for the Agence, I think we should be treated to lunch by she who manages the office, or at least by le Flirteur (her husband) not short of a bob or two, but then he also has his floosie to maintain. Team Tuesday is not necessarily a good day for me, particularly if I have the honour to sit next to him who grew up in Jarnac, François Mitterand's old town, and who has a love of devouring all things to do with offal with a passion only a Frenchman could turn into culinary ecstasy. Normally I jump at the opportunity. He has a comfy car and he's a 'cool dude,' who introduces me to some beautiful singing as we drive through the countryside. Thanks to him, I fall in love with Carla Bruni's voice one day and buy the C.D. he's been playing, on my way home. I'm not, however, quite so enamoured to be allocated to his car when he's been eating leathery brown, skin bubbled, tripe. The stench is nauseating, even to me, a great lover of garlic! Worse than being asked to accompany him after a tripe or kidney, liver or andouillette feast, is when I'm instructed to travel with she who manages the office, practically a chain smoker. Very occasionally, I get to drive, though they seem to have serious reservations about allowing an Englishwoman to be in charge. They probably don't like my vehicle, either. I drive a German car, a Volkswagen Passat, bought in Italy, taken to England, and now back on The Continent, here in Poitou Charentes. The VW's a fantastic automobile for us, but the French are very nationalistic and if it's not a Citroên, Peugeot or Renault, I gather their street cred's a bit suspect. Ah, but I do have a Peugeot as well, but small and no good for an offal eater, a chain smoker, and an ex policeman who's used to chasing such things. It's the kind youngsters race around in rather than sit in sedately.

Andouillettes, in case you're wondering, are sausages made from tripe and other repulsive such things. I bought some once for Spouse, not realising what I was doing, nor what they were. One sausage looks pretty much the phallic same. He's a carnivore extraordinaire, and the oven turned into a bomb site, almost exploding off its hinges as he lifted the grill pan out amidst an inferno of complete disgustingness, sparks of fat flying into the kitchen, just stopping short of the ceiling. We wouldn't even let Megan eat them, caring for our dog a lot more than the French obviously care for their own human digestive tracts! Never risk them, and be warned. They often appear on the daily 'formule!'

We'd paid for our food, been given our schedule for the afternoon's property visits, lest some of us got lost amongst the vines and sunflowers, and were ready to leave the restaurant, when all of a sudden the owner locked the door and refused to let us out. We were informed of a gunman or two threatening havoc outside, although none of us could see anyone waving weapons around over in the Square.

90

Back to the table, the only ones left in the restaurant, we waited and we waited and we waited. Eventually the Police arrived and gave us permission to leave. Surprisingly, I wasn't in the least bit frightened. None of us seemed to be, probably disbelieving what we were told was unfolding outside, and what we could neither see, nor hear. Hesitantly, though, all eyes focussed on alleyways and shopfronts, we got into the cars and on that occasion I was more than happy to sit beside the tripe eater (it wasn't actually on the menu that day).

Just outside Beauvais, at the bottom of one of the hilly approaches to the town, is the house of an historian's dream and I'm only an amateur. The imposing cast iron gates, probably eight feet tall at their apex and painted in pale blue, are nothing out of the ordinary for properties in my secteur. I enter many, but none that quite reveal what I'm about to see next. This has been an extremely large and rather imposing maison de maître, obviously owned by a very wealthy family in its heyday, which would have been before the War. The grounds have become overgrown with knee high weeds, but I plough through them to the front door. The first thing I see is a flag pole, a huge flagpole, deliberately placed in prime position between the door and the first set of floor to ceiling opening windows, now rotten with age. There's no flag flying, and probably hasn't been since the Nazis either took theirs down before fleeing, or the Allies threw it on a bonfire, just like the Huguenots did to the head of John the Baptist, not far away from here in Saint Jean d'Angely.

The ownership of the house has skipped a generation, possibly to escape inheritance tax, and the current proprietor meets me in the garden, arriving after me. She's in her mid forties and tells me that it was her grandparents' home. She takes me into the kitchen, much as it would have been back in the 1940s. From having the freedom of the whole house, undoubtedly hosting parties for fellow wine makers, corn growers, perhaps merchant traders from Cognac, what followed was to change their lives completely. Fortunately they passed the story of what did happen down to their granddaughter, who's now sharing it with me. It's going to take a long time to write up this property, and I don't care how long that is.

The couple would have been relatively young when war broke out, and I'm not sure why le monsieur wasn't called up to fight, but it doesn't seem relevant to find out, and I want to learn as much as I can before she goes back to work in St Jean d'Angely, so I restrict my questions to what went on in the house itself. Perhaps her grandfather was just a little too old, perhaps farmers were excluded initially. It doesn't matter. He joined la Résistance instead. And what does matter is to hear of his bravery, his wife's bravery, and their children's, contracted to silence. And they were not the only ones.

The Germans didn't take long to establish control in Poitou Charentes, helped of course by General Petain with his government of collaboration in Vichy, pretty much on a parallel line with Beauvais. The area needed regional control centres and Beauvais became one of them. The German Commandant needed a home to retire to after his day's work at the office in the town itself. Before his troops actually arrived, an aerial trip was arranged for him and looking down, he spotted the unusually tiled roof of this maison de maître.

"That will do nicely," I hear him saying.

92

And thus the property was seized and the grandparents became his kitchen slaves, not only kitchen slaves but general household factotums. Forced to give up the graciously proportioned reception rooms, the bedrooms and connecting dressing rooms, they were allowed to move into the barns and outbuildings and turn them into accommodation for themselves, but that would have cost money. I have a hunch they slept in the kitchen, but granddaughter isn't sure. That bit never came up in conversation when she was little, and if it did, she obviously wasn't listening at the right moment. Here comes my reason why!

There was a problem, and it was énorme! The couple had been sheltering a Jewish family with several children, ranging in age from babies upwards. What to do? Most French houses, and virtually all old ones, have large greniers (attics) and that was where they were hidden. By day, as soon as the Commandant left for work, they were allowed relative freedom, at least of speech. I picture the mother helping Madame prepare soup, make bread; and her husband assisting Monsieur brew the cognac they almost certainly would have had the equipment for. But they never would have dared step foot outside, and as soon as it was time for the Commandant to return, they would have retreated to a world of silence in the attic. I imagine a baby crying, a toddler coughing, and wonder how the adults managed to control such things, and how they entered their secret domain. Then, as I'm shown round upstairs, I see a loft hatch, but if I can see it, the Commandant would have seen it.

"But it was not there during the War. The entrance to the grenier was in a very different place, and well hidden."

So well hidden, I fail to find any trace of it, no matter how hard I try when she leaves me alone to measure up and take photographs.

The Jewish family lived like that for a whole month after the Germans took over Beauvais, and this house in particular, and my opinion of the ghostly little town changes somewhat, becomes more understanding and less critical. The secretive air must be hiding many a story, mostly not wanting to be told. I am tall, fair skinned, and maybe I'm taken for the Enemy I remind them of. Perhaps, but I'm yet to find out the darkness of the other side of the coin, just perhaps there lurk a fair few collaborateurs around every crumbling street corner. I'm told over and over again not to discuss what happened during the War, but I can't resist asking, and why not? If history hurts, then surely that's all the more reason for discussing it, for learning from it. The answer I'm frequently given, is that one minute I could be talking to a résistant, the next to a collaborateur; to someone with a history of outstanding bravery, the next to one who was happy to play second fiddle to Vichy, and there were many, especially amongst the French Police, the Government, and the Railroad Companies. It's a delicate path to tread with the many who lost loved ones. It's a hard, very fine, line to cross and I try to recognise the boundaries! My life in France represents a huge learning curve, constantly creating a pattern of intrigue and arching through reticence, judgement, questioning, acceptance (not of everything!) and finally a deep sense of belonging, comfort and happiness to be here. But it takes time, as do all things worth having!

The local Maquis were finally able to arrange safe escorts for the family down to Marseille, and a boat to safety, and I'm full of praise and admiration for the previous owners of this remarkable house. I imagine the German Commandant snoring the night away in deepest slumber, perhaps with a local girl in bed beside him, and the Jewish family just floorboards above. What a remarkable testament to the lengths courage can be stretched, despite the odds!

It's a very long way from Beauvais sur Matha to Marseille. I shall give it my best. An easy house to 'wax lyrical' about, after all! The splendidly tiled roof has been renovated without changing its intricate artistry, and the property at least has new electrics. A basic form of central heating has been installed, rooms on the first floor partitioned to create more, but the kitchen! Pretty much non existent, as many of them are, but a blank canvas can be a good canvas, especially when it comes to the most important room in any house. It's a joy to create a new one, rather than accept another person's choice. I see it as a good source of potential income, a chambres d'hôte able to offer three gîtes from its outbuildings. There's even stabling, and two acres of land, plenty for an in-ground swimming pool, and the grenier! How amazing that would be, sleeping within so much history.

I can't wait to bring punters here, and know it won't be on the market long. Although I don't clinch the deal, I'm the only one who knows what happened within the ancient walls of this home and for that, I'm grateful. And now I'm off to my next historical gem, but it's not one of such honour and decency!

House shared by French Owners, German Commander and Jewish Refugees, secretly under one roof for over a month

12 Collaborateur in Matha, Owls & Toads

Matha's got a lot going for it, small, but full of charm and character. The little, almost Italianate, piazza in the centre reflects the sunshine bouncing off the walls of many of the light stoned buildings. There's nothing gloomy or run down about Matha, unlike many of the small towns I visit on my rounds. It has a bar in the centre, with tables and chairs outside to soak in this sunshine, and a park with a shaded tree lined walk, tennis courts, flower beds, and even a soccer pitch. Better than the park for dog walking, are the grounds of the little château which takes pride of place in the centre. The vast lawned area is regularly used for vide greniers (jumble sales held in the open throughout France, especially on Sundays). All that's left of the château is its tower, but it's the kind from which Rapunzel may well have let down her hair for her fairy tale lover. A third area good for walking is next door to the town's cinema and sports' hall where I do yoga one night a week, badly!

I lie on the floor and instead of zonking out, think of the following day's clients, which completion is about to happen, what merde is about to hit the fan. I stick with it, and get the yoga teacher's ex-husband's house to sell. It's a great town house with a large garden, in need of a bit of T.L.C. I sell it to a builder from the Channel Islands.

A double whammy! I put it on, and I close the deal. The commission structure for we who are self employed is split 50-50. When a sale is achieved within the Agence, whoever has introduced the property to the market gets half, and whoever sells it (we're allowed to sell out of any secteur) gets half. This means that I'm in with a chance of all the allotted commission, not everything the Agence gets, far from it, but my percentage share of the total commission received. When I think back to the pittance my commission was in Hereford, I'm staggered at current generosity, but then I have no salary, no security.

The houses in Matha range from young family new builds on a still developing estate, to little old terraced properties, some seriously grand town houses, a small block of local authority retirement apartments, and a few rather naff 'they don't know what they are' houses, the kind added to and subtracted from as time evolves. It's one of these that I'm instructed to put on the market.

It's anything but attractive from the outside, and the garden's a mess. Zilch kerb appeal, then! As soon as I step over the threshold, I wonder what it is that's striking me as so odd. Something isn't quite right about this place. The owner is very pleasant, and turns out to be a secondary school teacher with a job move to a lycée in some far flung city. The good many books and grand piano give credence to this. I ask how old the house is:

"It was built in the early 1940s, but we have only been here for a few years."

I'm not buying this. France was deeply in the War then, and money was scarce. Way too scarce to install, let alone source, superb quality marble flooring throughout the ground floor, continuing up the amazingly curved art deco staircase. It's wide enough for two or three people to pass en route, and the woodwork is solid mahogany. Art deco windows continue to add to my suspicions. It turns out they are not unfounded. I press him for further information and he's willing to tell me that the original owner was a collaborateur. He must have been very good at his dirt dishing trade. He was paid in goods and workmanship. In other words, the Nazis built his house for him, and with quality materials no doubt produced with slave labour. The marble flooring and fireplace look as if they are the finest from Massa Carrara in Tuscany, which was on our tourist trail for houseguests when we were living nearby, after our time in Como. It sticks in my mind that maybe it, too, was hacked out of its Italian mountain with slave labour under Mussolini's orders. It was Carrara marble which Michelangelo used, and of course can still be gawked at in his statue of David in Firenze (Florence) and in many other famous works of his in the Accademia di Belle Arti. So many that David's hard to find. He's at the end of the hall, just keep walking! I found him a bit of a disappointment, but then I'm a Philistine and don't much care for sculptures.

I continue to write and take photos, carrying with me in my thoughts the house near Beauvais sur Matha, a mere 8 kilometres from here, with its family of Jewish refugees living in the same house as le Commandant, for a whole month. I take some relief from knowing that le Collaborateur missed such an obvious opportunity for a seaside villa in La Rochelle into his bargain. Or did he? We shall never know, nor will we ever know how many others in this little town slept with the enemy. I shall look out for marble and mahogany c. 1940s!

I'm working with two companies who send me British house hunters, and the Agence then includes them in the commission package if and when they buy through us. I have to stand my ground here, as she who runs the office would do all in her power to cut me out, if only she could. It seems she can! Like many people, those I'm about to see have been spreading their wish list amongst several agents, including both of the British referral companies I am delegated to deal with, exclusively, within the Agence here in Cognac. They form the major part of my bread and butter, unlike she who has become a friend and who is salaried, and thus has a very much poorer share of the office commission than I do. In other words, she comes cheaply!

Driving down through the Vienne, they decide to call into the office which sends me clients, off their own bat. So far, so good. They are given my name, sent to meet me in Cognac, to ask for me specifically, and told that I will look after them. They don't say, perhaps don't realise, that they already have an appointment with me in Cognac, made by our referral agents in England. Ummm! (I wonder if they've twigged that I am one and the same person. It's not as if I'm called Anne Smith or Jane Jones!) I'm out with clients, so of course she who manages the office pounces on them big time, and immediately gives them to my newly made friend and colleague to be her very own clients, not mine! Newly made friend does the right thing and 'phones me on my mobile, giving me the chance to return to the office tout de suite and take issue with the dragoness. The plot thickens, with he who lives where la Famille Mitterand used to live being given the property which I put on the market, with my own bare hands and camera, within my very own secteur, and to which newly made friend and colleague is now heading, my instruction nicked in my absence! The secretary has been told to transfer the listing! This is outrageous and I am livid. Of course they buy it, don't they?

Good luck to them. Ballans is just another dull and dreary place where time has stood still, and many of the houses have been left to become dilapidated wrecks. In summer the vines redeem its attractiveness, but in winter it turns into one of those sleepy rural French villages of nuclear fallout ambience. The local people live behind their closed shutters and hardly a sound is heard, save for the guns of the chasseurs. That, however, is not the point. The house is clearly in my secteur, and these people have already been booked into the office diary no less as my clients. I miss a double whammy and both referral agents (the buyers are registered with both companies) we deal with lose out on any share of commission they thought may be coming their way, as well. My two colleagues take my share of the goodies, in one case not a lot, but in self employed 'cool dude's case, my 50% . Of course, I should have got 100%!

This is not the first time there's trouble at t'mill. She who runs the office hates the head of the referral company in France we have an arrangement with, and it's reciprocated with equal contempt. French woman has me into her hallowed smoke filled room and yells that she's:

"Not being dictated to by that abhorrent (it's the same word in both languages) madame in ...."

and tells me that I am to stop working for her and to work exclusively for the Agence. Her husband comes in on the scene, back from his latest trip to Morocco, and stands by his wife, not doing that very often, or so it seems to the rest of us. His stock phrase, virtually every time he sees me, is:

"You must tell Madame ... to go to 'ell and you must come and work for me."

So this is nothing new. The pair of them will do anything to rob others of what is rightfully theirs. They are not in business for love, not even for the love of each other. That becomes more plainfully obvious with every passing day, and there are times when I do, actually, feel sorry for his wife.

I'm in English woman's office 'up country' and she's banging her fist on the desk, screaming with all her might that she's:

"Not taking orders from that f...ing little French tart."

Ain't life fun! And here I am, pig in the middle of two warring women, both of whom I need to keep the peace between. It's not easy. At the end of the day, I'm self employed and can walk either way.

I walk in to the Domaine du Breuil, the gracious and historic home of the Rémy Martin family and now a country house hotel on the outskirts of Cognac, with a couple of reservations to make. Part of the service I provide is to organise accommodation for house hunters booked in to see me. I've tried various British owned Bed and Breakfast establishments, but it's not been a good idea. Either they drag old ruins for sale out of the woodwork of their villages, for which they may get a backhander of the odd bottle of cheap wine or two, or they have hordes of yapping dogs or kitchen counter cats. Worse still, they may smoke into the bargain. And bargains they are often not. Le Domaine du Breuil is a perfectly proportioned large house, complete with imposing steps leading up to its front door, approached from a splendidly sweeping driveway. It sets the scene admirably, and the room rate is often no more than a B n' B would charge. What's more, the restaurant is par excellence. I know! Several of my clients treat us to dinner. Work's not all about commission earned.

It's also about passing clients on to those I become associated with when I do manage to make a sale. What comes next is totally unexpected, but hugely appreciated. I'm invited to lunch with one of the Notaires from Ruffec, not the man in the sumptuously sewn silk suits, but his Partner, equally charming in his own way. We meet at his office and he drives me through the gloriously rolling countryside to the east of Ruffec, to Le Moulin de Condac. I'm in heaven, I'm back in la bell'Italia in an absolutely authentic Ristorante Italiano and it's truly superbo. The high level of comfort, of pure opera as we're welcomed into their fold, is perfetto. The owners are genuine Italiani, from Calabria. I eat a salad of langoustine tails, and follow it with spaghetti di aglio ed olio, con noce (garlic, olive oil, and walnuts) and it's divine. We share a bottle of Bardolino, and I pick up a house to sell. It's one of his father's portfolio, which I'm told he manages from his château. I'm about to visit my first château without having to pay an entrance fee. Wow! Italy always brings me luck. Why am I living in France? How did that happen? At this particularly moment in time, I'm glad!

His father is one of the most unassuming men I have ever met, but his talent shows through when he walks towards me, picks a leaf off a shrub, sits on a stone wall, and plays the most exquisite music from it. He's dressed like a country peasant, and we're not in his big house, not yet, that comes later. For the moment we're in his village, north east of the little town of Néré and not far from where the Charente meets the Deux Sevres, meets the Charente Maritime. He owns what seems to be the majority of the properties in this deserted outpost from civilisation, and what are not his, are his brother's. The few people who are around, doff their imaginary caps and bonnets at him, and he politely bon jours every one of them. He's obviously a good landlord, well respected. He hands me an enormous bunch of keys, directs me to the gates of the substantial house I'm to measure up, the buildings I'm going to entice the buyers with visions of turning them into an artist's studio, a pottery workshop, or perhaps just a couple of regular gîtes, and leaves me to mon métier (my job). He informs me he will meet me later, and disappears into what must be one of his tenanted hovels, as some of them sadly are. Perhaps I can persuade him to bring his village into the twenty first century, but I somehow doubt it.

He returns as promised and asks me to follow him to where he lives, for us to do the paperwork there. The driveway seems to go on forever, but he could be taking me the long way round. The château has been splendid in its heyday but is looking a bit tired, and the grounds could do with tidying up. The setting, though, is very lovely indeed. He lives alone, estranged from his wife. No wonder he serenaded me with the leaf! The main entrance hall is stacked with furniture, in pride of place a plastic garden set. He asks me to follow him into the kitchen, where he offers me a glass of wine. I decline. I'm working. Unrelenting, and perhaps thinking I don't like what he's offering me, he leads me down to the cellars. The first one, he tells me, is full of vinegar and is where the toads live. He seems happy to provide a home for them, and opens a bottle of vinegar for me to sample. I politely try as small a drop as I can get away with, not liking any kind of vinegar unless I'm eating caprese (sliced mozzarella cheese, basil, and plum tomatoes, liberally sprinkled with extra virgin olive oil and balsamic vinegar). The second cavern is vast, and has the most magnificent vaulted ceiling and individual bays. There must be several thousand bottles of wine down here, some of them born a considerably long time before I was! He moans that his lawyer son helps himself to a bottle every evening. He's living back home with Dad whilst his own matrimonial home is being prepared. He says his stocks are rapidly depleting and he won't be able to replace them. As far as I can see, there won't be a problem for a good many years yet.

We return to the kitchen and I accept a glass of fruit juice, and take it with me to the round plastic table in the entrance hall. This guy obviously doesn't like living the life his home could allow for. Plenty of good furniture exists, but he's obviously more comfortable at his garden set! We do the necessary paperwork for the house in the village, then he shows me the rest of the château. There are beds everywhere, even on the first floor landing. I'm told that his lawyer son is a great table tennis player and that the house has been used to host many players from as far away as China. He's immensely proud of his family.

They are not the only occupants he's proud of. Way up in the attic, after we've walked along 'miles' of corridors, passing umpteen bedrooms en route, he stands stealthily by a door and motions to me to be extra quiet. Slowly, very slowly and very deliberately, he opens the door and I take a few quick steps backwards. There before me, in all its splendour, is the most beautiful white owl I have ever set eyes on. And it's not alone. There are eight of them in here, perfectly free to leave whenever they want, but why would they? The château has been theirs for as long as he can remember, certainly since the servants who occupied this room would have left. A window is left ajar for their comings and goings, but perhaps they've seen Santa in flight and use the chimney in the corner of the room. I wonder if there's a nest or two in it. There's no furniture in here, nothing really at all, just the fireplace and the owls, and the beams they use to perch on. I imagine the châtelain (owner, lord of the manor and villages beyond) feeding them mice by hand, perhaps taking them toads from the vinegar cellar, but I somehow doubt it.

He's reluctant for me to leave, but I have work to do down in Cognac and it's a good hour south of here. I'm in the most northerly reaches of my secteur and know full well that my southern colleagues will not be in the slightest bit interested in visiting any of the properties this lovely gentleman is about to give me to sell. It will be my secteur in its entirety. I know they won't even be included in the Tuesday caravane's schedule. The future's rosé, a very nice wine, especially if it comes from Provence, or the Loire! We bid our au'revoirs and I promise to come back soon with clients.

I do, and for being prepared to venture so far afield, he gives me several others to market. Word spreads quickly, and I'm instructed to sell properties in another village not far from the château, but where the houses are mostly privately owned. The journey up here comes with much beauty and many advantages. As I get nearer, I see groups of deer wandering through the fields, some of them running, some stationary. I see masses of very large hares, and lots of impressive game birds sweeping over the newly harvested fields, decimating the local rabbit and mice population. I also get to know the people who own the little bistrôt in Néré, which becomes a useful stopping off place for lunch.

It has the added advantage of being British owned, and they run a lending library of English language books. Oh what joy!

German Officer's trunk in Varaize

13 Enemy Liaison in Varaize

My next instruction comes from the owner of a semi derelict
house in the little village of Varaize, not far from St Jean
d'Angely and very near to our own Commune of La
Brousse. It's another place my Cognac colleagues and
competitors won't be in the slightest bit interested in
visiting. It's a fair sized property, with its staircase still
intact, always a good start. The roof seems to be in
reasonable condition, and the rooms are all generously
proportioned. The garden stretches to almost half an acre
behind the property, and at the end of it are two more
ancient buildings, roofless, and looking as if a bomb may
have hit them. They have no windows, but the stone
structures of both are still in place. All this is located in the
little village square, with its imposing church at one end.
The boulodrome at the other end of the square is in full use,
and I see this whole set-up in a few years' time, proudly
renovated and providing good accommodation for a couple
developing a Bed and Breakfast business, with two very
generously sized gîtes at the bottom of the garden. There are
unlikely to be fairies. The Germans would have frightened
them away!

They've been here, that's for sure. I find an abandoned
German car amongst the ruins, and I know they've occupied
the main house, when I come across a German Officer's
trunk in what would have been the living room. It's locked,
shucks, I want to look inside. The key is no doubt back in its
Homeland, if its owner has survived to tell the tale. There
are lots of tales to tell about Varaize, and I've already
discovered one of them on a previous visit.

There's still a bakery in the village, which I use from time to time, and even a caramel maker. I've never been in a sweet factory before and, seeing me pass by, he invites me in. It's fascinating. He proudly explains how he makes the deliciously smelling toffees he's currently producing. However, I have no idea of what I am to hear later on from one of the other villagers. Word has got round that I've been asking loaded questions, based on the stone plaque on the wall of the house at the village crossroads. It serves as a poignant reminder of this little community of people when the War came to their front doors:

Ici est tombé le 14.6.44 à l'age de 21 ans Paul Etournaud Combattant F.T.P.F. Mort pour la France.

I'm told that the 'bon bon' maker's daughter slept with the enemy, and during her liaison with a young German soldier, told him that the baker's son was in the Résistance. He was shot. She had a baby with the German and their child (if rumour is correct) lives in East France somewhere, possibly Alsace. It was an Alsacien Regiment which was billeted nearby. She herself still lives in Varaize, perhaps she left and came back, but she's now an old woman and pretty much in solitary confinement from what I gather. Of course, this is all hearsay to me, may even be just village gossip, but the plaque is evidence that Paul Etournaud was indeed a Résistant.

As I go about mon metier here in Poitou Charentes, I come across more and more plaques on walls, commemorating the bravery of many young Frenchmen. I wonder what proportion of them were handed over to the Germans in this way. One of the oldest tricks in the book, sleeping with the enemy! The better the sex, the easier they'll find it to talk, disbelieving anyone who cajoles them into bed could be so cruel, although I somehow doubt their skills of seduction, German men no more noted for their passion than the British. But these girls' young French lads were away fighting, many already dead, and who so attentive could do anything so ordinarily alien to human nature as these tall, well fed (they weren't on the Russian Front, and Poitou Charentes still had plentiful supplies of corn, cows and cognac) and more powerful invaders? But it was war and we must remember that, and not throw the first stone, at least not until we've searched the sand beneath.

As I return through the fields to the Agence, I suddenly drive through swarms of mosquitoes, appearing as if they are airborne clouds of mist encircling the car at low level. My mind is awash, not with the 'mossies' and working the windscreen wipers at full speed, but with what I'm learning as I drive to these remote little towns and villages, trying to keep a balanced view on what I hear. Perhaps the ugliest tale I'm told, and which supposedly happened not far from Varaize, is when, not all that long ago, a German car pulled up outside a house on the main road to St Jean d'Angely. The owners assumed the people inside the car were lost, and emerged from their home to offer the driver and his wife help with directions. This was, after all, about half a century after the War ended, and most people have been trying their best to not necessarily forget (that's a tall order for many, and I don't believe these things should be forgotten) but to forgive, to understand, and to move forward united:

"No, that is not the case. I just want to show my wife the spot where I killed my first Frenchman."

His reasons for revisiting are perhaps best not asked.

The mosquitoes have gone, but the sound of guns is now all around me. It's Wednesday afternoon and that means the Chasse is out in force. It's a generic name for one and everyone who hunts, and Wednesdays and Sundays are the given days for World War Three to sound as if it's breaking out. On Sundays, we try and leave Esset as early as we can in the morning. Megan's labrador mum is a working gun dog, but Megan has all the characteristics of a slightly nervous at times collie, which is what her father is, a working sheep dog on the adjacent farm in Wales to her mother, one of the Sandringham Strain no less. She hates bangs and one of the good things about living in France, in the sticks of the Commune of La Brousse, is that we are so far away from civilisation that we don't have to suffer the fireworks on Guy Fawke's Night, and then on New Year's Eve, in Hereford. We spend our first couple of months rejoicing about this, until September comes and gunfire spoils our Sunday peace, and terrifies Megan, who refuses to step outside the house. So we go to the beach, the nearest one a forty minute drive away at Châtelaillon Plage, but the distance seems nothing and the roads are virtually empty. C'est la France.

The first couple of times we do this, she remembers what she's left behind and has to be coaxed out of the car. She's a highly intelligent wuffit. It becomes a real problem, but we eventually overcome it and she's ecstatic to loll in the sea like a polar bear between ice caps. It becomes a regular Sunday outing, but I work on Wednesdays, so she and Spouse are left to sort it out between them. I imagine she spends most of the day under a bed. She's lucky, many dogs here are not.

As soon as the chasse season starts, not only are people accidentally shot out in the field, some fatally, but an English lady from a neighbouring village ends up in Urgence (Accident & Emergency) in St Jean d'Angely, from driving with her arm out of the car window and suffering a stray bullet hitting it. The local papers are full of chasse accidents happening every week, and I'm not at all surprised. Most chasseurs (hunters) stay pretty much next to the road, too lazy to venture far from their cars. This is sheer stupidity, and highly risky for both ramblers (don't do it) and passing motorists alike! Completely lacking in lateral thinking (more an English characteristic than a French one) they also fail to realise that their dogs may get run over by passing vehicles. Thus, driving on chasse days comes with many dangers, not only to the 'game' they are supposedly attempting to kill, rather than themselves, but to all the rest of us. Stay home, or go to the beach!

Many a French hunter cares not about his dog. He may think he does, but this is not apparent. He may be slightly more attentive to it if he only has the one, but many of them have a whole kennel load. These poor creatures more often than not live in the most despicable conditions, often with bedding less kennels (some straw if they're lucky) and so much shit in their runs that they have no choice but to walk on it, feed on it, and relieve themselves on it all over again. They live this way for most of the year, only experiencing freedom during the chasse season, and then only once or twice a week. No wonder so many of them get lost!

Our village notice board has pretty much a weekly bulletin of chasse dogs found abandoned and in the Maire's holding kennel. It's his responsibility to take strays in, before handing them over to the police, who in turn hand them over to the dog pounds. If lucky, the dogs have a slight chance of ending up with the S.P.A. (equivalent of the R.S.P.C.A.) where they are kept until new homes are found for them. Some don't get this far, often killed on the roads before they are finally rescued. Sadly, this is not a rare sight.

Fortunately, not all French people treat their dogs this way, including those who shoot, and our immediate neighbours certainly treat theirs well, both father and son with house dogs trained to the gun. However, in my job, I see more and more badly treated dogs, specifically in the countryside. I ask one of my French colleagues about this, and she tells me repeatedly that:

"The French often have two dogs, one to kick and one to cuddle."

She's not far off the mark, as I often realise when I'm measuring up a garden with a kennel at one end, and in that kennel may be the most beautiful English Setter, German Pointer, local hunting dog, all affection and 'get me out of here eyes,' and then Madame will emerge from the house with a yappy little Yorkshire Terrier or some such under her arm. How does the big dog know he's not for loving? It never ceases to appall me, upset me deeply, but I think I've covered this ground already, so I'll shut up!

14 Offally Awful Lunch, Divine Chocolate Shop

I've had a good run of instructions, so I need to concentrate on finding some clients to buy them. It's Tuesday, and we have no less than eleven properties to inspect, so with the ones I've brought to the market place from up in my 'Northern Territories,' which are predictably not included today, that amounts to a pretty impressive portfolio amongst us. We set off after our morning sales' meeting, which comes after the thirty three kisses, so it's getting on for ten o'clock before we're even on the road. We all have town properties to 'show and tell' as they do in primary schools these days, so it's lunchtime before we know it. Heading off east in search of the feast which may be awaiting us, she who runs the office books us into a seriously uninviting canteen type place beside the main road to Jarnac, a gorgeous little riverside town and the home of Courvoisier cognac.

The owner's a nice enough chap, very cheerful, very polite, shakes all our hands, pas de problemo. Popular with the resident Expats in these parts, he kindly arranges log deliveries for them. However, I can't understand why we're not driving the extra ten minutes into Jarnac itself, where there are several perfectly acceptable and good restaurants per se. Called le Grizzly, this is not somewhere Yogi Bear himself would be keen on patronising, or maybe he and Boo Boo would. After all, bears are carnivores. The formule is the stuff hairy workmen may enjoy, but those of us with more delicate palates most definitely struggle. It's all offal, and lapin (rabbit) and gésier salads, which translates as a mound of gizzards scattered on top of the lank lettuce leaves the rabbit would have been partial to eating before being put in the pot. They refuse to make me an omelette, so I struggle with a plate of pickled grated carrot and celery from the buffet, declining the spread of fatty charcuterie. I leave hungry and with another ten euros thrown down the drain. Oh for some decent pub grub, or just a delectable mid-day sandwich from Louise's fabulous little place in Church Street, Hereford. Prawns and rocket in wholemeal bread would do nicely, and maybe a piece of carrot cake. Yum!

I'm beginning to get increasingly sensitive to criticism. My colleagues can, and do, criticise the English on a daily basis, to my face. Woe be tide me if I dare to utter a single negative remark at, or towards, the French and especially their food. They can reduce me to internal tears in an instant, and there are times when I feel my defence mechanisms breaking down under the strain of it all. It's not easy being the minority, the one and only minority. Suggestions on how they could improve their cuisine? Forget it! As I'm sitting amongst my carnivore extraordinaire colleagues, watching tripe and various other forms of animal intestines being devoured with great gusto, I imagine the list of questions I'd pose, were I able to:

Why don't the French use the saucers provided to put their wet tea and coffee spoons on? It's so much easier to wash a saucer, than a table cloth!

Why do they only have silly little tea spoons to eat their puddings with, even if they are fruit pies? Why not a decent sized spoon, and a dessert fork?

Why don't they use side plates? Why do they use the same plate and cutlery throughout the meal?

Why are they allowed to place raw meat and cooked meat for sale in the same tray? (Oh yes they do!)

Why do they consider it polite to lick their knives between courses and then use the same knife to cut the communal cheese? (I see this on a regular basis!)

Why can't men and women have their own 'loos?' (Do we actually WANT to see men pee? I don't think so!)

Why don't they wash their hands after they've used the 'loo?' (Watch this one, it's the norm, especially for men!)

It's all a bit much, and my thoughts trail off into how this has all happened.

"Allez ooop" shouts the boss, and we all jump to attention and follow her out of the restaurant, finished or not. She chooses her 'favourite' female of the day, usually the youngster, links arms with her, and they swagger off to her car together. I get to sit next to he who's just eaten tripe, again! Lucky old me!

It's not as if I can open a window, not unless I want to be eaten by the swarm of mosquitoes buzzing all around us. And there are vinegar flies everywhere, tiny little black dashy things which stick to pale coloured clothing like glue. They also get into picture frames! But this is cognac country, and the vines are everywhere. Colleague who speaks English thinks I'm decidedly odd to be so enthralled with them, and shouts at me:

116

"You're crazy! How can you say that? They just look like fields of sticks."

They may well do in winter, but now they are a beautiful kaleidoscope of purples, whites and greens. I find them magical, majestic, marvellous!

We stop in Jarnac, where we should have been all along in my opinion, and inspect a house put on by the tripe eater. Oh what heaven, it's the work place and home of a chocolatier, glacier, and patissier (he who makes chocolates, ice creams, bread and pastries) and the strong smell of chocolate is such sweet relief. With a delightful looking little restaurant right next door, and lots of tempting shops in the immediate vicinity, this is an elegant home in the making, perfectly equipped for sophisticated town living. Complete with two living rooms and four bedrooms above the shop, and a stone's throw from the River Charente, I can't wait to write it up. Whoever buys it will be able to lease the ground floor, hopefully to another chocolatier and croissant maker. He who eats all things offally awful has put it on at less than a hundred thousand euros, including our agency fees into the bargain! I would have probably gone in at double, but then I don't really know Jarnac sufficiently well yet. I vow to change that tout de suite and it won't be a problem. I like the place, a lot!

The next property we see, is the actual home where former President François Mitterand was born. A very unassuming little town house, it is nevertheless an historian's gem. It's in total need of renovation, a mere two main rooms, a kitchen, and a shower room on the first floor, but with a double garage beneath, complete with a men's urinal and wash basin. This, of course, means there's a plumbing system installed, be it somewhat primitive. I imagine this to have been a workshop at one point, long before cars were owned by ordinary folk. With its own terrace at the back of the house, ideal for sipping a glass of Courvoisier after a hard day at the office, or a day's sightseeing along the River Charente, this won't take long to move, either. The price? Less than seventy thousand euros, our fees included. Come and buy!

Join the exodus of Brits leaving Blighty. It won't last forever, I doubt for more than a decade. The tides eventually turn. Although I occasionally get younger buyers, mine are mostly in their sixties and newly retired. Move them forward ten years, and they'll want to return to the bosoms of their families. It's what happens! I've seen it from my desk in Hereford, returning Expat waifs with little money to spend, sadly swapping stone piles full of character, complete with stunning swimming pools and glorious scenery, for 'shoeboxes,' just to be back near their loved ones.

I've recovered from the grossness of the greasy Grizzly's food, and with the aromas from the Chocolatérie still dizzying my tastebuds, am happy to sit in whichever car I'm allotted to. I just hope we get back to the Agence quickly, at least before the working day ends. I have clients to call, appointments to make. I'll be burning the midnight oil, too, writing up the houses I've seen in Jarnac.

The following morning, I arrive at the Agence early, to be met by blasted holiday makers; "ooh, look, that's a nice house. Let's go in and ask if we can see it." Now they're behind me, waiting for me to turn the key in the lock and follow me in. I'm not very happy about this. I tell them that the owners are on holiday. It's a lie, but a necessary one which usually works. Not with these two, who see through me on my last try; "what, all your owners!" I lose, I apologise profusely and palm them off with lots of lovely brochures and a promise to see them again, when they've sold their house in Northampton. I know I've lost the plot with them, but also that they haven't the slightest intention of making the move to France. It's easy to spot time wasters, and we seldom get it wrong, trying to remain polite as we wish them away, and not always succeeding, like now!

I dash round to the Domaine du Breuil to pick up the couple I've booked in for a whole day's serious house hunting. They have an appetising budget of seven hundred and fifty thousand euros, give or take a hundred thousand, and this is just to be their country pad. Life can be so unfair at times, but then who'd want to slave away in London when life can be spent meandering through vineyards by day, and swimming under the stars as the sun goes down?

We start off in the middle of the Grande Champagne region of the Southern Charente, where all the major cognac producers own most of the land. The scenery is spectacular in places, and here, nestling at the bottom of a hill, surrounded by hectares of luscious vineyards, is a glorious old cognac estate up for sale. The views are outstanding, whichever way I look, and particularly in one direction over towards the ancient castle ruins at Bouteville. It's only a few minutes drive to the little town of Châteauneuf sur Charente, which will supply all their daily needs, and they'll be in Angoulême in less than half an hour. The TGV will offer them several choices of travel times back to London. All sorted. Move on!

The main house dates back to the sixteenth century, when France was ruled by the mighty Bourbon Dynasty. Their kings became less popular as time moved on, but Henri IV especially left an impression still seen by many of the French as highly admirable. Responsible for the Edict of Nantes in 1594, Protestants were now at liberty to worship throughout the Kingdom, hence the growing population of Huguenots in Poitou Charentes. Henri, himself, was one of them but became a token Roman Catholic when he succeeded to the Throne.

If you're ever in La Rochelle, visit the Protestant Museum in the centre of that glorious coastal city. Protestantism is still alive and well throughout the whole Région, and we even have a French Protestant Church in Matha. There's also one just along the road from where Mitterand was born, in Jarnac. Henri did a great deal for the silk and cloth manufacturing industries in the northern cities of France, drained the marshlands of the south west, including the Marais Poitevin, just a bit inland from La Rochelle, and encouraged vast waves of economic activity. He not only gave orders for several châteaux to be built, but gave his blessing on a rich, rural landscape of country house elegance and style all over the Country. Thus, many grand houses sprung up wherever there was wealth, and cognac is a far from new beverage!

Personally, I rather like a soupçon (a little) of Hennessy XO from time to time, and often pass through their vineyards as part of my normal working day. The Hennessy Museum in Cognac itself is on the tourist trail for our visitors, although Spouse usually has that pleasure. One of us has to work! The Hennessy Family has been in the Charente since the seventeenth century, and fled here as part of what is generally known as The Flight Of The Irish Earls. Oliver Cromwell, our own great republican (oh yes, England actually had a short spell without a monarch) caused so much mayhem in Ireland that those who could leave, left! A bit like the Potato Famine two centuries later, although not quite as good a comparison to make, given the vast discrepancy in the little matter of available money to spend by the emigrants. And so the Hennessy Clan moved to France, very sensibly so, given their success ever since. Their home is very lovely, but not in the slightest bit pretentious, and when the elderly Madame Hennessy died recently, her husband had flowers put on every single grave in the local cemetery where she is laid to rest. I think back to our time in Hong Kong, when every Chinese meal ended with round upon round of 'yam sings' whilst copious amounts of cognac were consumed in half pint tumblers. It always baffled me how men of often such little physical stature had the capacity to knock it back and remain standing, but that they did! Rémy Martin seemed to hold the Hong Kong Chinese market back then in the 1970s. It was before the Dutchman from Segonzac started trading! However, it was a very dear Chinese doctor friend of ours who introduced me to Hennessy XO. Thank you, Jon!

We spend all morning at this beautiful cognac estate at Bouteville and my clients are totally entranced with everything they see, not only the main house but its glorious swimming pool, two gîtes and six barns. It'd be a snip at half the price, and as it stands, probably costing less than an artisan's terraced house in Notting Hill, or a four bedroomed Edwardian villa in Leytonstone. It's on the 'up' you know! If you work in 'the city,' you'd be daft not to buy there. Tube right to Canary Wharf, and a short hop to City Airport.

With a lot to think about, they suggest lunch, their treat, nice people! He's a golfer, so what better place to take them to than Cognac Golf Club, method in my madness, which often pays off. Many a deal has been clinched whilst sipping a refreshing glass of cold vin blanc on the sun terrace overlooking the 18th hole, with its backcloth of rolling countryside beyond. It's exceedingly lovely, and was the original home of the Martell Family, yet more cognac barons. My clients are happy. I'm happy. How could I not be? What a job!

The food is generally excellent here, with the exception to the rule already mentioned, when Spouse and Son-in-Law got very excited at the prospect of a traditional English Sunday Roast. Lunch over, and it's 'up north' again, this time only slightly, but north of Cognac nonetheless. To an equestrian estate in Macqueville, within budget and complete with several excellent stables, indoor and outdoor schooling rings, gîte, pool, and over two hectares of land.

The house itself is a traditional maison de maître of great standing, and its presence is glorified by the sweeping driveway leading up to it. This should impress! Actually, it doesn't! Having worked in the country house market on both sides of the Welsh Borders for several years before coming to France, I realise only too often that these equestrian mansions are often the scene of domestic laissez-faire inside, and this one comes into that bracket. It only needs a facelift, easy enough to do, but these clients are not prepared to even lift a paint brush, or have somebody lift one for them, so it's onwards and upwards to Bagnizeau, passing through Matha en route. I know the next one is immaculate, perfectly presented at all times, and in tip top condition throughout. It's one of my own instructions, a heaven sent 'double' if I can pull it off. Let's give it a try!

Bagnizeau is a bit of a British Outpost, so I'm hoping this won't put my clients off. I have to point out the advantages of having key holders they can converse with, people to help them settle in before their French takes off adequately. It seldom does, but I shan't tell them that. It's also a rather cluttered village, with several grand houses lurking behind almost hidden alleyways, and lots of little old houses of more humble origins. But this means it's an easy place to find an army of cleaners and gardeners, and they'll need at least one of each variety.

The main house is upside down, with the ground floor giving way to two very large bedrooms and a magnificent bathroom, reminding me of some of those from our Far Eastern adventures, not least The Oriental Hotel in Bangkok. The tiling is exquisite, imported from Bangladesh of all places, and the fittings are glorious, no other word for them. It gets even better upstairs, directly entering a baronial living room fit for a duke's country retreat. It oozes style and pure sophistication, good planning, and yet comfortable family living, and this is very much a family home.

The magnificent dining table seats a dozen with space to stretch arms in between courses, and the piano displays family life through photos taken in Ceylon, some of them shot before Independence allowed them to rename it Sri Lanka. The kitchen is a chef's dream come true, and the lady owner is one expert curry queen. I know. She has us to dinner on more than one occasion. Her husband is still 'out East,' so she's doing everything solo and it's all becoming rather silly. More bedrooms complete upstairs in the main house, but this 'estate' can sleep a good many others. There are no less than four more houses, and not one, but two swimming pools. One's reserved for family use, the other for the gîte residents, who also have a games' barn at their disposal, complete with BBQ and Bar area. It's amazing, within budget, but do my clients like it? Nope! Lost again!

Three top of the market properties to see in one day, spread many miles apart, is all that's ever possible to fit into a day's viewing. My hopes pin on the first one, and they're flying back to London tomorrow, which means they've no time left to see 'the Competition,' at least not this visit. I drive them back to Cognac, silly really, given that Bagnizeau is just a few minutes from La Brousse, but it's all part of the service. I drop them off back at the Domaine du Breuil, and decide to pop in and say "bon jour" to the owners, "bon soir" actually. Because they are such delightful people, running an establishment par excellence, I've given them seventeen bookings this year so far, and some of those have been for stays of more than just the usual two or three nights. With the bookings come lots of dinner reservations for them, too, and Spouse and I are often invited to join my buyers on the nights of their legal completions. The food is fabulous, a pure delight with every mouthful. Hence I'm over the moon when I'm presented with a letter of introduction to their sister hotel, a brochure, and an invitation to spend a weekend there, gratuit. It looks stunning. I can't wait to book it
.

So off we set for The Lot. That's a Département (county) further down in South West France, in the Région of the Midi-Pyrenées. Wow!

Typical Charentaise Maison de Maître near Cognac

Gambetta, Cahors

125

15 Cahors, The Lot, Rocamadour

We leave early, but take our time driving down, stopping at a little café en route. It's Saturday morning, but the place is typically deserted. It's exceedingly hot, so much so that the atlas I've left on the dashboard of the car has fallen apart in the short time it's taken us to drink our coffee. The binding has completely disintegrated. I shall have to buy a new one, but it's all we've got for now. We by-pass Bergerac (stayed there before and were totally unimpressed) and turn due south, direction Villeneuve sur Lot. Villeneuve is famous for its prunes and its hazelnuts, and for keeping the English at bay during the Anglo-French wars. Even Richard The Lionheart lived nearby! It's a bastide, a walled hill town with great fortifications, and makes a lasting impression from whichever angle it's viewed. We don't stop. Hunger's setting in. We find our way to Tournon d'Agenais, another one of many of the bastides the Lot is famous for, and well worth visiting. It's very beautiful, and we're reminded of Tuscany, of Volterra in particular. Both towns, thousands of miles apart, offer spectacular views over the countryside below. Overwhelmed by its beauty, and wondering why we didn't settle here, a normal reaction to professional nomads such as us, we buy baguettes and beverages, and refresh ourselves on a bench by one of the old stone walls, soaking in the amazing atmosphere, and vistas.

Next stop, Montaigu de Quercy, where we wander around the little town and get our bearings to reach the Château de l'Hoste. It's the perfect country retreat, oozing rustic charm mixed with modern day finesse. It's also the first hotel in France where we've found tea and coffee making facilities in the room, which itself is énorme. With every little attention to detail accomplished, superb level of comfort, a bathroom big enough to walk around in (unusual in French hotels), comfy slouching into chairs, and a balcony to complete the feeling of well being, this will do very nicely, thank you Domaine du Breuil. It's divine, the grounds, the swimming pool, and dinner later on.

On Sunday, we find an outdoor market in Montcuq. Spouse is in paradise, able to buy all the spices he can't up in St Jean d'Angely, or Cognac, or Saintes. The whole little town is incredibly atmospheric, colourful, and everything a French Sunday morning market should be. We adjourn for lunch in the town square, which is actually round! Montcuq is to all intents and purposes a naturally evolved amphitheatre without the lions. Ah, but we see horses. Their riders dismount and tether them to specially provided posts just a few feet from the terrace where we're having lunch. They go inside the restaurant, much to my surprise. I'd be wanting to sit where I could see my horse, but obviously horse rustling is unknown in these civilised parts. It's all amazing and I could stay here all day, forever, but we have our sights set on Cahors.

Cahors is the capital of the Quercy region, proudly straddling the River Lot. Its famous bridge, often shown on wine bottles and nowadays only passable on foot (it's mediaeval so I guess they're afraid of it collapsing) is a splendid structure of square towers and soft looking gentle arches. It's a bridge to remember, but then I'm passionate about bridges. Good old King Henry IV is remembered in the town centre, but so is Guiseppe Garibaldi. He's the Italian guy who got together with Camillo Cavour (he was a count) and Guiseppe Mazzini. The three of them redesigned

Italy, led the Risorgimento which unified the various kingdoms, and in 1861 created Italy as we know it today. Perhaps Cahor's most honoured hero, though, is Léon Gambetta, presumably of Italian stock originally. Many of them are! He was the chap who was largely responsible for the creation of France's Third Republic in 1871, following its Emperor's fall in 1870 at the start of the Franco Prussian War. Poor old Napoleon the Third! We sit and have iced cold tea in the square, beneath Gambetta's statue. If it were evening, we'd be drinking the local vino, full blooded, deep red, very smooth, and unfortunately very alcoholic! Cahors wine is delicious, I love it, but it's not one to imbibe without food.

We take the opportunity of staying with ex Hereford friends after we leave the Château de l'Hoste, now living in Lascabanes, not far from Montcuq. She and I used to dog walk together on the Bishop's Meadows, next to the River Wye. Sadly, Sally, their beautiful old wuffit died shortly after they moved to France, and Megan has a friend looking after her back in Esset, so we are dogless when we meet up again. They have a cat, so do we, but of course the cats never met! Their house is in an idyllic situation, surrounded by glorious countryside, but it's a bit isolated. A bigger change from Hereford than Esset is for us, but they've owned it for several years and are très bien installé (well settled).

Next stop for us, Rocamadour! We can't pass by and not detour into it, so we head off the motorway from Cahors and follow the signs. We get it wrong, and end up on the opposite side of the precipice. No worries, it means we can see it in all its cliff hanging splendour, admittedly from afar, from the restaurant terrace, but I've more chance of soaking in its ambience than I had in San Gimignano! On our way to Pisa Airport one famous morning, we stopped at the gates of the town with its fourteen towers, short of time, and I was told I had:

"Five minutes to take a look."

Fat chance! Spouse is a travelling moron at times.

Rocamadour should be cited as one of the Wonders of the World, and I've gone and lost the tourist tray I bought. Shucks, I really liked that tray. We'll have to go back there some day and buy another one, choosing the correct side of the gorge to follow to find the town itself! Because we've got it wrong, I can't say much about it, but it clings to the cliff majestically and is famous for its shrine dedicated to Mary, Jesus's mum, and constructed by (not very well known and I have no idea who he was) Saint Amadour. In 1166, Amadour's body was found, still intact, and from then until now, Rocamadour has been an important place for pilgrims. Looking at the steepness of the climb to reach the top of the rock and its abbey, I imagine many of those thus moved by such things, will win several months off their time in Purgatory, that's if they believe in the place! Joking aside, it's well worth a visit, located just off the main north to south motorway, about three quarters of the way down France. There's no point in giving the name of the motorway, as numbers and names of them seem to change pretty much annually in France!

We decide to take the B roads back home, passing right through Sarlat la Canéda, a very pretty town and one loved by the British in Dordogneshire, where we now are. Passing the River Dordogne and its rocky outlets complete with caves and megalithic dwellings (very impressive and you can't miss them) we eventually arrive in Riberac, just in time for an afternoon cuppa. Riberac is full of Brits, so many that on market day not only are the customers speaking English, but the stallholders frequently ARE English. It's the place to come if you need a plumber, an electrician, a 'builder' (aren't they all) but check their credentials first! There's many a man who's employed a man who hasn't seen a man about getting legal, and hospitals can be very expensive, and equally unsympathetic, when an illegal immigrant has fallen off a ladder, even if they happen to speak the Queen's English!

Time off work's fine, and it's been great fun, but as we cross the border into Charente Maritime, my mind turns back to the Agence, to the morrow. St Jean d'Angely comes quickly upon us, and I have clients booked in for me at Cognac, looking for premises large enough to provide a home cinema, complete with the real seats, a candy floss maker, and a champagne cooler for those who don't like choc-ices. Funnily enough, the first house I'm planning to take them to is owned by a couple itching to move down to The Lot, to where we've just been. They live in the back of beyond, not far from Beauvais sur Matha, so a little bit more noise is unlikely to bother the natives. They also have one gigantic barn, absolutely perfect for converting into a cinema.
A demain (bring on tomorrow).

16 Rouillac Market, Kennels & Fleas

They not only decide to buy the house in Ranville Breuillaud (to give it its full name) on the spot, but aren't really up for viewing any others. Two lots of happy clients, and they are all mine. Makes a change! Of course, it leaves me with the ghastly task of 'phoning the next RDVs and cancelling them, never a pleasant part of the job. I drive them back to the Domaine du Breuil and leave them to explore Cognac, suggesting both the Hennessy Museum, and Otard's, once the home, indeed the birth place, of King François the First. Both of the museums are close neighbours, down on the banks of the River Charente. François belonged to the Valois Dynasty, the ones who reigned just before the Bourbons.

He was born in Cognac in 1494 and was quite a warrior king, defeating the Swiss at the Battle of Marignano (between Milan and Pavia) and then the Italians in Milan itself. His luck continued, and he went on to defeat the Italians in Naples. However, his own demise was not long round the corner, when he met his downfall back up north again in Pavia, resulting in the signing of the Treaty of Madrid in 1525. Not happy about having to do this, he turned his eyes eastwards and palled up with Suliman, the turbulent Turk, and the pair of them went on to create mayhem together. He had some good points, and appreciated the arts, giving his patronage to Leonardo da Vinci amongst others. Like most French people of means, he adored his châteaux and commissioned Chambord in the Loire Valley, and Fontainebleau, on the River Seine in the Département de Ile de France. That's the one which takes in Paris at its centre, and is also home to Versailles, so you could do them both on the same trip. Remember France is a big country, though, so don't try and do them on the same day. You can't!

One of the pleasures of my job is to roam the countryside looking for 'AV' signs. Translated, 'AV' means 'For Sale' and it's becoming more and more the norm to sell property this way in France. This is driven by the buyers, who pay all the agency and legal fees on real estate transactions. Hence, if they can buy privately, they save themselves a lot of money, especially as some agencies charge 12% and occasionally more. We come in quite cheaply, averaging a mere 7%, but that can represent a lot of money saved if they avoid us. Legal fees range from 6% up to 20% and these are not avoidable. It's not just the purchase price buyers have to take into consideration, but they do need to be able to hold their own with the French Language if they wish to pursue the 'AV' route, and very few can do that. Of course, if the sellers are English speakers, then no problemo, but few of them are and those who exist are usually happy to use agencies. Most selling Brits are elderly and far from computer literate, thankfully! The Rural French and technology? Naaah, a long way to go yet and they stand no chance in these deserted outposts, where Broadband has yet to arrive. So, it all provides the chance to add to my portfolio, and it's a nice day.

I head for Rouillac, an up and coming town north east of Cognac and host to one of the most famous open air markets in Poitou Charentes, on the 27th of every month, come rain or come shine. Don't go if you don't like seeing hundreds of caged poultry struggling to stay alive in the summer heat, or freezing to near death in winter. The temperatures here come in two extremes, very hot and very cold. We even have stalactites and stalagmites in our garden every January, brrrrrr . And in summer, the water in the pool is so darned hot, it's certainly not the place to cool down. Inside the house beneath the ceiling fans is our only escape, with the shutters closed to keep the cool in. Few realise this when they choose to buy here, and we fell into the same category. There's many a retired couple who wished they'd chosen Inverness!

Rouillac is not in my secteur, so I carry on to Sonneville, which is. It's all very lovely round here, and I stop the car and watch a field of donkeys. One of them is lying down, with all the others gathering around her (?). I worry, but I needn't, and the next time I pass by (2 days later, deliberately) I see her on all fours, accompanied by her foal. It just goes to show how much a collection of animals can work together, whether they be a flock of sheep, a herd of cows, or whatever a group of horses or donkeys are labelled. I often stop and watch cows grooming one another, snuggling up together, sometimes a couple licking each other. From what I can see, they mostly have a good life in France, until they are killed! I am frequently saddened, though, to see horses and donkeys left in endless solitary confinement here. They are pack animals and need company. If I had an spare acre or two, I'd adopt a couple myself.

No 'AV' signs in Sonneville, but I spot a beauty in Neuvicq le Château. The clue's in the name, and what's left of the original château remains in pristine condition and is used as the Mairie (town hall) and Bibliothèque (library). The house is a stone's throw away, and the owners are perfectly happy for me to market it for them. I do it there and then, sales documentation, clipboard and camera all part of my travelling kit. This will appeal to the British buyers, just a couple of minutes from the bakery, and the morning baguette seems to be of utmost importance to the vast majority. Goodness only knows why! French bread goes stale by lunchtime. Most of us make our own or buy it sliced via visiting house guests, along with the tea bags and baked beans they bring out.

I have one more stop to make before I leave Neuvicq, and it's at the Balluet family's cognac distillery. Their products are a fraction of the price of Tony Blair's Frapin, Hennessy's XO et al, and taste wonderful. They've been here since 1845 and I can't recommend them highly enough. For us locals, armed with cash, they'll give us 2 for 1, knowing we'll continue supporting them. I put two bottles of their forty year old nectar in the car, but not until I've tagged on to a small group of tourists, and left some of my visiting cards by the till.

Neuvicq is too near the teeny little hamlet of le Breuil Batard not to call in and have a cuppa with some of my first clients. They've transformed their already pretty from the outside Charentaise home into what the 'French dream' is all about, and it's now delightful inside as well. I'm welcomed with open arms and am happy that they are happy! This is not a couple I'll have to avoid in the supermarket, and they've become good friends. We sit outside the old pigs' quarters half way down the garden and now cleverly disguised by flowering bushes, and look across the garden to the Romanesque swimming pool in progress. It's stunning, a perfect square, just like the print on their dining room wall.

This garden was the pits when I sold them the house, and the first thing they had to contend with was a plague of fleas. The motley group of chasse dogs, as ever confined to outside kennelling, must have been home to millions of them. I had no idea. No-one had, until the outbuildings were disturbed, and then the whole house was swarming with them. The infestation spread at such an alarming rate, causing such great itching in the process, that Professionals had to be called in tout de suite.

Quelle horreur, mais c'est normale!

Montcuq on Market Day

17 Team Tuesdays & Foul Formules

It's not only fleas some of my buyers have to contend with, although we who bought in Poitou Charentes back in 2002 also inherited enough to support several flea circuses, as well as beams semi rotten with ancient woodworm infestation. Serves us right, we should have bought in Italy! The next one is alive with bees which have spread their territory from the outbuildings to the main house. They must have been dormant when I measured up the property, as I saw none, and the owners said nothing. Of course not, they needed to sell!

This is particularly embarrassing as the house is in our village of Esset, where I naturally begin to get a fair few instructions. It's utterly charming, a typically large Charentaise family home, in an elegant Bourgeoise style, and recently modernised into the bargain. It comes with an open barn, several outbuildings, and a two story cottage, ideal if my current potential purchasers wish to bring Granny with them! They don't; she's not old enough yet. The swimming pool is a large in ground one, and the generous garden will be ideal for children used to living in an apartment block in the Far East, not quite the snazzy Hong Kong of my youth, but where there's an equal amount of modern day pollution to cope with. Their father's here on his own, and we meet up in Matha initially. He's very relaxed and easy to get on with, delightfully describing his two young children to me. I immediately put my big size 7 feet in it and say:

"At least he's not called Arthur"

when I'm told his son's name is Stanley. (Apologies to all those who are!) A tad embarrassed himself, and offering a wide grin, he annouces:

"That's his middle name!"

They are all coming back, the Wilfreds, the Alfreds and Sidneys; the Elsies, Maisies and Daisies. Poor kids! I laugh as I inwardly recite Stanley Holloway's poem about Albert and the Lion:

"There were one great big lion called Wallace ..."

Oh no, please, don't do that! And next time round will be the Dereks, Erics, Normans and Kens; the Doreens, Paulines, Maureens and, oh no, they couldn't, not Beryl and Horace. Names, forever as cyclical as the weather, or the economy!

Current client's wife has set him free, with strict instructions to buy a house in France. Oh yes, he's on his own, and I find this highly unnerving. He's not the first client in this situation. I tot up a fair few of them, including the one with the house alive with fleas in Le Breuil Batard. No way on this earth, or any other, would I fall for that one and I can't imagine many women who would.

He only views one other property, and doesn't like where it is. Nor do I, but obviously I have to do my best for all my selling clients, even those in the villages between Matha and Cognac, many of which are depressingly dowdy and run down. He says he'll do the deal on the one in Esset with the bees he's not yet found out they'll be sharing it with. He's happy, I'm happy, his wife's happy with the photos I insist he emails to her from my office, and he signs the paperwork. Phew, another double! I make an appointment to visit the sellers for them to sign the copious number of pages in the sales' documentation, and they are over the moon. They get the asking price, in line with virtually every sale we make this year.

The market's good, but it's got to fall soon. I've worked through two booms and two recessions in my working life in England, and suspect a downward spiral here in France any moment now. She who runs the office is oblivious to market trends, just as she seems to be totally oblivious to her husband's philandering. She's not the only office philanderer, though. The youngster's playing away, too. Silly girl!

I try and broach the subject of the economic predictions for the housing market in France, as far as British buyers are concerned often fuelled by huge City bonuses, but they are beginning to dry up. About time, too! I'm totally against the philosophy behind them, but have to admit that many of my sales would probably not have happened without them. C'est la vie (that's life).

We're team lunching, it's Tuesday again, and we're in a restaurant in Cognac which my colleagues think is Italian. It isn't. The pizzas are dreadful, and the pasta is congealed. The ambience is cheerful enough, the place is always clean, especially the 'loos,' but if the food's lacking, what's the point of nice decor? Why we use the Duguesclin so often, I have no idea. The chap wasn't even a Charentais. A noble Breton, he defeated England's Thomas of Canterbury in a duel in Dinan, or so legend has it. I didn't know old Thomas had even crossed the Channel, but the statue in the fabulous mediaeval town of Dinan is obviously proof that not only did he, but that he lost the battle.

There's a guy at the next table eating tagliatelle with his fingers. She who runs the office picks her nose, in full view of us all. Not only does she pick it, but she then examines the snot, obviously sufficiently hard for her to throw over her shoulder. I joke not! My mind wanders uncontrollably back to what I find hard about living in France, working in France, having to keep quiet about in France, and feeling forever English. It's not a good day, but Tuesdays seldom are.

He who eats tripe has put a joke in my mailbox. I find it when we finally get back to the Agence. It's a penis, a 'stiff willy.' Am I supposed to laugh? It's pathetic, and he instantly loses any brownie points he's gained. Of course it's nothing to when he pees in the front garden of a house we're inspecting. And then, to cap it all, a young male colleague follows suit, and just as he's about to do the same, he who used to be a policeman sees me giving him the 'evil eye' and thinks better of it. Youngster who's already cheating on hard working husband, not only finds it all amusing, but as the afternoon progresses asks he who eats tripe to stop the car, and hurries off to shamelessly relieve herself in the village church yard. I wonder if Molière wrote about such things!

She who's become a friend tells me the story of how, when they were living in England, they took her father to London to see the sights, as one does. On approaching Buckingham Palace, he asks to be let out of the car. Thinking he wants to photograph the Queen's 'Des. Res.' they oblige. He pees! Oh yes he does! Her English husband would have joined ranks with Queen Victoria in being "not amused!" It is, however, a story which continues to amuse many.

"Allez ooop" nose picking boss shouts, and up we shoot. I walk back to the Agence. Enough's enough! But, sadly, it isn't. I'm yet to find the 'stiff willy' in my mailbox! It gets worse. The following morning, I discover a pornographic shot of a naked woman, bum in the air, a fat one of course. The stupid bit of rubbish meant to annoy me, also comes with some linguistic caption I don't even attempt to read. I bin it, pretend it doesn't exist, and whosoever's the culprit can sulk as much as he likes. He's not winning this round and he deserves no less than being sent to Coventry! Of course that means the lot of them, except the lovely guy who's gay. How come they're always so nice!

18 Americans in Weobley

The War brought many new people to many new, far flung, countries for them. In Weobley, that's in Herefordshire, a regiment of African American soldiers was billeted there. Weobley is an idyllic, picturesque, village, solidly white only population back then, and statistically pretty much now. To play on words, it's one of the County's famous 'black and white' timbered ones, and for the Anglo-Saxons and Celts (it's Welsh Border country, not far from Offa's Dyke) a huge shock was upon them. I was instructed to do a market appraisal (that's a valuation, but we're not allowed to use that term any more) for an elderly lady selling up her fourteenth century mini manor house, right in the centre of the village. But the gates were anything but that old!

Wrought iron, tall, and certainly not more than fifty years of age, I was told that her father had them installed during the War. Nobody in Weobley had seen a black man before, let alone one in uniform, and they were terrified lest their daughters should lose their purity. Hence the gates! I passed a pleasant morning there, and was instructed to market it. The house was magnificent, oozing with period features, and I loved it. I especially loved feeding a lamb she was looking after, a first for me. It was black, woolly haired, and just adorable. Read on, the connection's coming .....

I'm now in a little hamlet between Matha and St Jean d'Angely, with people wanting to move into Saintes. That's a Roman town, straddling both sides of the River Charente. It's full of interest, has what's reputed to be the largest

Roman amphitheatre in France, after the one in Nîmes, and a fascinating collection of Roman artefacts in the museum down by the River. It also has some rather swish shops, a theatre, and of course the Law Courts, where my journey into estate agency in France all began to take shape. We go to Saintes ourselves fairly frequently, and Spouse would like to move there. I'm not so sure, but at the moment that's totally irrelevant. His raison d'être is no doubt to be near the English Shop, run by a delightful young man from North London, ex Sainsbury's. With his endless supply of Asian herbs on the shelves alongside HP Sauce and Bassett's Liquorice Allsorts, Spouse is in seventh heaven. For me, it's the huge collection of English language books, paperbacks a euro a throw. Oh alright, and Cadbury's 'Twirls' and the purple nutty caramels in 'Roses.'

The house I'm in is extremely difficult to find, but I eventually get there. Inside, it's a treat. Not to my own style of decor, and a little bit over the top in colour and clutter, it is nonetheless immaculate and many will like it. Personally, I prefer magnolia! I'm sure the guy keeps calling his wife 'darling,' often out of context, but better than some of the alternatives I get, and I'm not talking 'eh, you!' It comes to the paperwork and then I realise why. Her name is Darlene. Her husband has me in hysterics when he describes how much easier it is to call her by her proper name here, than it was when they were living in Lancashire:

"You can just imagine it, looking for her in the aisles of our local supermarket, calling 'darling,' as that's what it comes out as. They don't do that in Leyland!"

She was given her name because, yep you've got it, her mother's social life during the War revolved around the local dances, with G.I.s from the nearby American Army Base. And Darlene, of course, is a regular Yankee Doodle name, as we who used to watch 'Rosanne' on TV all know.

The run-up to the War also brought many Italians and Spaniards to France, escaping Mussolini and Franco. My next house is in St Jean d'Angely itself and is owned by a charming Spanish guy from Alicante, brought to France as a young child . This is an interesting man, and I listen intently as he tells me all about his daughter, secretary to Sarkozy, whose parents were also immigrants. She, of course, has no allegiance to Spain, but her father wants to get back to his roots. Many do, of his generation. They have none of the fears of their parents, and seek the warmth and year round sunshine of the Spanish Costas. This one will sell fairly quickly, to a regular French family in all probability. It's not for the Ingleses. Not yet. Perhaps when all the old ruins have been bought up, or when those who've bought them grow tired of constant maintenance bills and headaches, chopping logs, collecting rotten fruit on hands and knees, they'll turn their heads to sense and sensibility. I hope! It's something we'll need to take on board ourselves, but for the time being we're enjoying our old stone country pile with its barns and cherry trees. We can't leave yet.
.

We've been invited to the local 'do' at the village hall in La Brousse. Rural communities in France excel at looking after their own folk, with regular meals laid on, and dancing until the small hours. It would be churlish not to attend!
It's organised by the local chasse committee, so I have mixed feelings about this. I convince myself that they will have kept to their quota of allowed 'game' to kill, and that at least it will all be eaten. The menu sounds amazing:

Potage (soup)

Filet de panga sauce Normande (fish in a cider sauce)

Sorbet

Gigot de chevreuil (leg of venison/roe deer) sauce chasseur

Haricots verts et champignons (green beans and mushrooms)

Pommes sautées

Salade

Fromages (selection of cheeses)

Framboisier (raspberry dessert, kind of a cake-cum-mousse)

Drinks to accompany all this:

Kir, Vin blanc et rouge, café, cognac, cassis

The price ? 22 euros per adult, 9 euros for the under tens, and there will be lots of them. It's to be a family occasion, as most of them are in France.

Starting at 8 p.m., we arrive on time. That's a big mistake. Nothing happens until the hall is nearly full, and that takes until 9.30 p.m. Only then, does the bar open. We have a lot to learn. It's all rather dull, and we are the only anglais who turn up. If it were a lunch time event, many more of us would crawl out of the woodwork, but it seems the rest of the Expats have obviously had enough experience of such things. Phew, it's almost 10.30 p.m. and we're allowed to take our places à table. It all starts to liven up, with lots of handshakes, a few kisses and general introductions, and then we are left to struggle. The first three courses pass with superb serving skill by the village youngsters commandeered to wait on the rest of us, and then there's a pause. Conversations bubble away, and then the dancing begins. We sit still!

The main course, the venison, eventually arrives around midnight and I try and stop my mind wandering off track to the baby deer I saw the other day, playing with two Breton Spaniels, chasse dogs not in the least bit interested in killing it, just having fun, celebrating their short lived freedom.

I give the venison a miss, already having had more than an elegant sufficiency and no longer in the habit of midnight feasts! The servers are having none of this, so I accept some haricôts verts and sautéed potatoes, a favourite of mine when it comes to what to do with spuds (I've Irish blood).

A neighbour spots me from a distance. He's a real charmer, a retired engineer from Paris, married to a Spanish lady, and oh what a mover he turns out to be. It's not the first time I've danced with him. He was at the summer barbecue, where he whizzed me off my feet and whirled me around the dance floor like a thing possessed. I'd wished I'd possessed just a teeny bit of his energy, as I was left with no choice but to oblige, and actually rather enjoyed being in his grasp. But that was daytime, a mid afternoon in the same village hall, and I hadn't eaten such a vast amount of food as I have tonight, and it's nearly one o'clock in the morning, for goodness sake! I survive, much to everyone's amusement, and applause, and we finally return to our respective seats and spouses. Mine finds it all one huge joke, many a year since he's used his dancing feet, probably not since dancing the night away in the Hong Kong Hilton, and no intentions of resurrecting them, even though he was quite a mover in his youth. Quel dommage (what a pity)!

After the salad, and the gourmet selection of cheese, there's another break. We're talking 2 a.m. the following morning now. The music loudens and with great ceremony, people are standing on their chairs, waving their white paper napkins around their heads, chanting enthusiastically with every turn. It's hilarious, and a sight to remember. Then comes the raspberry concoction, a bit sickly, and it's almost 3 a.m. I pass on it. We give up and go home, to be told the next day that the last revellers left at 5 a.m., several of them with babes in arms and children sleepy but high on adrenalin. There's been no drunkenness, goodness only knows how, no fighting, no noise as they've returned to their deathly quiet stone houses, just a lot of fun and mega good behaviour. Why can't we Brits be the same?

This is one of the many sides of France I grow to love and totally respect, one of the reasons to be grateful for living here, and not wanting to leave. Perhaps it's because they all learn philosophy at school, from the age of five or six years old. It's that old devil called love again, 'do as you would be done by.' Love comes in many forms, and where there's love, there's respect and joy. Much of that has seems to have been lost in the U.K. and becomes more apparent with every trip I take back. It no longer feels the same country I grew up in. Too much rushing around, with too little human contact en route, too much dreariness, too much litter, too much hedonism! I know, it's unfair to compare totally different entities, but that's how it seems!

19 French Humour, Missing Blighty

The stupid jokes keep coming! They remind me of my teenaged years when boys were still boys; when vegetarianism was something to be ridiculed big time, and jokes mercilessly played on the few of us who were. But I'm talking about men in their fifties now. French humour is very childish, mostly only participated in by men, and more often than not involves lavatories and lower body parts. This morning's is another pathetic pig picture in a sexual pose! It's there, in my banette (mailbox) and goes directly into the secretary's bin, herself sarcastically grinning as I chuck it in, obviously titivated by it herself.

I'm not surprised such things feature so heavily in their vocabulary. In my favourite little café in Matha, usually with immaculately clean facilities, friend who speaks English asks me where the 'loos' are. It's the Tuesday Caravane and Team Lunch . With no sense of direction at all, she returns to the table. I take her. Before we even get close, she says: "we're here, you can smell it." This is highly unusual for Pinocchio's, so I politely inform the owners. A young lad is sent in tout de suite to clean them. They should have sent a young lass!

It's just a few days after I've taken clients into the little café in Sonnac, a couple of kilometres east of Matha and a popular village with les anglais. I sell several houses there in my time. It has a lovely little tree lined square in the centre, and the much sought after bar/tabac/morning coffee place they all yearn for. Unfortunately, the day I picked to use it, I was horrified and so were my buyers, who settled for a house near Cognac instead. The Sonnac café doubles as a small grocery store and fresh meat shop, hardly big enough to call a butcher's. The meat counter was right next door to the 'loo' with no wash basin in sight, not anywhere! The toilet itself was tiny and absolutely, stenchingly, filthy. The meat counter was in full view of it, and cooked charcuterie (ham and other cold meats) slap bang next to the raw meat, no division in place, right there in the same trays. Not only that, I saw precisely one knife to cut both raw and cooked food, and he who ran the place had nowhere nearby to wash his hands, or the utensils of his trade. I'm fighting a losing battle, having wanted to go to war over it before, to be told I'd get nowhere fast! I shan't use it again, and am beginning to accept that 'Health & Safety' does not exist in France.

The clients I had with me in Sonnac were Expats returning from The Middle East, as a fair few of my buying people are, and now renting a gîte whilst they house hunt. They have rescue dogs, acquired here in France, one called Angus. He was shot, and when they found him and took him to the Vet's were told he had five bullet wounds in his back. The Vet also told them that the poor dog could have been part of the latest dog cull, by the police! I'm deeply shocked by this. I still can't accept the truth of what I'm hearing, but where there's smoke, there's fire. It seems that this sometimes happens, rather than rounding up strays and taking them to the animal rescue centres. I guess it's easier to fire a few bullets and leave them where they fall.

Angus had just been left to die, in the field near their house, but now he's fully recovered, totally devoted to them, and happily settled with their other rescue dog, Barney.
France has a huge problem with the way some of its dog and cat population is treated. Every summer, thousands are abandoned when their owners go on holiday. I get used to

seeing the posters, pleading with people not to do it. It doesn't only apply to pets, either. In the canicules (heatwaves) of 2003 and 2004, many elderly Parisiens were abandoned by their families and left to die, alone in their apartments. It happens annually, but those two years were HOT.

2003 was a tough one for me. Youngest son celebrated his 30th birthday, in Saxty's, Hereford, his siblings there but not his parents, marooned in France! Daughter sang solo in a concert in London, and we were not there, although I did get to see her at the rehearsal. Eldest son and fiancée were cracking on with renovating the delightful little town house he himself had bought a few years earlier, and we weren't there to help. All those normal family things abandoned in the move to the other side of the Channel, so near, yet so far away. It's what happens, and is precisely what a lot of my buying clients are due to discover. They feed the market for the Agence, often selling up within the first three years. It begins to follow a pattern, a bit like the 'Seven Year Itch' of marriage. If they survive the first three years, they're in with a chance of staying the course until old age grabs them, when they invariably return to their roots, penniless, bereaved and lonely!

But for now, we are still here. It's another day at the workhouse, another Tuesday Caravane, and the sun is shining. The house we look at after lunch is in St Même les Carrières, named after the workers in the quarries surrounding the town, although I've yet to actually discover them. It all looks rather lovely to me. It's a great little town, with shops and restaurants, a school, and even a bus depot. Bus passes aren't valid here, so don't get excited! We arrive ten minutes early, which is not acceptable. C'est la France and to arrive less than fifteen minutes' late, is not what they do, unless they are from Paris. These owners clearly are not, and their surname's Italian. She's obviously not Italian herself (none of that Italian warmth here, then) and she makes us wait, the whole lot of us. He who eats tripe paces restlessly through the garden, coming back with a present in his hands for me. A foetal bird!

The property is beautiful, perfectly presented, lots of original features lovingly preserved, a 'posez les valises' (move in with just your suitcases) house. She who runs the office scours at me and my enthusiasm, takes me to one side and tells me to stop saying how nice it all is. Of course, how absolutely stupid of me. If I sing its praises, how can she then ask the owners to reduce the price? As well as stupid at times, I'm also forever foreign, and no matter how well I integrate (which I do) will never be taken for anything else.

At the next house we visit, I explain that I'm English and will be bringing lots of anglais to their home. The owner stands to his full height of not much more than my own:

"I know. I can tell from your complexion!"

I take it as a compliment.

We pass through Bourg Charente en route back to Cognac and the bird presenter waxes lyrically about his favourite restaurant here, La Ribaudière. I trust his judgement, despite his liking for tripe, and add it to my list of places to go, should I sell enough houses, or take seriously wealthy clients out for the day. He's worried, though: "where are les anglais?" Perhaps they've read the news and taken the first 'plane back. Two swans have been shot by chasseurs at

Chalais, who are to go before the Tribunal at Angoulême. A cat has been shot 50 metres from its house. The law says 150 metres distance is ok for killing!

I stop in Matha on the way home and see a former neighbour. Her alcoholic husband died a year ago and she's moved into town.The change is dramatic. Last time I saw her, she was searching for snails to eat. Now she's radiant, weight lost, nicesmile, happy, confidence regained. We shake hands. Such a difference! Shakespeare was exceedingly clever entitling one of his plays 'The Merry Widow.'

Belle Maison Bourgeoise, St Jean d'Angely

20 Ships, Slaves &'Shit'

I write up the details of the house in St Même les Carrières, making a point of revisiting and learning more about the town itself. The stones from St Même were used to construct the Statue of Liberty, rather poignant given how America and France sometimes see themselves linked philosophically, even though at other times they're considered to equally hate each other. I read that American supermarkets are currently ridding their shelves of French cheeses, banning Bordeaux wine, and foie gras (quite right, too) after one of George Bush's political faux pas. Liberté, Fraternité, Egalité.

The American theme continues, with a short away break to Nantes and Saint Nazaire, where the latest Cunard cruise ship, The Queen Mary 2, is under construction. Her maiden voyage is scheduled to cross the Atlantic to New York City. We cross the bridge over the River Loire, one of the longest of its kind in France and perhaps the most elegant, although we've yet to cross the one at Millau, down in the Midi-Pyrénées. 'Tin Tin' was 'born' in St Nazaire and remains one of the World's most famous cartoon characters. The Port also has a darker side to its past, part of France's own Triangular Slave Trade.

 In my earlier life, I taught. Whilst training, I was given a class of sixth formers to teach the Slave Trade to, for a whole term. A Liverpudlian by birth, I had masses of information to hand (and a head full of memories) from the Dockside Museums. It came in very handy in Rural Gloucestershire! My pupils were a mixture of Liberal Arts and Science A level candidates, doing the history component of the trendy General Studies course. I rounded off the term with a debate on slavery. The room almost exploded with the passion of youth, the Science boys all in favour of the 'yes' motion, the Liberal Arts' girls' 'take me to bed' eyes diminishing to almost tears at the thought of the boys approving of slavery! Many budding romances collapsed that day!

Nantes is a wonderful city. The former capital of Brittany, in the days when it was an independent Kingdom, or Queendom as was the case in Queen Anne's days, the castle still reigns supreme as its centrepiece. Nantes cathedral is glorious, the museums amazing, and there are several superb restaurants to choose from. We have the best meal in France so far, on the terrace of the Restaurant Le Pont Levis, sitting in the sunshine opposite the main entrance to the castle. The food is exquisite, the chilled Chablis sheer nectar, and the price? Who's counting! We'll make up for it next week, but for now .... The gateway to the Loire Valley, the City's a mixture of old world elegance and a modern success story, and often voted the best place in France to live. We fully understand why and shall revisit, that's a certainty.

Holiday time for all the world, but not exactly for us! Instead, it's hard labour and mega expense again. But this is family, and we are no longer living in la bell'Italia where we had no fewer than 19 house guests in our first twelve months by Lago di Como! And did we take a holiday? Forget it, any spare cash we could have accumulated went on supplying our visitors with copious amounts of food and wine, sophisticated and cultural sightseeing, and 'going Dutch' on lunches out when we'd normally only be having a sandwich at home. And then there was all the extra electricity and water consumption, not forgetting having to run a taxi service for train and 'plane pick-ups, leaving neither money nor time for ourselves. Not that it mattered. Spouse was away working in Tanger and Istanbul most of the time, so travelling when he wasn't in the air himself, was not something he would have agreed to do.

For me, living in Como was a perpetual holiday in its own right, and not all of our guests were free loaders seeking free holidays! We were warned about this several years later, before disembarking here in France. A neighbour in Hereford had a maison secondaire in Normandy and told us the only way to stay solvent was to tell everyone the house was a ruin, but that they could put a tent up in the garden. He and his wife got no takers! But I like people, so it's been the price we've paid over the years. Also, having personally taken so many people to La Scala's Museum in Milan, I've been granted a free ticket for life:

"Signora, you are so good for business, you do not have to pay."

(Don't get excited, it just applies to me!)

Our youngest child arrives with 'other half' and our first grandchild, and 'other half's' child from his first relationship. Marriage seems to have flown out of the window these days, and 'living tally' as we used to say in Liverpool, knows no social boundaries. Daughter, with our water born baby granddaughter in her pushchair (I was there, I took the photos as she swam to the surface) and I leave the two men and honorary step grandchild (preferring to stay with Daddy and Grampa) at home, and drive off to La Rochelle. We've arranged to meet youngest son and his

154

own 'significant other' down at the Harbour. He's also not married and unlikely to be. He doesn't believe in it.
Youngest does get round to marrying, but it's not destined to last, and the first divorce enters the family. Eldest is already a married man, so one out of three is an achievement in itself in this modern age we live in. C'est la vie!

Daughter hobbles around the Old Port in obvious discomfort, which worsens as the day progresses. Big brother and 'significant other' have flown in and taken the bus into the city, a doddle of a journey, airport to seaport ten minutes and ten euros, actually it's eleven! Daughter struggles with a lunch the rest of us thoroughly enjoy, apart from when the wine list arrives à table. The cheapest bottle is 63 euros. Son laughs and says we'll be drinking water. It's his treat. Our children look after us very well. We're lucky. I don't believe the wine waiter, though he's clad as elegantly as befits such an establishment of this grandeur and obvious affluence. Lobster and champagne apparently are the 'norm' for les Rochellais, especially those who frequent this fabulous restaurant down at the Harbour, one of Les Grandes Tables du Monde, owned and run by Christophe Coutanceau and right up there with Raymond Blanc and Michel Roux. "It just looked inviting m'Lord" may not quite do the trick in the bankruptcy court!

"But I'm local" (obviously in my best French).

The waiter is squirmingly apologetic and brings us 'the other list!' We choose a bottle of perfectly acceptable Sancerre for just 28 euros, and settle for a carafe of 'château la pompe' (tap water).

Tomorrow comes, and with it more pain and discomfort for the one who's given us our first grandchild, way ahead of both her brothers, but at the respectable age of 27.

She and I arrive at the Urgence (A & E) of l'Hôpital de Saint Louis, in Saint Jean d'Angely. I'm forbidden entry. Oh no, I'm not. I force my way in. Daughter speaks Italian and German pretty much like the natives, but her French is not as good as mine. There's little else that I'm better at than my three children, I have to say, but français is definitely one of them. I've already learned that to get results in France, one has to scream and shout as well as shove, so I heroically do all three. Shrinking violets fade into insignificance in this chauvinistic country. It's how French men like women to be, and French women play to their pipers, but I'm English for goodness sake, and we know how to stand up for ourselves!

 I've already learnt this lesson in the workplace. I had a point to make in a monthly sales' meeting a while ago, one which two of my colleagues fully supported but asked me to bring the issue up. Nobody listened to me, I was totally ignored, until I was told that I would get nowhere until I shouted and banged the desk. It worked, and the motion was carried, but what a horrible way to learn and not one I enjoyed!

It's 13:50 and there's hardly a soul around. We're escorted on to the ward and left until 14:10, not long but with not so much as a 'bon jour,' just a grunt to stay put. Blood pressure and pulse readings are taken, and we're left again, this time until 16:30, not a soul in sight, and precisely one section of the previous week's 'Sunday Times' we've brought with us, as our only source of diversion from the pantomine we've entered. Ah, but I do see someone else, a man I take to be the cleaner as he seems to spend all his time wandering around aimlessly looking for dust. But he's le DOCTEUR! Really? So why couldn't he have seen us sooner? He speaks to my daughter:

"Doucement, doucement."

It's a regularly used phrase here. It means both 'softly' and 'slowly,' and that's what living in Rural France is all about. He's not even French. Same problem in France, then, having to import hospital staff!

After a fair amount of stomach prodding, he summons a very fierce and unfriendly nurse. She's fat, needs to go on a diet, and like many French (and British) women of a certain age, has a highly unflattering butch hairstyle in the most ghastly shade of orangey red, exposing even more fat. She obviously hates our English guts, and I can't say I'm particularly attracted to her, but my daughter's fate rests in her chubby great mits, which are now attaching a cannula with unnecessary force.

The poor girl has no fewer than six phials of blood taken. We're alone again until 18:50, when we're told she's not pregnant. We know that, but we didn't know they'd sneaked in a pregnancy test. Action at last, as she's wheeled down to Xray, reappearing at 19:05 for yet another tedious wait. By this time, both she and I are totally stressed, hungry into the bargain, and at the point of shouting to be let out of here. She's not the only one who shouts. Daughter is desperate to relieve herself and drags the drip she's attached to in the direction of the 'loo,' situated way at the other side of the ward. Ever grumpy nurse shouts out, at the top of her Gallically screaming voice, that:

"l'Anglaise in Cubicle 3 needs to pee!"

Le Docteur promptly reappears on the scene which he's not
actually left, still spending most of his time doing precisely
nothing. Obviously few accidents happen in St Jean on a
Sunday afternoon! He addresses my daughter, with not even
a smile on his face:

"Madame, vous êtes pleine de ca-ca."

(That's French for constipation!)

The fun's not over yet, although my daughter is laughing
hysterically at this point, and I join in. It's infectious! It's
Sunday, the chemists are all closed, especially at 8 p.m. The
big stroppy nurse telephones the gendarmerie (the police
station). The police person telephones the duty chemist, who
telephones the hospital to tell us which one he or she is, and
where the pharmacie is. The nurse tells us we can leave. I
ask her for directions to the designated pharmacist's:

"Non Madame, vous devez aller au Gendarmerie."

(I'm speechless!)

So off we go to the Police Station! But not before we've
begged the nurse with the short hair and ghastly disposition
to remove a very empty looking cannula from a very sore
looking hand. It should have been removed hours ago, but
this is France: 'lentement, lentement' (another way of saying
'slowly, slowly'). The policeman chuckles as he looks at the
prescription, which we duly take to the chemist, who's there
with his dog (of course, it's Sunday walky time) and we
finally arrive back in Esset to a barrage of questions, and

much laughter when Daughter declares she's "pleine de ca-ca." It's a diagnosis she lives on for years, and she's not as polite in translation as I'm being right now!

The rolling hills of The Lot

21 Yoga & Apple Eating Rat

"Consider your uncles.
 Visualize your basin.
 Close your orifices."

Three instructions given to us by Geneviève, our yoga
teacher. Her English is quite good, but she's hoping to
improve it, hence she's split us up. From starting the term as
a mixed group, she now has different classes, one for les
femmes françaises and the other for les femmes anglaises, so
bang goes yet another opportunity to parler the lingo and
make new friends. So here we are, a group of five Brits and
one Belge, all good friends already.

The hall's massive and the view's worth coming for, over
open fields and great dog walking territory. There's also a
children's playground, small but functional and too far away
to be able to watch little people swinging and sliding. We're
fully stretched out on the hard floor, with mats way too thin
to offer much protection for ageing bodies on cold tiles.
Instead of lying semi comatose, eyes closed (not mine)
humming yoga chants and sending the World into oblivion,
my mind's full of deadlines I have to meet, clients to serve,
new territory to explore, and I really want to be outside in
the sunshine. Why did I sign up?

At the moment, the only parts of our bodies touching the
floor are our ankles, but she's got me going, thinking about
my uncles! I have one left (my mother's brother) into his
eighties now and living in Melbourne, still playing in a jazz

band, though. He was the 'black sheep' of the family, so no wonder he ended up 'Down Under.' His working life took him to Kenya, but the Mau-Mau Uprisings put pay to that, so he transferred to Papua New Guinea, preferring to live amongst cannibals. Oh yes, the last reported case was in 1971 and Vincent was definitely working there then! Apparently we taste good cooked with bush cabbage. I think I'll stay en France and move on to visualising my basin. We've just installed a new one upstairs in what was the old hay loft, we've replaced the old yuchy orangey pink one in the downstairs' bathroom, and I recently cleaned the teeny one back in the office in Cognac. Which one shall I focus on? Ah, my own basin! O.k. then, here I am, doing the old squeezing and clenching and kneeling on all fours now, as instructed. A sight for sore eyes no doubt, and only one of us has the slightest chance of getting a 6 pack (not me)! Now the time has come to consider our orifices. Oh dear, could she get more explicit? More squeezing and clenching, holding them all in and counting huge strings of numbers until we give in and zonk out on our mats for meditation.

We're instructed to close our eyes again. I try, I manage to, and she takes us on a journey to the beach, a day at the seaside from dawn to dusk, the sound of the waves taking our stress away. She's good at this. I very nearly fall asleep, and dream of having her as a personal stress reliever. Can't afford it though, will have to sell a lot more houses. She's a lovely lady, the nicest I've had for yoga, and I've tried three different classes in France now. One was in such a tiny hall, the nauseating smell of body odour put me off staying the course. And then came the lady who tried to turn us all into circus acts, backward wall walking, excruciatingly painful leg crossing, très ridicule!

Back to work the following morning, I drive past the French Air Force base just south of Cognac. A rugby match is in full play, but a fighter jet momentarily stops the action. Then comes another, always flying in pairs on their practice flights. They zoom over our house in Esset, and I never cease to charge across the garden in pursuit of them. It's our only excitement out in The Sticks!

I'm en route Archiac, a pleasant little town cum large village pretty much half way between Cognac and Jonzac. There's a superb château in Jonzac, a town well worth visiting, and it's sufficiently close to Bordeaux for those searching a city buzz once in a while. I've a sale going through on a house at Saint Palais du Né, a hamlet amongst the vineyards, and I'm meeting my buying clients there. The chap's already decided it's a done deal, has signed the 'compromis,' but it'll be the first time his wife's seen it. I'm crossing all fingers and toes that she likes it.

I'm gagging for a coffee, and I have time, so I stop in Archiac and use the little Bar. It's spotless, and very welcoming. The sun's shining, and there's a mini market outside, attracting locals and tourists alike. The Bar owner looks decidedly Mediterranean French, but turns out to be an Italiano. He's also a poet, and proudly presents me with a copy of his latest book. I'm taken aback by his generosity. His wife comes on the scene, toddler in her arms, and we while away half an hour ensemble. She's française, the child a delightful blend between the two. I'm their only customer, but lunchtime beckons so they'll need to get busy for the market day rush. I do my 'grazie mille' and my 'merci beaucoup' and head up the country lanes to Saint Palais.

Client's wife's happy, phew! She loves it, and the sale progresses to plan, four more happy clients and a bit more dosh for me. I'm self employed, remember, and the market's not going to hold out with asking price achievements for much longer. I can feel it in the air, and with the fewer number of clients arriving from the U.K. Buyers are already beginning to negotiate, and sellers are beginning to realise they'll have to do likewise. It takes a long time to convince them, though, and the majority of my French selling clients insist on holding out for their price, no matter how many years that may take. Doucement, doucement! (Slowly slowly, and often it is precisely that). Also, more and more estate agencies are taking on native English speakers, so the competition is getting fiercer and harder.

The atmosphere is spreading to the office, too. The monthly sales meeting is horrendous, with myself, she who's married to an Englishman, and the lovely secretary all excluded from the first part of the meeting. Upstairs, they are all massacring the secretary, eaves dropping and picking up snippets of the assassination. She runs out of the building in tears, leaving the two of us behind to tell she who runs the office what has happened. We are told to join our colleagues, and witness an abhorrent show of hand waving, screaming, and high pitched voices, all adding to the drama they've created. Three of them are at war and won't let the battle end. The rest of us remain silent, including the ex police man, who will have seen it all before. We have no idea what anything is about, and dare not ask, do not want to ask. I'm merely understanding about half of what they're saying, all defamatory and getting nowhere fast. It's now really hotting up and he who's usually a diplomatic smoothie, is getting seriously hyper. She who runs the office is performing like a tragedy queen on stage, and young male colleague and ex police man are now obviously bored witless. Young girl whom female boss is grooming for greater things is evaluating and assessing everything she hears, remaining silent now into the process. Perhaps she's afraid her 'affair' may be exposed.

She who runs the office is now screaming:

"Merde alors!"

and is hitting the table with such vehemence that she's likely to damage her hand, especially as she's given to wearing enormous dress rings, and today is no exception. She's really fuming, and lights up a cigarette in our presence. Mais c'est interdit, alors!

Ah, we're told at last, the two of us who were excluded earlier. It's all about the commission structure, and giving clients presents. Surely that's supposed to happen the other way round? I'm getting the impression that some of us (not me) have been passing over little amounts of money to friends for leads, as in "I'll tell you where there's a house to sell if you give me some of your commission," which of course is strictly interdit (forbidden). Times are tough and obviously getting tougher. I make a mental note to look at my contract in depth. He whose family knew the Mitterands, gets up from the table and storms out in a mega huff, hopefully to find the secretary and give her a hug. They're old friends, and he's a charmer, able to cajole any lady with ease.

But, oh yuch, we all have to lunch together, and almost everyone chooses TRIPE, apart from young secretary, now suitably calm and calmed, and tucking into raw mince, adorned with a sloppy egg. Please God, get me out of here!

I do get out and decide to stop outside the sports' hall in Matha on my way home, just to catch my breath after a pretty senseless sales meeting and lunch full of offal and awful disgustingness. My mother was half French, and as a child I can remember her devouring white tripe floating in milk, in a favoured restaurant near the Market Hall in Bolton. I think it was the U.C.P. Company's retail eating outlet. I never understood how she could do it, but now I live in France, I can. I never realised the effects of nurture over nature and she must have been brought up to like the stuff, despite her delicate and tiny body size. She also liked fatty ham and pickled cabbage!

All is well again, and I walk beside the stream, taking in the clean air. And then I see it. A huge, great big, brown rat. Happily swimming along, very purposefully, with an apple in its mouth. Obviously has a family to feed, so I worry not. It's not bothering me, but I'm glad it's here in Matha and not near MY house. I'm a tad concerned, because this is the stream beside the children's play area, but what can I do, and who would listen to me? Nothing, and nobody!

I head for home, via the back road which leads eventually to Aulnay. The sun and the moon are on opposite sides of the maize, the sunflower heads have turned black, but it's all still very special, very lovely. The early evening change from dusk to dark in our part of France is spectacularly beautiful. I'm lucky, exceedingly so.

22 Cultural Differences

The atmosphere's not improved and now we have split camps. It's been a week since the shouting match, the hard anger, the sadness of a previously successful team at war. The Market's beginning to slump a bit, so the Tuesday Caravane's a small one and we've finished for the day. It's time for some lunch. He who introduced me to Carla Bruni, he who had a dog that pulled a sledge during the wine harvest, and myself go as a threesome to Le Pilou Pilou. I'm delighted I've been included in 'their' camp. Apart from anything else, it's one of my favourite places. The rest all disperse to Le Globe, one of my least liked restaurants in Cognac, especially its ghastly communal 'loos.' They're welcome to it! My two companions are true gentlemen when needs be, and when one in particular isn't putting pathetic schoolboy jokes in my mail box. I could easily fall for him, and am learning to take it all on the chin at last, but he'd have to stop eating tripe! Or maybe the other one would be a better bet, less mischievous but more subtle. Glad I don't have to choose, but once a lady stops flirting, life becomes rather dull!

French men, especially these two today, excel at appearing completely cavalier with women when other men are present. On such occasions, their manners are truly impeccable and they are a joy to be with. I imagine they revert to type as soon as they arrive home. English men of a certain age do! Lunch is excellent, and nous sortons très satisfait (we leave very happy). It makes a delightful change from the dreadful formules we're forced to suffer week in and week out in the country restaurants, where culinary expertise is almost always sadly lacking.

By the following Tuesday a reserved politeness has established ground, and we set off amongst the vineyards for a full caravane. The first house is in Mareuil. It's beautiful, and I comment:

"Gosh, what a lovely view over to the church."

She who's married to an Englishman tells me to:

"Stop being such a snob. I've lived in England long enough to know that only snobs say 'gosh.'"

(We like each other, really, so I pull back the tears).

It's not the first time I've been criticised for my use of language. I've already been in trouble for saying:

"Puis j'avoir?"

That, too, is considered snobbish, and only used by the hoy-palloy. I'm told to say :

"Est ce-que je peux avoir?"

Total nonsense! Why say six words when two and a bit will do the job just as well? Both mean 'may I have?' and I know which version I'm going to continue using. I shall never win, not in France, not in the workplace here, not even admiring what it has to offer. At times, I feel that I'm in the most civilised place in the World, and at others that I'm in Hicksville. I guess it's normal to feel ostracised.
The French women I work with are lovely one minute, bitingly cutting the next. When an outside lady is in their midst (yours truly) I'm reminded of primary school children

in a playground, young girls smiling as they trip others up on the hopscotch pitch. They are a strange race. Or maybe it's us who are strange. They are certainly very different. In the basement of a house close to Cognac Golf Club, we come across a 'loo' in pride of place in the middle of a vast space. She who runs the office actually sits on said 'loo' majestically and makes rude gestures, admittedly still fully clothed. My colleagues find this hilarious, and follow suit. He who eats tripe takes photos, not just one, but as many of the others he can get to pose for the camera. I walk away. Discretion is the better part of valour and childhood humour needs restricting to childhood, especially toilet humour. But don't they just love it, thrive on it, base all their jokes around it. Body parts, sex, and B.O.! I'm thinking of that podgy little git, Napoleon:

"Do not wash, Josephine, I am coming home!"

Driving around the Charentaise countryside, I come across villages with the most unbelievable names and wonder if I'm going to be able to keep a straight face when I have clients to view properties in these locations: Ars, Arse en Ré (but that's the posh one on the Ile de Ré), Le Prat, Herpes, Bollocks. Yes really, and that's a word I can never in a million years utter. I'm a good convent girl, remember! Oh, and there's a Condom further south!

We women are adorned with les ananas (pineapples), perhaps slightly preferable to having 'a standard handful.' Be careful not to ask for une banane (a banana) in the company of men. It's their description of an erection. Funny, that one. A banana's usually bent! You'll never think of maccheroni in the same way again, either. It, too, means the same as a bent banana! Even a parsnip is likened to a sexed up banana. Now we're on to flowers. A camellia can be used to describe a mistress. I guess that makes sense, thinking back to the '60s song: 'comeh, comeh, comeh, oh comeh camellia, you come and go, you come and go oh oh oh.' A marguerite can mean a condom. And even shell fish don't escape. Next time you eat moules, just remember to be careful whom you tell, or they'll think you're referring to what we women have, and men don't!

With all these cultural differences racing around in my head, I'm wondering whether I'll survive the next village 'bash' we are persuaded to attend. The menu reads well, starting with a Kir (white wine and cassis) on arrival, although that isn't actually the case, as everyone has to have arrived before the arrival is declared and the kir is distributed. We make our way to the table, the only anglais to have turned up again, and are served smoked salmon by the village youngsters. Then we're given hake in a butter sauce, served with leeks. It's delicious. Spouse goes on to enjoy roast beef in Madeira sauce, and I enjoy the accompanying vegetables, just for a change! Haricôts verts (of course), and sautéed potatoes (I love them). Mixed green salad leaves greet us next, followed by a selection of cheese, and we finish off with the usual raspberry gateau. It's all excellent, and I'm glad I came. Wines are served course by course, and then the cognac bottles come out. We have a producer just down the road from our house. La Brousse is surrounded by vines. La vie est belle, quelquefois, mais pas toujours! (Life's good, sometimes, but not always !)

The amazing thing about tonight's soirée is that it's free, the Commune's annual 'merci beaucoup' to us all. The day's started with the Memorial Service at the tiny cenotaph opposite the chapel, with its picturesque avenue of trees.

Dressed formally for this particular 11th of November, and carrying copies of the Marseillaise, we are prepared, and feel proud to be representing Angleterre. Both our fathers served in the Second World War, mine mostly in the Far East with the Royal Navy, and Spouse's in the Merchant, crossing the Atlantic with supplies and dodging German 'U' boats. Both now dead, we owe it to them to be here. Our Scottish neighbour attends with his Colombian wife, the four of us the only étrangers (foreigners). There's no band playing, so we struggle with the French National Anthem to the accompaniment of a transistor radio. Then everyone goes home, to recharge for the evening.

The atmosphere tonight is fabulous. The sadness has gone, but not forgotten, and now it's time for celebration, for victory and for freedom. The dancing between courses means the meal takes several hours, but we're getting used to that. The white napkin demonstration is phenomenal, but I'm surprised that the old chairs take the weight of those standing on them, waving and chanting something I shall never know the words of. Maybe its origins go back to the days of la Résistance, and the napkins are the flags of freedom. I don't know.

I dance, of course I do, with my retired engineer from Paris. Spouse doesn't do dancing any more, and he used to be so good at it! My head's back in 1970, the pair of us flirtingly gyrating to 'Cecilia .... you're breaking my heart ...' on the dance floor of Dee Sailing Club, Heswall. Next came marriage. No proposal, no ring (two failed engagements and one very near trip to the altar, had left me with no more hankerings for such prenuptial razzamatazz). Just a joint decision after a fun filled night! Swifly came the little Church of England in Thurstaston; the bright lights of Hong

Kong; the stress of London; the fields of Lancashire, Lincolnshire, and Herefordshire; the joy and beauty of Lake Como and then Tuscany's Lunigiana; and now France, totally unplanned but it's beginning to feel good. It's been a long journey, but I've arrived at last!

Bastillle Day, Matha

23 Snakes to 'Civilisation'

Autumn's well and truly established itself, with black headed sunflowers still not cropped, wandering pheasants, orphaned young deer learning to fend for themselves, the odd wild boar entering the village at night, and lost chasse dogs racing breathlessly along the roadside, hoping to catch up with packs or owners. They're not the only dogs to worry about. On our excellent Vet's recommendation, we've had Megan vaccinated against a horrendous tick disease which plagues certain regions of France, including Poitou Charentes, also Dordogneshire! Other dogs we hear of have already been infected, and several have died, including five known to myself. One other I know caught the disease but recovered.

Our immediate neighbour's dog was poisoned. He was Megan's friend, Oscar, a beautiful Breton Spaniel. Poisoning happens quite a lot in Rural France, usually affecting cats, but sometimes dogs take the bait. To the French, it's a way of keeping the rat population down, and if cats and dogs wander into barns where tempting dishes of raw meat are doused with poison, then the rodent assassins don't care. I love dogs, and am desperately upset to hear that two magnificent large ones have been stolen from clients near Rouillac. Taken from their garden, in broad daylight from all accounts, the likelihood of their return is not good. Apparently it's just another aspect of rural life one has to factor in, although is more likely to happen to thoroughbreds, than mutts. Lock the gate!

The snakes and lizards of summer have all retreated. The last snake I saw was impressive indeed. I was just about to turn into our driveway, when a very large greeny-brown slippery thing slithered at great speed across the road in front of me. I was taken totally by surprise, initially thinking it must be a rubber tyre or something similar, blown off course by the wind. I stopped the car, moved forward a tad and then reversed to see if I could find it in the undergrowth. I couldn't! Now it's too cold for them, Gemima misses the lizards. Her Italian feral roots obviously included them in her diet initially. Watching her catch them, usually from teeny gaps in our stone walls, is quite something. Then it turns to a somewhat disgusting sight, as she emerges with them swaying from her jaws in an effort to escape. They don't! Fortunately, she's not a wanderer and normally stays within her own territory. I think I'd be on the next boat back to Blighty if anything happened to her, or to Megan.

The owners of the next house I take clients to are indeed heading for the Port, but I'm not sure which one. At first, I can't understand whereabouts in the World they're mentioning to me. It's sounding like 'mon raye al.' Silly me, Montreal! They emigrated to Canada back in the '60s, raised a family there, and then got homesick for France. The children, all Canadian of course, refused to accompany them and Madame is now missing them too much to stay in Cognac. It happens, but usually it's the Brits who have to cope with such loss.

An estate agent, especially a female one, can seldom remove the 'agony aunt' sticker from their forehead, and so it continues. I have clients escaping drug dealing children; miserable marriages, second time round marriages (sometimes third or fourth) filled with hope for the current one to succeed; failed businesses; repossessions; and job losses into the bargain. Many wait until elderly parents die and then make the move to France, die themselves, and leave non French speaking other halves to cope through an endless mire of paperwork they haven't a cat's chance in hell of sorting.

I'm not a 'facilitator' and my French is not of the legal variety, so I steer clear of translating legal documents, well clear. What I can, and do, help with are taking clients (after completion) to schools to register their children, to doctors' practices, dentists, vets, insurance offices, banks (especially those with English speakers amongst their staff), and to D.I.Y. stores so they can begin their arduous task of repair and renovation. I get into trouble all the time for doing this, and am frequently told: "ce n'est pas votre responsabilité," to which I relentlessly try to persuade all my French colleagues that if we make it our responsibility then we will get more clients. To them, I'm making more work for myself, and they consider me totally stupid for doing so, failing to see the rewards. They are incapable of grasping the fact that satisfied customers will recommend us to others, and that not only will we get more buyers walking through the door, but more sellers instructing us. She who runs the office doesn't buy this one bit, even though one of her stock phrases is:

"Il faut manger" (one must eat).

For me, it's a case of not having to hide behind supermarket aisles when I hear English voices, lest they be dissatisfied clients who've received no help at all in their settling in, aka from the majority of my competitors. I don't have that problem, and delight in building up my network of morning coffee and afternoon tea stops, not forgetting our delightful weekend down in The Lot.

I brace myself for a trip back to England. It's been a while, and I'm missing my family, just like the rest of us. Spouse drives me to La Rochelle Airport, where we have an excellent lunch in the restaurant, 'L'Escale Atlantique.' We often drive over here on Sundays with Megan, and watch the 'planes land and take off as we're tucking into what is consistently good food, perfectly cooked and well presented. After lunch, we beach walk at Châtelaillon Plage, forever special to me, and to Wuffit, who basks in the sea like a polar bear when she's not chasing balls and airborne kites across the sand at phenomenal speed. The Airport's restaurant is popular during the week, too, with French Air Force pilots and crew en route to wherever they're going, and to local business people. Most of the anglais just buy a sandwich at the bar, forever timid to try something new. Perhaps they're reluctant to eat oysters and langoustines etc. immediately before flying. I'm not, and choose a plateful of succulently plump prawns, large ones, followed by sea bass. Spouse eats oysters and then carré d'agneau (lamb). We round it all off with crème brulée and coffee, and have shared a bottle of Sancerre. I'm all set for the flight to Stansted.

Oh dear, perhaps I should have just had a sandwich. Is it going to get bumpy? The captain announces that we're running late, at least ten minutes late, but doesn't give any reason why. Eventually, as we approach the Essex runway, we're told we're in a queue and it'll take another ten minutes to land. What about the fuel, I wonder? We seem to be floating aimlessly in an otherwise calm sky. The Ryanair fanfare begins to play. Err! I thought we'd be late, but

175

actually, we're not. Clever marketing and a bit of kiddology get us to our destinations on time. Thank you Ryanair, I think you're great! And if you take away your services, sure as eggs are eggs, the housing market will tumble in France. It's already happening where flights have been cancelled and we do not want that to happen here in Poitou Charentes. Keep flying here, please!

I spend a day solo in the British Museum, never having visited it before, and I have a wonderful time. The snack I have at lunchtime is expensive, as much per head as we paid for a three course meal at the Airport in La Rochelle, a fraction as good, and not even a meal, but it fills a gap and it's fun people watching while I eat. I spend a couple of hours wandering around the Ancient Greek, Abyssinian, and Egyptian sections and am totally enthralled. Then I seem to walk for miles, every turning revealing something fabulous, and make use of the randomly provided sitting areas to write post cards.

It's nearly 6 p.m. and Daughter's going to walk through the door of the Gallery Café any moment. She looks stunning, and I'm so proud of her. We adjourn to a pub nearby, we both love Guinness and she's had a hard day at the office, whilst I've been adding to my education! We have a dinner date with one of my oldest friends and her husband, over from Toronto. We meet in the foyer of their hotel, the Montague On the Park, in Bloomsbury. Friend looks fabulous, still with her long dark hair. I've gone white already, but actually I find it rather fun! The meal is absolutely fantastic and I can't believe how cheap it is, and for such quality. At less than twenty pounds per head for a three course meal, in London, in Bloomsbury of all places, it's silly money. We wouldn't get that in a decent French hotel, but then where we live there aren't any theatres for the hotels to lay on budget 'pre theatre dinners' for. There aren't even any theatres. Celebrating how little we've spent, we take a taxi back to Daughter's West London apartment. It's the first time I've seen it, and it's delightful.

It's a good trip so far. I've been picked up at Stansted by eldest 'child,' spent a couple of nights with youngest, and will be with middlest before setting back to France. Mission will be accomplished! I've factored in a sentimental trip back to Hereford, and take the slow train through the Cotswolds and the Malvern Hills, stopping at Ledbury before meandering through the cider orchards lining the track all the way to Hereford.

It feels good, and I factor in lunch with three of my old work colleagues. Not one of the four of us is still with our original firm, but it feels as if we're all still together as one team. We eat well at The Left Bank, sometimes referred to as a 'modern monstrosity' overlooking our old house on the Right Bank, but I happen to have liked it, except when disco music fired itself across the River at midnight when it was home to us! It feels very emotional. I'm persuaded to go and say 'bonjour' to the old boss. We shake hands vigorously and the warmth between us is still there. We had a strong professional relationship, fraught at times, but it lasted a good many years. He taught me everything I know about estate agency. I'm forever grateful. I hesitate as we say "au revoir," and move a couple of doors along King Street to where one of our team of four is now working. She has some documentation in French I've agreed to help translate.

I've not seen any sun all the time I've been in Blighty and it's beginning to get to me. I count two stars the first night

I'm in Hereford. In La Brousse I'd be counting two thousand. A man has thrown himself into the River Wye near our old house and apparently he's the third in two weeks. It's taking an hour to cross the city, sometimes longer. The train back east is filthy, with food all over the floor, including a rotting banana skin. I alight at Worcester, into a very run down station in a pretty run down city (except around the Cathedral, of course) for lunch in an old Methodist Chapel, where the food is mediocre and the music too loud to hear oneself speak. I head back to the station, all ready on track for getting back to France and civilisation. En route to London, on yet another filthy train, I count three pheasants, three young deer, and one rabbit, all munching away in the fields, oblivious to the whizz of metal hurrying past. I break the journey at Reading, to spend a couple of nights with youngest son. He has a fabulous flat, très chic, with a little balcony. I sit and watch a squirrel in a tree and begin my translation, but it's hard without a dictionary. We have a marvellous meal at The Griffin in Caversham and my spirits are uplifted again. It's a super pub, great grub, lovely location, home to swans on the Thames.

The train to Paddington takes no time at all, and I'm back at Daughter's flat. I've taken a taxi, too scared yet to take the Tube. How pathetic! But I'm not alone. It's what life in Rural France does to us, especially we women. The taxi driver's filled me with fear about crime in East London, where he sometimes refuses to take passengers. But this is Kensal Rise, not at all far from Notting Hill, and not at all bad from what I can see. I remind myself that East London is well 'on the up' and reckon he'll soon be singing its praises, especially when the Olympic Park developments entice Russian oligarchs to buy up all the new real estate under construction. They and the Chinese, making sure that the 'locals' won't be able to afford anything themselves, that's my conclusion! London is not for me, never was, and I doubt it ever shall be.

However, I love its many parks, not only the famous ones, but relatively unknown Roundwood in Willesden, and slightly more fashionable Queens in Kensal Rise. Roundwood wins with its floral displays and amazing gates; Queens with its nature trail.

Onwards and upwards, into the sky back to Rural France tomorrow. I can't wait. Bring it on! Bring me some sunshine; bring me some peace; bring me an evening free of police sirens, but skies filled with stars. Bring me more clients so I can stay awhile longer in my newly adopted country. I'll put up with the downside, honestly I will! The downside, which one would that be?

Cat takes refuge from the Chasse

24 Wild Boar Hunt in Chizé Forest

The local grapevine is reporting some shocking news. A man from our own Commune has been shot by his brother-in-law, in a nearby village. It's an accident, killed whilst out shooting game, and he won't be the first of this season, or the next, and so it will continue until the Chasse wakes up to the dangers it creates. Health and Safety is pretty much non existent in France, and this is just one of the areas in which it needs to adopt some. I try and avoid driving through the countryside when Chasse signs are displayed, but it's not always possible to do so. A clue is to look for burly men in shiney orange jackets, and white vans parked by the roadside, waiting to store 'the kill.'

Today is no exception. I also try and avoid driving through Chasse areas on Saturdays, but I have a house to put on the market and it's in the most northerly reaches of my secteur. I head out on the D121 towards Aulnay, passing through the busy little village of Cherbonnières. It's one of the few which has managed to retain its baker's and its butcher's, a small post office which opens for a couple of mornings a week, and there's even a little electrical shop in the Square. Straddling the main road, it's not a picture post card village, but is forever popular with les anglais, as is nearby Aulnay. It's blessed with a fair few shops, a small hotel, and an acceptable restaurant in the middle of the town. Spouse and I use it when we meet up with friends from 'up north' in Tillou, a very pretty little village with some delightful walks we share with them from time to time. Aulnay also has an outdoor market once a week, a doctor's practice, a dental surgery, and pretty much everything an incomer could need. I introduce a fair few of my buying clients to its charms and conveniences on my house hunting travels with them, also the restaurant of course. It's one of the few around which does good formules at lunchtime, and has clean 'loos!' But I'm not stopping today.

I turn off for Dampierre sur Boutonne, its château still not repaired after the fire it suffered a few years ago. This is a great shame, as it was once on the tourist trail. And now the fun begins, or rather the fear! I turn off and drive through Saint Severin, continuing towards my destination, La Croix Comtesse. I'm suddenly, without warning, entering the Réserve Nationale de la Chasse. Oops! I'm not liking this, but daren't turn back. I've come so far and will have to grin and bear it, hoping I'm not the latest fatality of some reckless chap with a gun. (I've not heard of women chasseurs in chauvinistic France, but perhaps they exist somewhere in the depths of the French countryside). It's not small animals like rabbits and hares on the schedule for today. Oh no, they're after much larger ones. How do I know? Because the tracks from the road into the forest are lined with the already mentioned burly looking men wearing bright orange jackets, hunters' knives slung from their belts as part of the kit, as well as guns. A white van is indeed parked every so many hundreds of metres, ready to accept however many boar or deer they have killed. I do not feel safe, far from it, but there's absolutely no turning back. Safety is not something which accompanies Saturdays in any wooded area when it's the large animal hunting season. Always better to go to the Coast!

I'm now deciding to eliminate anywhere further north west of Aulnay from my secteur, after today of course.

Eventually, I emerge from the forest and arrive in the small hamlet of La Croix Comtesse, not an attractive place and I can't find the property I'm supposed to be putting on. The few locals I bother to ask don't understand me, and I certainly don't understand them. The very last house looks a cut above the others, so I stop and ask the Saturday gardener. "Madame, they do not live here. They live in Villeneuve la Comtesse." It's not the first time this has happened to me, but it's only a few miles away, direction the main A10 which cuts this part of France in half. West for the Atlantic, East for the forest. After all that, it's not really anything les anglais will buy, the Caravane certainly won't entertain adding it to the Tuesday list, and nor will any of my colleagues bring their own clients this far from Cognac. It's been a complete waste of time, and I could have done without the excitement of driving through the Chasse! I politely suggest they instruct an agent in Niort.

Loulay is just a ten minute drive south, and the bar in the centre is always welcoming, so I stop for a coffee en route home. We know Loulay quite well, coming to the annual Christmas Show put on by the Expats. Some of the entertainers are first class and several have amazing voices, especially Trevor, the leading man, with his unforgettable rendition of Sinatra's 'I Did It My Way.'

I'm refreshed, calm again after fearing for my life (and the lives of the wild animals being hunted) and stop in Saint Jean d'Angely to do some supermarket shopping before heading home. It turns into an eventful Saturday. Spouse is entertaining our next door neighbour, who tells us with great enthusiasm that when we were out last weekend, a wild boar stopped outside our gate:

"And what happened to it, may I ask? I'd've let it in!"

"Non, Madame, you would not. He was very strong; he would have killed you."

"So did the Chasse kill him (the guy's a chasseur)?"

"Mais zut alors, of course we did not. We have killed our quota for this year. We said 'au revoir, monsieur' and let him go."

I want to believe him, so I do! Our Commune's quota for this year is three wild boar, a few deer, but as many hares, rabbits, and pheasants as they care to shoot, but I'm relieved to hear that they do indeed respect the quotas set.

This weekend is turning out to be challenging. It's Sunday morning, I'm on my way to St Jean d'Angely again, and forget to take heed of the speed cameras. The next thing I know, I'm sitting in the back of a police mini bus sized vehicle in Saint Julien de l'Escap being interviewed. It's Sunday for goodness sake, and I'm on my way to St Jean's inaugural church service in our Parish the size of Wales. I plead both ignorance and innocence, but stupidly speak to them in their own language. I should have stuck with English and may have got off the ninety euro speeding fine. I'm told to consider myself lucky, because I am not going to have points taken off my licence, which they are at liberty to enforce. The gendarme takes great delight in telling me she's giving me a present, because she could take six whole points off me. This turns out to be a gross exaggeration, but it settles my nerves and I carry on to St Jean, annoyed with myself for being so unobservant. It turns into a very expensive church service for me, but gives everyone a great topic of conversation over coffee, which I can just about afford on this particular Sunday morning!

Evenings are turning darker and colder earlier, and the log fire is a welcome friend after the stress of the last couple of days. It won't be peaceful for long, though. This is the time of year when hedgehogs invade the garden in their masses, munching their way through the copious amounts of windfalls we have from our apple and pear trees. It's Megan's favourite month, and it's normal to find myself searching the outer reaches of the garden for an almost totally black dog in a pitch black night, looking for dark brown camouflaged prickly creatures she torments hell out of. It turns into a highly inconvenient nightly event, searching for dog searching for hedgehogs, with a search light!

One of her other joys is to chase the hens which saunter over the dividing stone wall separating Annie's flock of coqs, breeders, and layers, as well as ducks and geese. Fortunately, the geese stick to making hissing noises from afar! Hens are an easier challenge, and Megan's collie genes make her an excellent herder and protector. Her labrador ones are not sufficiently tuned enough to retrieve them, even when frightened into frozen statues! It's not quite the same with the adventurous owls which fly tormentingly from beam to beam in the barns. That's when Gemima joins in, taking a break from feeding on her supply of slivery little lizards amongst the masonry. Oh, the pleasures of country living, forever exciting and joyful!

25 Stalactites & Stalagmites

They *descend* from the barn roofs and *ascend* from all the guttering and outdoor water pipes. Brrr !

It's turning cold and the log fire's glowing every night. We live in the second sunniest region in the whole of France, but that does not mean it's the warmest. Far from it. Our summers are extremely hot, but our winters are desperately, bone chillingly, cold. Our two feet thick stone walls (inside and out) are great sound absorbers, but don't seem all that efficient at warmth retention. Very few houses have central heating, and ours is not one of them. We make do with electric, calor gas, and paraffin heaters to supplement our enormous chimneys and burning oak. Friends go to bed wearing hats and socks, and the locals live behind closed shutters pretty much from November through to March. (Some of them live behind closed shutters all year round, in summer to keep the heat out).

It's also exceptionally wet, even more so than it was in July, when we suffered weeks of violent thunderstorms and lightning strikes. However, winter has its rewards. The vinegar flies have gone, the last plague lasting a whole week and invading framed pictures, light coloured clothing, and the insides of all the windows. They're a product of the grape harvest, but an unwelcome one. The sunsets are amazing, with glorious full moons filling the sky before the sun has left it. Michaelmas daisies and marguerites adorn the hedgerows, there for several weeks now and still producing buds turning into an array of colourful flowers.

The days are still graced with sunshine, but the cafés have put all their outside furniture away. My concession to the cold nights upon us now is to change the summer duvets to winter ones, and Spouse closes up the pool. Visitors will return in Spring but until then we shall be home alone, huddled by the log fire!

Winter Frost in Esset

I worry about the dogs forced to live in make shift kennels outdoors, often just old cognac barrels, and about the horses and donkeys not given any shelter. Whenever I can, I do my best to influence those who'll listen, and hope that both television advertising and children's comics will do the same. People romanticise about moving here, likening it to England fifty years ago. And then they do a reality check, and search for hot water bottles!

No worries, we have some Christmas cheer around the corner and set the scene with a carol concert in Cognac. I organise a meal afterwards, for eighteen Expats. It's a great success and the Taj Mahal does us proud. It's a joy to savour the flavours of India again. Spouse is doubly delighted when he opens a discussion about chick pea flour with the owner. He's from Leicester. Of course he is! We leave the restaurant with two bags of it, so now we can have our own onion bhajis at home.

The Day itself passes uneventfully, but that's how I like it to be. I belong to the 'Christmas is the most boring day of the year' brigade. The French obviously feel likewise and celebrate it little, not even in the shops. That's fine by me! January arrives and brings with it the most phenomenally strong winds, too strong for snow to settle, so we feel as if we're back in St Moritz without the white stuff. Work is pretty much non existent. There are no buyers around, hardly any new instructions, so those of us who are self employed struggle. The Chasse calls us to a meal in the village hall the following month and with mixed feelings from me, but wanting to dance the night away, we attend:

Potage avec Pearl de Japon (I don't know what it is, but it looks like frogspawn)

Assiette de fruit de mer (lots of yummy prawns, not so yummy bulots (think rubber) all surrounded by crab claws, lots of them, and a few langoustines

Pavé de Dorade, sauce crevettes (sea bream in a shrimp sauce, delicious)

Sorbet pêche de vigne (peach sorbet)

Gigot de chevreuil (leg of venison), haricôts verts (of course), pommes sautées

This, of course, is the raison d'être of the evening, helping consume the quota of deer they've been allowed to kill. Feelings aside, none of it is wasted and all of it is shared. I'm brave. It arrives in casserole form, and is truly delicious. Of course I feel guilty afterwards, but enjoy it immensely whilst eating it.

Salade

Fromage (large selection of cheese as it happens) and even more baguettes

Framboisier (raspberry gâteau again, they must have a secret supplier)

And all the usual aperitifs, wine by the course, coffee and cognac to finish

This time we have to pay, but it's only 22 euros each and

that's all inclusive!

Why can't the restaurants perform as well as the village halls always do, and as cheaply? It's a question I continue to ask, but nobody seems able to answer.

Farmers are busy in the fields and the size and stature of the machinery they hire from the local co-operatives is impressive. The ploughs return and I'm invited up into one of these huge things. The bird's eye view is impressive and it's great fun to ride in the cab. Perhaps I should change jobs. Naah, too much like hard work. Estate agency is easy, at least compared to what these guys do.

March winds give way to a glorious April, with our lilac tree in full bloom, the uniformed rows of maize in the field opposite growing shoots, and our fruit trees promising good crops. We have our own little orchard, which yields copious amounts of cherries, those delectable black ones, some not so interesting red varieties, lots of figs, and the blasted apples and pears I'll have to pick later in the year as they fall to the ground. The hedgerows are a glorious mélange (mix) of bright red poppies, purple clover, marigolds and buttercups galore, wild violets, and cowslips. Also, some blue flowers I fail to identify. Perhaps they're cornflowers. That would make sense! The crickets are singing, the lizards emerge from the stone walls, the bats return to our barns at night (so do the owls, much to Megan's fascination and Gemima's frustration) and enormous hedgehogs emerge from hibernation. It's Spring!

26 Slave or Leave

It's not all love and loving it at the grindstone in Cognac, though. She who runs the office and her estranged husband are in the throws of selling their franchise. It will affect us all. The person who wants to buy them out comes to meet us. A long and boring morning begins and we brace ourselves for the inevitable. Boss picks her nose throughout, examining the contents once evacuated, and chucking it over her shoulders as usual. He who's to become the new owner picks the skin off his fingers, gathers it into piles, and chucks it on the floor. Like, where's it going to go? Who's going to pick it up, ditto the dried snot? It's the same with smokers. Who's going to pick up their fag ends? And are the empty packets they throw out of car windows going to disintegrate into the concrete? And are they going to miraculously soak into non-smokers' lawns? I think not!

Secretary seductively smiles when she thinks she needs to, and sulks when she's not having to impress. There are no happy bunnies here this morning! He who eats tripe goes ballistic when proposed new owner suggests targets, muttering something about not needing carrots to make him be successful in life. He makes it clear that no carrots will be dangled under his nose, ex policeman says likewise, the matter's dropped and we all breathe sighs of relief. (This is France, not Taylors, Haarts, or Connells back in England!) Ex policeman is asked for his prognosis for the following year's trading. He smiles sweetly (he's a lovely guy), bids us all a good sales year and then shuts up. I want to clap, but resist the temptation.

All those on the salaried payroll stay dumb, obviously wanting their salaried bread to remain buttered. I take the floor and grieve that none of my instructions have been included in the last two months' sales figures, despite one of them going on the market at over a million euros. She who runs the office obviously wants to take credit for it, but I'm not going to let her over ride me on this occasion. I ask "pour quoi?" (why) and she just shrugs her shoulders, a national trait with les français. I grab the official sheets, amend them, and pass them to the new chap, sitting there aghast. The anglais are supposed to shut up and put up, but I've learnt to go beyond the barrier. He hands them to the secretary, reluctantly asked to amend them. I've won! The gain, however, is to be purely temporary.

We discuss the Caravane and I point out that we rarely go northwards from Cognac. I meet with the usual objections, but emphasise that we drove 28 kilometres south last week to the first property, and over 40 the previous week, so can someone please tell me the difference? They probably can, but they don't. Boss just gives yet another Gallic shrug and states:

"C'est comme ça (that's how it is)."

Young man sitting opposite me actually agrees. He who eats tripe joins the boss and does the shoulder shrug. Ex policeman, always polite, says nothing but smiles in guarded recognition. Meeting over, individual fates unknown, we all retire to le Duguesclin, including newcomer.

Nobody seems to have taken to him, so there will be lots of troubled times ahead. I pay 11.85 euros for a rubbish pizza, which the Italians would chuck in the Tiber (except that's in

Rome and the pizza holds pride of place in Naples). I'm being a bit unfair here. I also have an espresso coffee for my money. New guy eats like a savage and it's disgusting to watch him. He has absolutely zilch table manners. I am not going to work with this man for long, I can feel it in my English bones. He makes it obvious that there are three of us at the table whom he hates: he who eats tripe, our charming ex policeman, and me! He blatantly sees us as threats to his empire building. We are, of course, the oldest and the most experienced, always dangerous thus to be. I make the decision not to do any more property translations. It's a service I've been providing free of charge. He can get stuffed and find another mug!

It gets nastier. Ex policeman is told he's no longer welcome to use the office but can still sell the properties on offer, calling in just to collect keys etc. He who eats tripe is a law unto himself and one which newcomer dare not take on. He's been contracted (but self employed like I am) to them since the beginning and if he walks, it will all collapse. He escapes Scot free. So, in a roundabout way, the three of us survive to live another day. But my fate hangs in the balance. I've already been kind of replaced. A young English girl has been taken on as a salaried employee, like she who's French, but married to an English man. They come cheaper, on very low commission rates. They will survive, without doubt. In an active market place, all are welcome and I'm happy to work alongside both of them. The more properties we can offer the Public, the more sales we'll get. The trouble is, we are sinking into a period of non activity. Old boss relinquishes the franchise but survives as manager. Unpopular new owner pokes his head in from time to time, obviously preferring to work from one of his other branches. Alleluja! Tensions escalate and the atmosphere is ghastly. I'm asked to attend a meeting with the new guy, who gives me a choice. Either I work for him full time, for which I'll be paid a salary (the French basic) but will lose a huge 32% of my commission rate, or I leave. Before making my final decision, I have a meeting with old boss, lay my cards on the table and get no response, just another Gallic shrug from her and a pathetically uttered:

"Je suis desolée (I am sorry)."

I reflect on some of the things which have happened to me in the three years I've been with this firm. I've had clients taken from me and given to salaried staff, not just once, but on several occasions. I've been pig in the middle between two women who openly hate each other's guts, whilst attempting to do business together. I've seen two short lived colleagues who've become close friends caught up in the same battle and leaving, too. One of them is still fighting for money owed to him, and I doubt that he will get it. He's planning a return to Blighty. I shall miss him, a delightfully kind Scottish gentleman with a great sense of humour.

I've seen referral agents providing us with clients, deals then closing in secret, so that less (or no) commission has had to be shared. Whenever I've been able to, I've fought on their behalf, including the warring referral agent who's long since severed connections with the Agence! Alas, I have failed on more than one occasion. These things plague my catholic conscience. I walk! But I take happy memories with me, and some weird ones.

I remember entering an embalming parlour on one Caravane, but was told not to worry because all the fluids were stored in the cellar and there was *no body* to work on that day. We were assured that the only coffin currently in situ was in another room, beyond the kitchen and, no, we did not have to go in there. A ghost 'lived' in the attic, but he was a friendly one! It struck me as slightly odd that a British funeral director should set up business in France, but his other half was French, and what a stoic lady she turned out to be. Rather her than me!

I remember the day when clients walked into the office and asked:

"Has there been a war, it feels like nuclear fall-out. Where is everybody? The villages we've passed through have all been dead, totally deserted."

"Nope, you've just arrived in France, in Poitou Charentes!"

They do not buy!

27 Job Move to Saint Jean d'Angely

I sign on at the local employment exchange, in Saint Jean d'Angely. This is fun! For a start, I'm English and am received politely, but with a certain amount of intrigue. I'm asked why I'm here and tell them it's just to keep myself in the System, having paid my taxes and social charges for the last three years. Of course I receive no benefits, none whatsoever. A charming middle aged lady takes me to the computer area and shows me how to work them. Once registered, I'm to come here every week and check out job opportunities.

"Can't I do that at home, from my own computer?"

Obviously such things are not commonplace here yet, understandably given that Broadband and Wi-fi haven't reached many places in Rural France. We have 'dial-up,' which is frustratingly slow but ça marche (it works).
I'm given permission, taken back into her office, and presented with a package of various administrative stuff I shall have to get my head round, and it won't be easy. My French doesn't really stretch to this kind of thing. I ask if I can go on the language courses provided for non French speaking immigrants. They're free of charge. She laughs, and reminds me that I've been speaking almost fluent French to her since I walked through her door. Ooops, failed again!

I am, however, offered the chance of attending a day seminar the following month. I grab it. A group of us gather round the horse shoe of tables in the conference room, and introduce ourselves. I've been through this kind of thing many a time and oft. A lady who looks decidedly French gives her name, also French, but turns out to be as English as I am. Next, we're asked what we've been doing and what we hope to be doing. There are some retraining courses on offer and the other English lady trains as an electrician. But not before trying her hand at estate agency in the outer reaches of La Rochelle. It's what a lot of Expats do, most of them untrained and unskilled, but good on'em. The women become realtors and the men become builders! Ah, but she's in the business long enough (not long) to tell someone in the office she's working out of, and who's already met me, that I'm currently unemployed. Wonderful!

After just a few weeks of computer clicking, I'm off to Rochefort for the day. I worry about my hair. It's ash white and maybe this new chap prefers brunettes. Naah, I'm not going to dye it, it's me, who and how I am, and I actually rather like it. I concentrate on my clothes, youngish without being tarty (never) and stick to navy blue. I treat myself to a new skirt, pencil lined tailored, wear my favourite ivory coloured shirt, and the tweed jacket with the navy velvet collar I bought in Switzerland ten years earlier and still serving me well. I feel safely confident. My feet aren't quite as enthusiastic. It's not often I wear court shoes these days, and they're rebelling big time. No worries, I have a pair of 'flats' in my briefcase (an expandable one I bought for a song in a shopping mall in New Jersey, also many years ago). It's come a long way, my American work bag!

Spouse and holidaying with us again daughter, come for the ride. We part company out of sight of where I'm to be interrogated. We agree on a place to meet up for lunch afterwards. If I'm kept longer, I'll buy a sandwich and we'll rendezvous down at the Docks, scheduled for the afternoon's fresh air and fun. Unlikely, given that every Frenchman stops for déjeuner (lunch) at mid day. Il faut manger (one must eat)!

It all goes smoothingly, ridiculously, well and I emerge with a signed contract of salaried employment for the Branch he's opening in Saint Jean d'Angely. This man doesn't believe in the self-employed lark. It's all or nothing. I have nothing at the moment, the market is dropping drastically, and hence the chance of being salaried is too sensible to refuse. He's also a decision maker, and I like that. He's tall, rugby player build, full set of large white teeth, well presented, and carrying an appealing aura of professionalism.

My commission rate, at 8%, will be a mere pittance compared to the 40% I've been used to for the last three years, but that fades into insignificance when taken within the package of salary plus social charges he'll be financing on my behalf. They are crippling in France and once started, must be paid whether money's being earned or not, for as long as one's registered. Self employment in a buzzing market works well, but in a broken one, it soon turns to disaster. I'm to report for duty in Saintes, his Head Office, immediately after the Easter holidays, for training before we open up in Saint Jean. By then he'll have finished building his team. The manager and secretary are to be Parisiennes taken from other Branches. There'll be one more negotiator, and she's likely to be the Parisienne he's seeing tomorrow. A small team of trois femmes françaises et une anglaise.

Rochefort is a busy port at the mouth of the Charente Estuary, and the little restaurant we've chosen reflects its cosmopolitanism, like its sister city of La Rochelle, a little further up the Atlantic Coast. Lunch is good, as expected. A

197

new job is always something to celebrate, and in this case it's more than that. Spouse is not yet 65 and I really need to keep working until he reaches that magic number.

France isn't the push-over the United Kingdom is, and benefits aren't handed out willy-nilly. Quite right, too! To get into the French health care system, for instance, one has to be 65 and in receipt of a British (or other) pension, alternatively work, or be a dependent of someone who does. In our case, that's me. Eventually, if we are still here, I'll become his dependent and be able to retire myself, at 59! In France, married people are fiscally treated as one unit. Even when in the System per se, it doesn't come free, neither to les français and nor to les anglais. 60-70% of basic health care treatment is paid by the French Government to all entitled to receive it, the balance picked up by individuals pretty much always having 'top-up' insurance, although it's not a legal requirement. France is reimbursed by the 'pillars of power' in Newcastle Upon Tyne for those in the British, rather than the French, System who are cared for in France. Woe be tide those who don't have 'top-up,' though! The remaining 30 to 40% can be hard to find! Those on the baguette line, of course, get it all free.

Thereby lies another tale, and there's many a Brit walking the streets of Poitou Charentes because he's not declared his income from brick laying! I'm reminded of a bridge playing partner who often spoke of "many a man walking the streets of Glasgow because he didn't know his diamonds from his spades," actually "because he didn't clear his trumps."

We can't visit Rochefort without catching up with the progress down on the Docks of the frigate 'Hermione,' the ship General Lafayette sailed across the Atlantic to help the

Americans defeat the British in their War of Independence. The replica we're now inspecting has been a work in progress for several years, and we've been watching it stage by stage. It's still very much a hull, but since last time we visited we can see the final shape it's to become. We can now feel the atmosphere, relate a little to the sailors, and to the engineers who created this splendid vessel. The steps up to the various levels get higher with every visit, indicating how much nearer it will be to sailing the exact same journey.

Alongside the dry dock 'Hermione' occupies, is La Corderie Royale (the rope museum) built in 1666, commissioned in the reign of King Louis XIV and one of the largest in the World. With maritime battles the order of the day, rope was one of the most needed commodities for all seafaring nations. Perhaps this ropery is also unique in being afloat itself, on marshland. We visit it yet again! The place is phenomenal, with no fewer than five hundred doors and windows and over eleven thousand floor tiles. The length in itself provides a good after lunch walk, stopping at various places en route to learn about everything from marine astronomy to navigational tools, not least rope itself. Still a working model, it's intriguing to see the small engines toing and froing along the central division. And of course, like all museums, it's a great place to buy post cards!

Rochefort isn't the only French Atlantic Coastal town or city which is linked to the American War of Independence. Benjamin Franklin got all the way from America to the South Breton Coast, only to be scuppered by bad weather. Hoping to disembark in Nantes, he had to change plans and thus he arrived in the little town of Auray. The year was 1776 and he was in France to muster support for the revolution Stateside, not realising that by doing so, the

French would rally more forcefully towards their own revolution, not far around the corner. And there was I, thinking it was only recently that it became fashionable to blame the Yanks! Auray has quite a lot of history for such a small place. Not many years after Franklin's landing on dry Breton soil, we Brits tried to help restore the French Monarchy, and one of the last battles against the new revolutionary forces took place there. Many of the French Nobility and their supporters were killed in the process. Why Auray? Because it was the home town of one of the anti-revolutionaries, Georges Cadoudal. A humble miller's son, he survived the battle, only to be guillotined for taking part in a plot to remove Napoleon from power. The year was 1804, just five years after the self made little man had finally and successfully seized power, and fifteen since the French Revolution had officially begun.

Just up the road from this port inadvertently made famous, is the village of Sainte Anne d'Auray, now a major place of pilgrimage for Roman Catholics. Even the Pope has celebrated mass there (John Paul 11 in 1996). It's all about Jesus's grandmother Anne appearing to a young man called Yves Nicolazic in 1623. Some say that Anne was a native of Brittany, went by boat to Judea, married Joachim, gave birth to Mary (she who remained immaculate) and then returned to France. There are even those who believe that Jesus visited his grandmother there. I am not one of them.

28 Initiation Day in Saintes

Saintes straddles the Charente in utter Roman glory, upriver from Rochefort. Its Romanesque buildings are magnificent, and the museum on its left bank is well worth visiting. Cross the river and climb the hill, passing fashionable shops and chic restaurants en route, the prefecture and theatre on the right, and then turn left at the roundabout. Follow the signs for the Ampitheatre and go there, you'll not be disappointed! It's one of the biggest outside Rome, but unlike Rome's, is likely to be deserted. Also, it only costs one euro to go in!

The office is large, light, and welcoming. I introduce myself, shown where the kitchen is and pour an espresso. I meet far too many 'equips' (colleagues) to remember the names of, but they all seem really nice! Saintes and Cognac vie for superiority like the Lancastrians and Yorks do, Saintes taking the biscuit in terms of architecture and history, Cognac for its commercial success with its drink of the same name!

A few of us are filtered out (the new guys and gals) and led upstairs to the conference room. This firm is on the up, obviously expanding. We have satellite branches in Rochefort, Surgères, Niort, and of course we'll soon be in Saint Jean d'Angely. The Trainer's come all the way from Nantes, obviously hired for his talents and for the occasion. Most of it is boring, and of course I understand a mere fraction of it, but nobody seems to notice. It pans out over three long hours (we're allowed a bottle of water each) and then we break for déjeuner.

The Big Boss treats us all to lunch at a lovely restaurant Spouse and I have used over the years, so all's well, but this is only the start and I'm the only Brit. Again! For me, it's another survival course, the only difference being jumping through psychological hoops, rather than physical ones. I know, the Marines do both! We're back in the classroom, more boring video presentations and white board scenarios, role play, and group work. No break for a cuppa (c'est la France) and we plod on until 6 p.m. when we're finally allowed out. The instructions are clear:

"You must report here at the same time next month. Then we will discuss your progress."

The French love their 'formations' (vocational training) but I happen to hate them! The car? Ohmondieu, I'm sure to have a parking ticket, and can't remember where I've left it, my head full of facts, figures, and frustration. It's fine. I retrace the morning's walk and have left it far away enough for no warden to trace. Phew!

It's staff only day at the new office, but only the manager has a key. We report for duty at 14:00 hours (why we're given the morning off, I have no idea) and arrange to meet on the corner of the Square leading down the cobbled lane to our premises. I arrive fifteen minutes early, the manager does likewise. The other two are late. She's hopping mad, accusing the locals of being backward and having no respect for punctuality. This is a good start. The other two aren't even locals, but both are from Paris. Well, it seems I'm wrong on that score. The secretary has been living in Saintes for the last ten years or so, and the negotiator is a born and bred lass from a rural hamlet on the outskirts of Saint Jean. But she's only just moved back here, from Paris ! A bit early to readopt tardy country habits, surely? They're both officially five minutes late, and have already blotted their copy books.

We hobble on the cobbles to the workplace, which is a semi derelict dump. O.k. then, this won't attract the punters. The builders move in the following day and work phenomenally well, whilst the four of us tread the streets with fliers announcing our arrival, and the date and time of our official opening. I'm not prepared for this, and my feet are killing me. I'm able to side track into a shoe shop and buy a pair of sensible walking shoes. That's better! The bank account isn't though. Tough, I need them!

I can't believe what happens next. There I am, clipboard in hand, fliers in a carrier bag, walking towards the ancient old clock Saint Jean d'Angely is famous for (as well as John the Baptist's head) and the very first couple I see are old selling clients of mine from Cognac. I'm aghast. They moved back to Norwich, so how come they're here? They even managed to buy back the house they'd left there, on the market again as part of a divorce settlement. And then they missed France. This time round, they're being sensible, ditching the country (they lived in the middle of nowhere last time) and insisting on buying in town. That's fine by me. We'll soon have plenty to show them, no problemo. I hand them a flier, they give me their details, and I make a fuss of Boston, their adorable Golden Retriever. I've missed him! They're just the inspiration, and motivation, I need. My new clodhopper shoes glide easily over the cobbles and I carry on, smiling and sure that it's all going to be fine. St Jean is on home ground, and it feels good to be working here. The sun shines more the further west one travels in Poitou Charentes, another bonus over Cognac.

We rendezvous back at the office and find the 'phones have been connected in our absence. The Big Boss and his sexy wife (ooh laa laa she's all baubles and bangles and lacey mini skirt above stiletto heels certainly not fit for the cobbles of St Jean) are here. She won't have any competition from our staid team of four professionals (no, not that kind), won't need to worry about her husband taking a mistress from this Branch, not that he does from any Branch. With her at home, he has no need! We all use the intelligence we've been given in different ways, n'est ce pas! They've brought some chairs for us to use amongst the mess, and vast amounts of peripheral stuff to get us started. By the end of the week, between treading the streets and driving the villages, I've six properties to put on the market. Cheating a bit, but there's no law against it here and I certainly haven't signed anything, they were all clients of mine in Cognac and want me to carry on marketing their homes. They were just waiting for my call! It makes more sense for them, too, as they are all a lot nearer to St Jean d'Angely than they are to Cognac, and now that I've lefthere, none of their other 'equips' will bother with them. That's a certainty!

I revisit Bagnizeau and take a whole afternoon writing up the main house and the 4 gîtes again. We adjourn for tea (in style) half way through and she tells me how she nearly lost her husband in the Tsunami which hit Sri Lanka. It's a terrifying account that I listen to, and not what the family had expected to happen for Christmas. He's still working in Bangladesh and is anxious for her to join him. She seems very uncertain about it and I'm not surprised. France is surely a safer and gentler place to bring up two girls. We become good friends and have several social evenings together, eating her excellent curries when it's her turn to host.

I go back to the little house in La Brousse I put on a while back, but at such a high price that it hasn't any chance of selling in the immediate future. Madame insists it's beautiful, but sadly it is not. She's desperate to move back to Alsace, to be near her daughter and grandchildren. Another granny home alone in the wrong place! It's clean (many are not) but too inconvenient for youngsters to take on, in terms of location and what it offers. They're beginning to catch on and will no longer accept long walks down steps and through rear corridors to reach the 'loo.' The 'oldies' are often glad to have an inside one at all, and it doesn't seem to matter if it's in an outhouse, or under a dining table. Most Rural Frenchmen pee in the garden anyway. Oh yes I have, I've actually seen a 'loo' under a table used for eating at, and I've seen another taking pride of place in the middle of the bedroom, two in fact. One of them was in a very swish modern house, and there it was, with no barrier, right in the middle of the room. I mean, would you?! Granted, the other was in an old farm house where 'granny' used to live. I guess she was so old she couldn't walk very far.

I was in a house with he who eats tripe once, one of his instructions in the centre of Cognac. The house was superb, fully renovated from its 'Edwardian' origins, 7 bedrooms and three of them had en suite shower rooms. None of them contained toilet facilities. I found the bathroom. Fine!

"But where's the 'loo'?" I ask. I receive a blank look back.

"What is it with you French, do you pee in the bidet?"

"Non, pas de tout. (No, not at all) We pee in the lavabo (basin)!"

The only 'loo' in the whole glorious house, with its amazing walled garden, beautiful swimming pool, and gorgeous reception rooms, was under the stairs on the ground floor. The headroom would have been insufficient for any man taller than me, 5'7", and I'd've clonked my Anglo-Saxon head every time I had to raise myself from the said receptacle. We are very different, private, people.

My revisits are in Fontaine Chalandray, Aulnay, Sonnac, Matha and Brie sur Matha, all popular with Expats but none quite so much as Sonnac, which has managed to retain its post office, and café cum general stores. Not that I'd advise anyone to buy anything in there, unless it came fully wrapped, having explored its facilities earlier on! If it's a treat you're after, then go to the Patisserie below ...

Sunday cakes in La Rochelle

29 Catherine de Medici and La Belle Hélène

The snakes are back! Just the odd one, but impressive enough to write about and remember, especially when they slither so close to our territory. Gemima is a cat, not a mongoose, and fortunately sticks to lizards. She can get those in her mouth, rather than a snake getting her in its mouth. Fortunately, they never find their way into the garden, obviously not liking the huge amount of gravel we have between gate and grass, so Megan remains blissfully unaware of their presence in the fields beyond. They move so quickly, I'm not able to photograph them, which is more the pity as many folk are under the illusion there aren't any in Poitou Charentes. Oh yes there are!

Word passes through Bagnizeau that 'the new English estate agent' from Saint Jean d'Angely is working the patch, so I pick up four more instructions there in less than a month, ranging from a hovel to a mansion. The same happens in other villages, obviously having been neglected in all real estate matters up to now, too far from Cognac, and even from St Jean it seems. But the times, they are a changin'. This time round, my manager is graced with both vision and lateral thinking and encourages, rather than blocks, my venturing out into the bush! She does the same herself, and her secteur practically reaches the historical little town of Surgères, half way between St Jean and La Rochelle.

Surgères is charming, has several towers left from its mediaeval fortress, surrounded by parkland; a busy indoor market; several independent shops; and a fair few restaurants, including a couple of superb ones we use from time to time. The Ronsard is a great stopping off place for dinner after depositing the never ending round of house guests at La Rochelle Airport. The return flights to England are splendidly time tabled for us to be driving through Surgères when hunger begins to strike. It's necessary, we're exhausted, and in need of rest and relaxation! For lunch time meals, Le Vieux Puis is a little bit of luxury. It's tiny, tucked away up a little lane, but in the centre of town.

Food features high on the agenda around here. In its time, the château was the home of Catherine de Medici and her lady-in-waiting, the young and beautiful Madamesoiselle Hélène de Fonsèque. The poet, Pierre de Ronsard (hence the name of the restaurant) fell head over heels with the young aristocrat, wrote sonnets galore to her, and was gutted when she married someone else! Next time you order a 'Pear Belle Hélène' for pudding, think of Ronsard and his Love because that's why it's called that. Of course he didn't stand a chance. She was a young maiden (or was she?) and he was already middle aged when they met.

That was back in the seventeenth century, but to me this town's history really begins back in 1152, when Eleanor of Aquitaine married Henry II of England, thus placing it in our grubby little English mitts. Louis XIV managed to reclaim it during his reign (1643-1715, blimey that was a long one, especially for those days) although I doubt that he had anything to do with it personally. Whilst his men were fighting The Hundred Years War, which didn't really last a hundred years at all (it actually went from 1337 to 1453 and that makes one hundred and sixteen no less) good old Louis, thinking he was a cool dude, was no doubt swanning around in the abject gaudiness of his palace at Versailles. He would have done better living in the Charente Maritime, here in Surgères, where the sun sure shines one helluva lot more than it does so close to Paris.

Still thinking all things culinary, Surgères is home to one of the largest and most important agricultural colleges in France, specialising in all things dairy. Remember, Poitou Charentes is famous for corn, cognac, and COWS. If you've an afternoon to spare, knock on the door and they may let you in. But not if it's July or August. Of course not, you may be on holiday, and so may they. Not the cows of course! If you're lucky, you'll be able to end your visit with a trip into the shop. Bring a cool box, there's a big selection of butter and cheese to buy, even cream. This is an item not usually easy to find in these parts, Brittany and Normandy pretty much having the market in cream and all things dairy. I have work to do, so I shan't be getting the TGV from Surgères to Paris today. (That's another advantage the place has.) Perhaps some day, though! It's a nice thought, but city life holds little or no appeal to those of us who have given up the bright lights for life amongst the vineyards and the cornfields.

The grand metropolis of St Jean d'Angely is quite sufficient for me, with the occasional trip to La Rochelle and the Ile de Ré. What could be nicer? I know, a 'Pendleton's Twicer, ice cream with a lolly each end,' eaten on a summer's day in a Charentaise village, by the poolside!

30 The Tin Man

This is an easy start, or shall I make it late morning? Much better idea! I'm putting our neighbours' house on the market, a beautiful barn conversion with a fantastic swimming pool set in their parkland type garden. They're lovely people, well travelled with interesting stories to tell, some from fascinating far flung places. Gladly, they're not moving far, just into St Jean d'Angely. But the house will have to sell first, and it's not a fast market at the moment.

Many of us are growing increasingly disenchanted with Esset, with the whole of La Brousse per se. The Maire's following the trend and allowing lots of new build properties to be built. In Poitou Charentes, this means ugly storage boxes with roofs on to all intents and purposes. They are not in the slightest bit attractive to look at, and some of them remain forever unfinished. There's a stupid loop hole in the law. Taxes aren't applicable until the property IS totally finished, which means horrible looking breeze block rectangles are blotting the rural landscape. I stare in disbelief at the foundations of yet another one directly behind their house and to be seen from their window, and go home for lunch.

Back in Néré and Villiers Couture in the afternoon, I return to St Jean with three more instructions. That's another four for the punters, and we're finally open for business. By the end of the first month's trading, we're doing well, with a great portfolio of town houses, country cottages, and a few grand rural retreats. Many of my old clients have found out where I'm working, but equally so I've 'phoned a good many. In no time at all, I find myself veering more and more into my old secteur again, the old and the new overlapping. I even get a redundant shop to sell in Macqueville, really Cognac's territory but they were too slow off the mark and all's fair in love and war! Macqueville is one of the few villages between Cognac and Matha to have retained its General Stores. The little church stands proudly in the Square, with seats for whiling the time away for the elderly not playing boules, and it's altogether a very pleasant little place to live. It's one of the few villages in this area which has what I call 'the light factor.' So many of them are dull and dreary outposts, with crumbling down houses lining the streets, shutters permanently closed to the outside world. The shop I'm instructed to sell comes with excellent, mostly renovated living accommodation, and really only needs the finishing touches. It's a good product, one which won't linger on the market for long.

Back in Bagnizeau, I'm writing up a little cottage for the second time of doing. This one has an intriguing history from a not very well known aspect of the German Occupation. The property itself is delightful, has great potential, a fair amount of space, comes with three double storied outbuildings, and windows on both floors. Bagnizeau is a good hour's drive from the dockyards of La Rochelle, and that's driving quickly in a modern car. By bicycle, it must be more like three hours, but that's working it out in today's terms, on a modern bike.

I'm now talking the 1940s, when a great many young men from the villages around here were ordered to work on the dockyards, and to get there under their own steam. Presumably they were given accommodation of sorts whilst there, not least in case they escaped en route either way. I discuss this with the current owners, charming people from Tarbes, down in the Hautes Pyrénées (that's the mountainous south west, bordering Spain). The man of the house insists, having been a child in Bagnizeau himself during the War, that the youngster living there then would indeed have cycled to and fro La Rochelle on a daily basis, but I continue to doubt that. I'm usually more interested in gleaming little bits of information about France's recent history than the French themselves are. It's dodgy ground to tread. One never knows if one's talking to a résistant or a collaborateur! Monsieur et Madame bought the cottage as a maison secondaire, returning to his roots for holidays. C'est normale, très normale ici. All he's able to tell me is that they found a clapped out old bicycle in the outbuildings when they bought the property, which triggered his memory to recall certain events, the teenagers turned into slave labour during the German Occupation, the docks being one of the locations they were ordered to by force. It's something to check out.

In my standard day in the life of an estate agent here in Poitou Charentes, I come across relics from this period frequently. I see stacks and stacks of abandoned German vehicles randomly left to rot in farmyards, ranging from cars to tanks and transport vans. I can't understand how the current owners can walk past them without hurting deeply inside. No matter which side they supported, the memories must be horrific. I think of the German Officer's trunk left in the living room of the house in Varaize. Perhaps the house was never lived in again after the War. That would make sense. I see museums springing up in local towns, displaying artefacts of war behind splendid glass panels, surreal in their detachment from the reality they were once part of.

Returning to Néré, I put the view with the mostest on the market. It's truly magnificent, absolutely gob smackingly beautiful. Through long range binoculars, and obviously more sophisticated equipment, it's possible to see right across to Rochefort. And guess what? The Germans were up here, camped all around, but really using it for the uninterrupted surveyance it offered. It's now the country home of a Parisien film maker, his young wife, two yappy little Yorkshire terriers (don't French women just love them), and one adorable proper dog. No secret which one I'm preferring. The man's utterly charming, and after writing up the house (nothing really special, but well kept except for the copious amount of mostly naff clutter, especially in the kitchen) he leads me past the old stone well (I wonder what's down there) and on into an enormous barn. Blimey, this is something else! Music's playing (apparently it does all day long) and I'm greeted by a mechanical tin man, larger than life and, yes, it's he who starred in 'The Wizard of Oz.'

Next stop, back in Matha. It's a day of mixed emotions, lots for the memory bank. This one also has a German connection, but not a war time one. Phew, I've had enough of those for one day! The current owner was married to one, but left him behind the other side of the French Border and moved back to her little home town here. Needing a bit more dosh to supplement the divorce settlement, she went to work as a 'carer' for a wealthy old Frenchman, who's now left her the bungalow I'm currently working on. Lucky lady! It'll sell easily enough at the right price. It's just a bog standard box which will appeal to starter-uppers and trading-downers alike. The position's good and we all know that's what it's all about. It's not for the British market, though, but that's ok.

Back home, exhausted and emotionally challenged after some of the tales I've heard, but it's all in a day's work and I'm not ready to let go of the clipboard yet. And especially not the camera, not with all the splendid scenery at my disposal to shoot, the only kind of shooting I do these days. I shot a bottle off a brick wall once, just once, back in the days of my youth. And, yes, I cleared up the mess afterwards. It was quite spectacular, actually, but having got the target once, I decided twice would be pushing my luck! Funny that my friend's parents were German and Italian respectively. The basement was its own museum to his father's (?) time in the S.S. I try and kid myself he was just a collector, a much nicer thought! I shudder when I think of it, especially as said friend went on to fight for the Americans in Vietnam, voluntarily!

Spouse has been cooking curry, at which he excels, both Indian and Thai (my preference) so all's right with the World. Where's that bottle of nice cold white? Voilà, c'est bon. C'est la belle vie en France.

Macqueville Church, next to the village shop, and
Bagnizeau Church taken from a client's house

31 The Latin Mass

I have a Belgian friend who still practices the religion I left behind in 1970. No longer having any emotional fears in that direction, I sometimes accompany her to church on Sunday mornings. We flit between the Abbey in St Jean d'Angely, and the Latin Mass up one of the back streets in the centre of Saintes. The Service is very beautiful and we can both still chant away in the language of our convent childhoods. Saintes has the advantage of an Indian restaurant there, for when the 'blessing' releases us. There's even a Chinese one as well, so it tends to win on location, as we patronise both!

This morning, we've come up with the not so bright idea of trying one we've heard of in the absolute back of beyonds, a church that is, not a restaurant. It's vaguely near the village of Asnières, en route between the two towns just mentioned. The Brits flock to Asnières for Sunday lunch in their droves, but we shan't be doing likewise ever again, at least I shan't. I've been there once, and vowed (excuse the pun) never again, despite their generosity with all things which come out of the Sea in shells. That was the time we joined a group of Brits to celebrate a birthday one of them was having. The wallpaper peeling from the walls, and the owner with a dirty apron round his middle, and a dirty tea towel suspended from his shoulder, was enough to put me off for good. A shame, as he seemed a friendly sort of fellow! But I don't do dirt, especially not in eating establishments, sadly often the case en France! The Group we were with went on to break apart big time, which was all very sad, very silly, and totally unnecessary. The trouble is, there's a tendency to develop a ghetto culture in Expatria, all perfectly understandable from an anthropological viewpoint. Few, however, seem able to restrict friendship to those with whom they'd have developed one back in the U.K. Drawn to the common language, the tendency is to pounce where perhaps they shouldn't. 'Twas always thus, and there's many a person out there who wishes they hadn't said "pop round for a cuppa!" Be warned, don't do it!

The church we're seeking turns out to be a devil (here I go again, oh the hold of it all) of a place to find, and has not a sign in sight. All I have are the directions I've acquired from a couple of très sérieux Roman Catholics from America, whose house I have for sale. They take their religion very seriously Stateside, no matter what form it comes in, and which branch of ultimately the one and the same thing they are drawn to.

We find it. It's outside, not even in, a small hamlet taken straight out of France circa the mid nineteenth century. The Mass is to be in Latin, nothing else will do for this congregation, the fundamentalist, thou shalt obey all rules, types. These people are far removed from those who attend Mass in Saintes, who are the refined, affluent, city types, très French chic. Saintes is a fashion show of elegance, affluence, and education.

Within seconds of arriving, in fact on the little walk up the path to the church itself, I realise why I became a Protestant. The phantoms of my Romanesque childhood are revisiting me! Friend and I are amongst a tiny minority who are not wearing mantillas. For those not in the know, they're the black veils we had to adorn our heads with in the school chapel every day, and were forced to wear on Sundays when we went to 'church proper' with our families. Actually, we had a choice on Sundays, velour school hats in winter, panamas in summer, or mantillas all year round.It was obligé to cover our heads, total lack of respect to let the gloriously thick hair of youth be paraded in all its healthy splendour.

There are well in excess of a hundred people here, the sexes pretty well balanced between the men and the women, and several (perhaps a dozen) small children. The men are mostly in suits (these are not poor people) and the women either look straight out of a 1980s' Laura Ashley catalogue, or a television documentary from America's Amish Community, perhaps even from the television series, 'A Little House On The Prairie.' Even the children are wearing hats, and the girls all have long, plaited hair, like their mums, descending to the waist beneath the bonnets they wear. Only one other woman is wearing trousers. That makes three of us! The skirts are all almost to the floor, in pastel backgrounds sporting pretty little pastel flowers, and they wear pastel cardigans, neatly buttoned to the waist, the sort made popular in the 1950s, creeping into the 1960s, when 'twin sets' were all the rage.

The servers on the altar are, of course, all boys. The female of the species rests in its given place in this little corner of Poitou Charentes.The man behind us reeks of aftershave, or maybe it's deodorant. He must be French! Why, oh why, can't they wash every day instead of plastering themselves with pungent sprays which do nothing to mask the body odour they're obviously trying to hide? It can be the same with English men of a certain age, of course, although not so many these days. Mega sales of showers, and television advertising, have seen to that! The over powering smell of whatever product it is he's using, nauseates friend and I, but we decide it would be churlish, unChristian, to move, so we stoically put up with it.

It's all exceedingly spookey, and there are statues and shrines everywhere. The 'Stations of the Cross' are particularly gory and yet their ugliness is fascinating. Rosary Beads are firmly held by many, even little children. I remember it all so well! The priest is now giving a sermon, in French. He's speaking very slowly and yet I can't understand a word he's muttering. I think his theme is about 'hope' as he uses the verb espérer (to hope) a lot. I decide that I shan't be taking communion, and I just want this experience to end as quickly as it started. We'd already been warned about it by a lovely joint friend from South America, who was made very unwelcome here. She just happens to be black. But curiosity has clearly got the better of us both. Others have said that many of the congregation are not only racist, but followers of Jean-Marie le Pen's daughter, Marine. That is something I shall refrain from expressing an opinion on. I can only speak as I feel here, today, and that's great unwelcomeness, silent stares, and zilch bonhommie. It's all creepily sad!

The nearest I've ever got to this kind of experience was in Columbus, just a few years ago, when I was over for a wedding our daughter bridesmaided at. My hostess took me to the Museum of Rural Ohio and this little church would have slotted in perfectly comfortably as an exhibit, complete with the old fashioned clothes of its congregation.

There's no chaleur (warmth) shown to us at the end of the service, and we are both in need of some. Nobody ventures forward with handshakes. They don't want us to join them. That has been made decidedly clear to us. It doesn't need a dice to throw. Off we head for the Indian Restaurant tout de suite, that's if we can find our way to Saintes!

We do, but it's well past midi and are wondering if we'll get served, arriving so late. C'est la France, remember! It's fine, they show us to a pleasantly positioned table and the food turns out to be delicious.

Shortly after 1 o'clock, a group of expectant lunchers walks in, to be told they are out of luck. We gasp in amazement. This attitude is très francais but never Asian, leastwise it never was. With only the two of us in the whole of the place, they surely can't say that the restaurant is full. They don't. They just announce that it is too late to receive them. So beware, if you fancy an onion bhajii in Saintes on Sunday, make sure you get there early!

We finish our coffee and head out into the cobbled streets surrounding the splendid cathedral Saintes is home to, then walk down to the River and watch the mini-cruisers loading passengers for an afternoon trip on the Charente. We'll do it one day ....

32 Food, Fashion & Fame

I'm with clients, sitting outside Bar National in Matha, taking coffee and discussing the day's viewings I've lined up for them. A charming British man approaches me, apologises for interrupting, but says he and his wife are wanting to sell their house and leave France. He's twigged that I'm an estate agent. They've been listening to me in action, and have decided to give me a try. That's fine by me, and I'm getting the impression they've been on with other agents a while. Always carrying my diary with me, we make an appointment on the spot and they leave with my card. I leave with great excitement, having been introduced to his wife and not failing to be inquisitive about her name. I ask, and she verifies!

Their house is en route Cressé, a good village, popular with les anglais because it comes with shops. These are getting increasingly more rare in Rural France, as are the bars and cafés most villages had once upon a time. Cressé still has one, owned by Brits. Spouse and I were treated to a meal there by two lots of lovely house guests staying with us at the same time. This turned into a highly amusing evening, so funny that its naffness paled into insignificance.

Neither the young couple from Vancouver (a cousin of mine and his wife) nor the family of four (old friends from our Hong Kong days) had set eyes on one another before, but we decided they'd get along together just fine, and they did. Spouse was an admirable host, whilst I carried on working to fill up the copious amounts of wine consumed, missing out on all the fun of the beach at Châtelaillon Plage and lunch at Saint Martin de Ré. It happens! As a 'merci beaucoup,' we were treated to a meal on the Friday evening, leaving me to make the booking, and thus the choice of venue. A client as fussy as I am when it comes to food and where to eat, had waxed eloquently on the joys of the restaurant in Cressé. Virtually everywhere else I tried was either fully booked, or closed, and so that's where we trundled off to. Big mistake!

The entrance bar had lots of people sitting on high stools, smoking away, and looking for all the world, especially the women (I'm tempted to call them 'Fag Ash Lills' but that may upset the rare few who still cling to the filthy habit) as if they'd be happier in TV's 'Benidorm.' Either there, or in the Rover's Return, that fictional pub made famous in the television soap, Coronation Street, and probably watched by many of those who do indeed take their holidays in Benidorm, or perhaps Ibiza. Anywhere where brainless boozers gather!

Oh dear, the vibes were not good for the evening which lay ahead. Owner turned out to be paralytically drunk and still in bed, obviously having had too good a session at lunch time. Wife appeared and showed us to our table, which turned out to be in what was to all intents and purposes the family living room, cluttered with toys and everyday apparel. Straight out of rustic mess, rather than shabby chic, the table was large and inviting, with plenty of space for everyone to sit in comfort. Our spirits started to lift, but not for long. Young lad, as in he who served, came to take our orders. He had not a clue, but it wasn't altogether his fault. We could have duck, or duck, or duck.

"O.k. then, we'll have duck, we'll all have duck."

Wine ordered, to the table it came, in a couple of ugly stone jars. Not what we'd asked for at all. The owner had obviously drunk everything in bottles and thought he could fob his clients off with stuff from giant sized catering cartons, decanted into country kitchen type recepticles. Wrong again! The vegetables arrived, two massive troughs of new potatoes (I like new potatoes) and chips, but all mixed together to form a mound too ridiculous to describe.

"Any greens, please? And what are you going to do about the wine?"

Two more massive troughs appeared, with volumes of over cooked, exceedingly sloppy, sliced courgettes. The wine? No chance, they'd not had time to restock! Ummm! It was a cheap meal (if it had been anything else, they'd've had a job getting any money out of us at all) and we laughed so hard that we actually enjoyed the sitcom we'd found ourselves in. The following day, in my local supermarket car park, Casino in Matha (no, not the gambling type, although that confused me one Sunday morning when we first arrived in France. What, a gambling den open on Sundays!) I met up with the owner (who'd not shown his face at all the night before) and his young employee, the pair of them completely dishevelled. I introduced myself and posed several questions, especially regarding the lack of wine on offer (boxed red and nothing else, not even boxed white), and the disgustingness of the vegetables.

"They were all we could get in the market yesterday."

I hear that the business has since closed!

More interesting to me than the house I've been invited to, lovely though it is, are the owners. Ex hoteliers from Dominica, they actually knew my sister-in-law's brother-in-law and his wife (work that one out) also ex the same island in the Caribbean. That, however, is not nearly as interesting as what I know now though. Outside 'Bar Nat' as we locals call it, when I'm introduced to his wife.

"Not THE famous fashionista, the best of the '60s?"

The Brand became one of the fashion icons of the decade, along with Mary Quant and Laura Ashley. One of the first dresses I ever bought was from Laura Ashley's shop in Bold Street (very posho shopping road, also good for its Chinese restaurant) in Liverpool. It was made from very fine courderoy and dyed vivid orange, way above the knee, tailored bodice and sleeves, then a flowing mass beneath. I think they call it 'Empire Line,' but I could be wrong, not being a fashionista myself. It was beautiful, I loved it, and wore it throughout my first pregnancy. I also had a Mary Quant dress (fake; I couldn't afford the genuine article), navy and white diagonally striped with a zipped front down to the waist. They called them 'easy accessibility dresses' back then. No idea why, as they finished nine inches above the knee! Unfortunately, I never owned a Biba dress, and can't even remember seeing them in Liverpool, strange given that Cilla Black was one of her customers. Even stranger, given 'the Pool's' prime position in '60s culture.

The house I'm in carries its own history, and also involves the Second World War. It comes to the market with several stone built outhouses (dépendances) and in one of them, I see a wall covered in graffiti. There's a German tank, and a swastika amongst the scribbles and sketches. Apparently a

German soldier was held here until the War ended. This happened rather a lot, I'm finding. I guess if they were considered dangerous, they were shot and promptly disposed of (perhaps down wells!) but if they were considered harmless, as many of them actually were, especially the youngsters, they were taken in and fed by the family in return for manual labour, grape picking, harvesting, looking after the family pig, the poultry, or whatever was needed to be done. The majority of the able bodied local men would have been away fighting, at least until General Petain's Vichy Régime took hold, and the women would have been grateful for fit young defectors pleading for succour, especially the young girls deprived of the lustiness of youth. Obviously kept under constant guard, lest this kindness be betrayed, and the families themselves betrayed, it's a little bit of war time history rarely mentioned. It was a risk many took, including people in our own Commune of La Brousse. The youngster taken in by villagers in Villemarange, the next hamlet along from Esset, is now an elderly gentleman, revered by many but not by all. Such is the legacy of war!

The fabulous swimming pool, surrounded by masses of colourful flowers, and a fully landscaped garden, together with the charm of this superb maison de maître, original features still perfectly intact, will sell this house smoothly. It'll just be a matter of time, and I can but hope I clinch the deal. It's amazing where my clients come from. Sometimes I pick them up in shopping aisles, sometimes in bars and restaurants, at the municipal pool in St Jean d'Angely (where I do aquagym) at church in Cognac, and BarNat in Matha! Spouse jokes that I'll talk to anyone, anywhere, anytime. It's a good 'job' that I do! Silence may be golden, but it doesn't do much for business and I'm not a Carmelite, not like my Great Aunt May. It was wonderful visiting her in the Convent at Upholland, Lancashire, as it always meant a bottle of pop and a packet of crisps at the pub after we'd seen her, outside in the car park of course, while parents sipped beer inside. Children weren't allowed in pubs back then. Nowadays, they've all but taken them over, some verging on kids' play centres!

Silent Walls, Hidden Dreams

33 Tea in Bohemian's Barn

A lady rings the office, just as we're about to close up for the evening. She wants to view a property for sale a few doors down the road from the Agence, a key holding job, so no worries. Fortunately not tonight, but "tomorrow night please." Even better, tomorrow night comes, but she doesn't. I wait, and wait, and wait. She's been delegated to me, as she's 'une anglaise.' No problem, I'll get the commission if she buys it! I've already been into the very swish appartment concerned, opened all the shutters, made it look all tickety-boo, and telephoned the owners to say that I'll be in there with a client at 6 p.m. or thereabouts. (They have a habit of using it themselves from time to time and leaving the odd unwashed mug in the sink. First impressions!) By 7 p.m. it's obvious said lady isn't going to turn up, but nor does she answer her 'phones (either of them) so I have no choice but to give her the benefit of the doubt. I give her another half hour, swear and curse at her, go back into the apartment and close the shutters, and finally get home in time to go to bed. Leastwise, that's how it feels. Oh, and I have to telephone the owners with the bad news.

I eventually pluck up the courage to ring her a few days later, trying to disguise my annoyance and disdain in the process. She's clueless, and doesn't realise just how inconsiderate she's been. Few of them do! She invites me for aperitifs, which I decline, but agree to go to her house for a cup of tea next time I'm in her area. She's in my secteur, not far from St Jean d'Angely, so no worries and a cuppa's always nice to have, especially (often only) when given by a fellow Brit.

I arrive in the middle of a heavy shower of thundery rain, and it's actually quite cold, goose pimply cold in fact. I've rung her first, not trusting this particular lady's mode de vie (lifestyle), and first impressions of the house are that it's rather odd. It's quite grand, but not at all in character with anything else in the village, more like a Victorian Gothic mini mansion. There's nobody in sight, so I walk up the flight of stone steps to the front door, knock, open it a little, to find a hall full of various types of footwear ranging from flip flops to brogues to wellingtons. Obviously she has a young family with her, and they've all gone out for the day.

I retreat down the steps, and in doing so, an apparition floats across the garden towards a barn. The lady's dressed in Bohemian chic, all flouncey and bouncey, and has swishly coiffeured silver hair from what I can see of it. She's wearing a towel over her head! She's slightly built, and could well have been a 'Pan's People' in her youth. She runs with dancer's feet! ('Pan's People' were a group of skinny young professionals who danced on 'Top Of The Pops' a lot back in the '70s.) She has presence, in an impoverished and theatrical kind of way. I hit the nail on the head when she sees me, is all over me like some kind of long lost friend, and leads me with her to the barn. This is all very well, but the blasted door's locked. It's now pouring down and getting colder. She has her towel, and I have my umbrella, but neither is enough to stop us getting soaked, a fact she seems oblivious to. We still can't get under shelter, when she asks:

"Can I take your umbrella? You don't need it now. You can stand under the roof, the bit that's sticking out."

She takes my brolly and disappears into the distance, leaving me there for a good ten minutes, wondering why on earth I bothered visiting this obviously somewhat eccentric lady, nice as she turns out to be. I ask if I can go with her, help her make the tea, lighten her load:

"Oh no, you can't. You must stay here. I'm living in the cellar! I don't want you to see the mess I'm living in."

O.k. then, I'll wait under the roof, the bit that's sticking out, even though it's perishing freezing and the sun's giving way to even heavier showers. It does that a lot in Poitou Charentes. She eventually reappears, not with a tray of tea but with a laundry basket full of cups and, thankfully, a cardigan for me. That's nice of her. She also hands me the keys to the barn, then legs it again, under my brolly, returning with a pot of totally cold tea of the dishwater variety. We sit in the farthest corner we can find, to escape the torrential downpour, and she explains that she rents the house out during the summer, so that she can remain solvent the rest of the year. Many do the same thing here, living under canvas in some cases while they make enough money to survive the winter in their old, cold, stone houses, which they shouldn't have bought in the first place. I have a fair few selling clients who move into tents and caravans, gîtes if their budgets allow, in the summer months. It's not such a bad idea!

I'm still here two hours later, but am fascinated to learn that her late father was an Eastern European Diplomat, wanted by the Communists for his war time activities, later to be granted a pardon in abstentia, presumably whilst the family was living in the U.K. Thus, he returned to his Homeland in the '60s, to be mysteriously murdered, in all probability by the Secret Police. Her mother very sensibly decided to stay where they had already been given sanctuary and protection, in England.

My mind wanders back to the story of my late sister Suzanne's Godparents, Polish Refugees fleeing the S.S. in the 1940s, her Godmother giving birth to twins in a forest en route to the safety of England, who didn't survive. Eventually arriving in Devon, her Godfather joined the exiled Polish Navy and thus met up with my father, serving out of Plymouth at the time. The two couples became friends. After the War, the Polish couple settled in North America, had a healthy daughter, Elizabeth, and a settled and secure life. It's funny that after 62 years of peace (for those of us lucky enough to experience it) all this war stuff seems to be visiting me in my daily job.

Even more bizarre is the fact that my chain smoking hostess for the afternoon's taking tea in the barn, just happens to have been the lover of a friend of mine's husband once upon a time, back in Blighty (I shan't say where exactly!) I'd already been told that this lady had "moved to the Cognac area," and now she's telling me that she still has "some bottles waiting to be collected by him." Fat chance of that! The guy's married to one of my closest friends now, and no I shan't tell him whom I've taken tea with, even though I happen to know him rather well myself, but not in that way!

Next stop, to see a lovely selling client of mine recovering from cancer. Just a courtesy visit, just to let her know we're still trying to sell the farm for her and her husband. Néré's a pleasant distance, enough to get my head together after the bizarre afternoon's tea ceremony in the barn. The rain's finished, and I know the route like the back of my hand. This is cattle country, spectacularly beautiful, gently undulating terrain with fields of magnificent herds. Disappointingly, I don't see any 'Herefords,' my own county's breed taken to America and Australia to start cattle farming in the wilds of Wyoming and Queensland, later throughout both continents, and stocking New Zealand. There's even an Australian and New Zealand Cattle Society in Hereford. What I do see around here, are fields full of Charolais, Limousins, and lots of shaggy Aberdeen Angus type look alikes, but I'm sure they're not Aberdonians!

My lovely Madame M takes me to one of the barns to see their latest bovine purchase, a fantastic looking young bull, a brown Charolais rather than a white one, but every bit as lovely. He's a little less than a year old, but has all the makings of a fine fellow at stud. Artificial insemination is rare in Poitou Charentes, but I'm sure there's many a cow out there hoping it arrives soon. He's only just arrived, so is restricted to the barn until he gets used to life with his new humans before meeting his new 'ladies.' Of course he won't be put to work this year, but he'll no doubt get the jist of what's expected of him. To stop him feeling lonely, they've put an older, experienced, bull in the other half of the barn, divided by a barrier hopefully neither will try and jump over. These are not cows which fly over the moon! No doubt le taureau (daddy bull) will sense the competition from the young garçon (boy), but not until he's told him all about the life awaiting him! How do cows communicate, I naively wonder?

Out in the nearest field to her lovely old stone farmhouse, is a much adored and revered vache maman (mother cow) with her latest babe, around a year old. I ask the age of la belle vache:

"Elle a quinze ans."

"Quinze ans. Non, Madame, ce n'est pas possible."

But it is, it really and truly is. Lucky lady cow, 15 years at home on the ranch!

It's been another day in the rural countryside now so close to my heart, but it's time to head back to the Agence, to check in before I check out again. A new system! Oh mon dieu, c'est ridicule, but it won't last long. There'll be a realtors' revolt, headed by the office manager, as in she who disappears most afternoons without returning to the fold. Perhaps she, too, is having une liason dangereuse. They seem to be quite popular in France, just as they were in Italy. We Inglese (English) didn't stand a chance, way too frumpy for our own good!

"You do not give off the right vibes," an Italian friend continually told me!

Shucks, and there I was, thinking I'd grab uno bellissimo italiano!

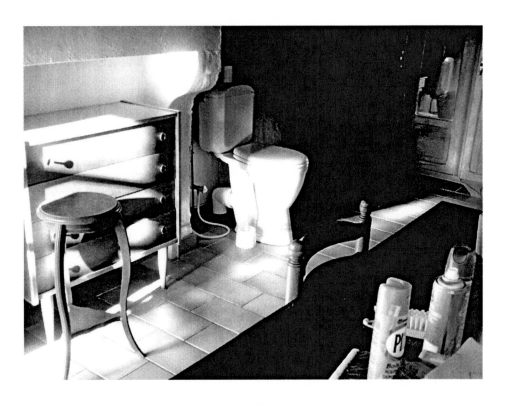

French 'convenience' in Charentaise living room

34 Army & Quiz in Beauvais

The modern day French Army passes through Beauvais sur Matha, impressively and in great numbers. It has to be Beauvais! It's early evening and Spouse and I are en route to a quiz night held in the Salle des Fêtes (village hall). Hitherto, it's been held at the home of friends who live a couple of miles outside, in the country, but numbers have grown out of all proportion and we can now fill a hall.

Expatria at play, all stemming from the Anglican Church in Cognac, and latterly its annexe at Saint Jean d'Angely. Back in Blightly, the good old C. of E. struggles to get 7% of its seats filled. Here in France, its flock is growing with every ferry load of new Brits heading for Poitou Charentes. Of course, if it weren't for the Vicar, who's ever so nice, they wouldn't come twice (that rhymes)! He's doing an amazing job and is providing a service none other could match. It's easy to be sceptical about the reasons this is happening, but it's better to set that scepticism aside and go with the flow, mostly very pleasant people. Tonight is no exception, but will we get to the hall in time?

This military presence is really quite alarming and reminds me of the British Army stopping the small world of Hay-On-Wye (where I was seconded for six glorious months) whilst they drove through one morning in various forms of military transport. It was a sight to behold, tanks and trucks, all forms of armoured vehicles, and soldiers galore, instead of the usual sheep heading for Hay's famous market. Of course, work stopped and we all stepped out into the little streets and waved them on. It's what one does! Hay is beautiful, but nothing much happens once the tourists have left, their arms bulging with second hand books. Were it not so far from the sea, I'd happily live there.

I'm taken back to Beirut in 1968. It was a particularly hot night, so I slept on the balcony outside my room, something I frequently did. Just before daybreak, I was noisily woken by the sound of tramping, marching, feet in the street below. There were hundreds of them, the Lebanese Army practising for a dawn invasion perhaps! Not long after Yom Kippur, this could have been feasible.

But this is Beauvais, and seeing French soldiers anywhere in these parts is rare. We have no choice but to stay in the car and await their departure. We're with friends from La Brousse, and the four of us wonder if we'll ever get to the quiz. We do, and we lose. It's not the first time. That was last year, when Spouse disbelieved my answer to when the London Tube began and scrubbed out my '1863.' Not only that, but he also decided I was wrong with my knowledge of William the Conqueror's wife's name: Matilda! We lost by two points last year. It could have been a tie break! However, this year we're losing hands down and there's no escaping defeat. Never mind, it's a good way of maintaining newly made friendships. I'm playing in a different team next time, though!

With a little bit of effort with 'parlaying le lingo' we're breaking new ground, and are invited for aperitifs (it's what they do) with other étrangers (strangers) in our village. They both happen to be as French as the locals themselves, but are not considered to be. Oh mon dieu, non, they are from Alsace-Lorraine, and that's even worse than being from Angleterre! To some of the more elderly residents of La

Brousse, this may well be the case. It was soldiers from Alsace-Lorraine who were part of the atrocities at Oradour, and other such events in West France particularly, stretching up into Brittany. The fact that the Germans had tactically forced many from their Border Region to fight against their own kind, is often overlooked. There's another couple in La Brousse, also from Alsace, and they too feel ostracised. I have their house for sale, so they can return East. They moved here escaping a wayward son. It happens, not only with the Brits!

We're in our new friends' house and it's as chalereuse (warm and welcoming) as they, themselves, are. This is going to be a long session. Hostess stays on soft drinks, Spouse and I drink the most delicious red wine from down near Bordeaux (Pomerol) and Host savours his favourite Scotch whisky. Megan is with us, and she drinks nothing! She's happy munching the aperitif nibbles all les français provide on such occasions. This seems to be the favourite way of entertaining in France, drinks and nibbles, and crosses all social stratum. We anglais love our barbecues, and this couple is more than happy to be included when long distance maison secondairers return in the summer and light theirs. On another occasion, we're invited to the home of other étrangers français, who sit us down to a mountain of sweet pancakes, and they are not Bretons!

It's all happening in La Brousse. The maison secondairers are back in force, including our next door neighbours from South West Wales. Lovely people, they're great to have the other side of the little lane the horses used to trot down, after they'd had their new shoes fitted in our old hallway. This is all very well, and we're pleased to see them again. What comes next, of course, is the removal of the winter cover from their swimming pool. Gemima Cat finds this too curious to resist, and spends one of her nine lives falling in. The first I know about it, is a yell from their garden that our cat's trying to learn to swim. Fortunately, it's a posho pool with Roman steps and neighbour is there to the rescue. I take home a very bedraggled feline and she never ventures their side of the wall again, at least we don't think so.

Pools pose many problems and I'm often retrieving dead frogs and, worse still, dead hedgehogs from ones in holiday homes left abandoned without covers. It's a win or lose situation. Covers can cause small animals to get stuck beneath them, as equally as they can act as visual prevention for falling in. Pool accidents are commonplace amongst children, and the Law states that protective fencing or other means of stopping unwanted entry are applied. This is generally adhered to, and is big business at the moment. The legislation has only just come into force. I'm told that helicopters are circling the summer skies to catch those who consider such safety measures unnecessary, but I'm not convinced. However, the fines are énorme. Swimming pool accessory outlets are booming throughout the area.

It's a bit like mains drainage. This was supposed to happen to every village throughout France, by 2005. Tell that to the 'frogs!' Smelly fosse septiques pollute many country villages when the temperatures rise high into the 30°s, attracting an army of amphibian frogs and toads to linger around .

Pools are a great selling point, though. Many buying clients refuse to look at properties without them. With 200 000 euros to spend, they may strike lucky. Below that amount, they can forget it. The maintainance is a daily job many fail to get on top of, and in my travels I see several which have turned into a yuchy, slimey, green mess. They are not for the faint hearted, nor for the lazy, although they are fabulous places to laze beneath the stars in, providing they are kept clean. But if you don't want visitors, don't buy a house with a pool!

The garden under snow!

35 Stilettos at Mill

I have French clients this morning, whom I meeting outside the Mairie (village hall) in Brie sur Matha, about as exciting as Ballans or Beauvais, and full of equally sad looking properties in various stages of falling apart, but bizarrely favoured by the Brits. The modern day français generally prefer to build their own, or buy nearly new. They also prefer to be in towns with facilities now.

I'm taking them to an old mill, owned by a couple from the Home Counties and who have no fewer than eleven children between them. Two of hers are in Estonia with their father, who's out there doing my job, selling to the English. It's competition we're learning to take on board, as more and more are turning their backs on the idea of relocating to France and buying in Estonia, Bulgaria, the Czech Republic, Montenegro, Croatia and all places in the 'New Europe.'

They arrive. Oh mon dieu, is she a dolly bird, une tarte française, complete with ridiculously high heeled stiletto shoes, totally unsuited for what she is about to see. Her husband looks after her like he would a china doll, taking her arm and steering her across the land. She pathetically hesitates at every house viewing hurdle, and consequently doesn't see much of what's for sale. Terrified of the two totally soppy boxer dogs, they're now dispatched to an old chicken shed between the house and the mill, which isn't a mill anymore at all. None of it remains in working order, and in fact I can't see what would have been any of it in the first place. This is a great disappointment, as there are indeed several old mills which have been beautifully and painstakingly restored, and I've obviously been too complimentary in my English write-up. I make a mental note to change the specification when I get back to the office. I must, or else there'll be many more wasted journeys.

The house itself is almost at the finishing stages of its renovation, and it's been done very well, beautifully maintaining its charm and character whilst introducing modern day comfort. Perhaps this will sell it. It doesn't, at least not this time. I ring the viewers a couple of days later, and am told the mill that's not a mill requires too much work, especially for one who doesn't own a pair of wellies, methinks! They do buy a mill, but one that's been converted, and they pay almost one million euros for the privilege of doing so. Sadly, it's not the one I have on offer at Pons, on the famous pilgrims' journey to Saint James de Compostella in Northern Spain. At 750 000 euros, it's a stunning property, with all the equipment superbly restored, and acres of delightful land. So why not?

"Eet as too many nayburrs." Shucks, lost again!

The next lot of clients, who aren't really clients, don't buy anything either. He's a colleague of mine, the lovely Scottish gentleman from the referral agents whom la Madame de Cognac has never liked. His equally lovely wife's still working in England, but comes over for a long weekend. He's on a mission to persuade her to buy in France, but she's not playing, at least not this time. They set off to look at one of the Châtelain's houses in a distant hamlet which is part of the rural Commune of Villiers Couture. It's a bargain, has lots of space, and could be lovely. They hit it early evening, when school's out, and rename it 'The Village of the Damned." His wife refuses to even get out of the car, as a gang of unwashed boys speed past mucking about on push bikes, and then another gang, this time on foot, harass a poor old hound out of the village. In a desperate attempt to break free from its oppressors, and exhausted almost to the point of collapse, the poor old dog finally escapes and the young thugs return to the boredom of sitting on walls staring into space, lost rural causes!

I ring my lawyer friend to tell him, who promises to ring his father, whom I hope will kick into action, and if he does it literally, I shan't mind at all! Because I'm a dog lover, of course I see more than most would, am attuned to more. On other occasion, I'm en route back to the office in St Jean, just arriving in Néré, when I see a beautiful black and white collie with 4 perfectly even white paws. He's charging frantically from one side of the road to the other, trying to knock at doors, and eventually lying down outside one of them. I stop the car and go into the butcher's, hoping he'll know who the owners are. He doesn't.

Nobody cares! An elderly lady takes her packet of meat, and is followed out of the shop to be joined by the collie. I hope it's her dog, but not so:

"Don't worry, Madame, he is only looking for a girlfriend!"

But I do!

Unfortunately, I've now been given yet another property in the same "Village of the Damned" and it's ghastly. The 'loo' is so dirty that the walls are splashed with human excrement. I ring the lawyer again, to ask him to ring his father, with instructions to the tenants of the hovel to get it cleaned, as well as sorting out his young village yobbos! Will I ever be invited to le Moulin de Condé again?

I'm back in Matha, at an ancient pigeonnier, that's where the pigeons would have been kept. It's such a splendid example, that the house almost takes second place. This would be the case if it weren't so lovely. This one is absolutely, stunningly, beautiful and will appeal to the luxury market, not that we have too many luxury clients right now, but one can but try. In one of the best roads in town, lived in by pharmacists and fellow professionals alike, it carries the cudos of a good address, although that's not as important in France as it is in England. Pharmacists, by the way, are often labelled as being the highest paid in France, way ahead of doctors and even surgeons.

Expecting to be greeted by English owners, in keeping with the surname I've been given, I'm surprised to be welcomed by yet another charming Frenchman and his elegant wife. The chap's a little bit older than I am, obviously born during the War rather than a few years after (like me!) I'm curious, so ask why he has an Anglo-Saxon surname. The son of British Ambassadorial Staff in Paris and his French wife around the outbreak of war, the rest of the family moved down to the Loire Valley. Then along came Babe. The Occupying Germans allowed the surname to be allocated to him, perhaps thinking it sounded French (it could, given the stretching of a yard or three of yarn, and providing it was pronounced with a Gallic lilt) but refused to register him with his father and grandfather's name before him, William. And so he became Réné, but only officially.
Our secretary wasn't to know that, and nor was I before I came. It's making a pleasant change from the rural north of my secteur, and I soak in the atmosphere of this stunning

home. It sells quickly, but I don't clinch the deal, not even having time to advertise it before one of my competitors sells it. Not a wasted afternoon, though, and it sells to friends of friends, a Methodist Minister and his wife, who've jumped ship to join the Cognac Crew. The current Anglo-French owners move up to Le Havre, from whence the lady of the house originally came. I can't imagine them in such a busy place after the peace and quiet of Poitou Charentes, but chaq'un son gout (each to their own).

36 The Rise of British Cafés

There we were, thinking the restauranteurs from the cafe of the disastrous night in Cressé had slung out their aprons for good!

A group of us has decided to try the new Irish Bar at Fresnau, not far from Matha. With friends having a relative staying, always a good excuse to go out for lunch, and a heavy week's work behind me, we set off to join others we know for what we've been told is traditional Sunday lunch. Oh, no, no, no ....

First impressions are welcoming, light and airy, and the clientele is minus its 'Benidorm' brigade. The tables are delightful, round for ease of conversation, and Elderly Auntie Joyce says "how nice." Don't we all! And then the fun begins, realising pretty darned quickly the connection between Cressé's past disaster, and Fresnau's forthcoming one. It can only mean the chef's one and the same!

'Traditional Sunday Lunch' is clearly advertised on the board, and sure enough, another culinary disaster awaits us! We have a choice of roast beef and all the trimmings (hah) or chicken, likewise. With great anticipation, we place our orders. The beef arrives without any Yorkshire puddings. The chicken comes without stuffing, bread sauce, cranberry sauce, and certainly not any little sausages or bacon rounds. Oh, and it's one DRUMSTICK per person, nothing else, no white meat per se, just one greasy drumstick. I'm nominated to ask for the accompaniments, to be met with distinct looks of sheer ignorance.

The vegetables, ah the vegetables, this is when we make the definite connection! A huge dish of semi frozen peas and soggy tinned carrots is placed in central position on the table, just one, but it's bucket sized. They are truly disgusting! What about some spuds! An Irish establishment without spuds! They've forgotten to bring them but, to give them some credit where it's due, another mound appears before us, not of roast potatoes, but of perhaps tinned ones momentarily chucked in oil and bunged in the oven. Oh, and may we have some gravy please? Just like Cressé, we are the only people actually eating here. No surprise there, then! The wine's some unpalatable wishy washy stuff, the type which comes in catering cartons, and is then brought to the table in tatty old jars, supposed to look chic. However, all is not lost. The Guinness, that divine creamy black stuff, is truly excellent!

The pud arrives; a slice per person of naff, revoltingly highly coloured cheap and nasty, very sickly, catering shop bought gâteau. Hugely disappointed, we decide to avoid all amateur Brits from now on, especially so called chefs!

It's completely understandable that the French often see the anglais as not only undiscerning, but unknowledgeable when it comes to fine food and wine. Were they to judge us by many of those who settle in France, and open such dire catering establishments, they wouldn't be far wrong.

That said, there are some very acceptable British owned afternoon tea cafés opening around us. These are different, and are springing up in several towns near to large British clusters of population. I patronise them at every opportunity, enjoying a slice of cake with a good English cuppa. To the

French, salons du thé are considered very upmarket, très chic, and they too seem to be enjoying English scones and carrot cake, and are spreading the word admirably. There are indeed British chefs working in top French restaurants, but these are also in a different kettle of fish. The British owned bars advertising 'fish n'chips' and 'traditional Sunday lunches' are generally better avoided, as we are learning fast and, in some cases, furiously.

We also have a reputation of drinking copiously, and it's unfortunately often true. This comes home to me rather sharply when I eat with work colleagues. It's perfectly normal for a bottle of wine to be shared between up to eight people, and not one more will be ordered. But the quality is superb, nectar with every sip. They are a refined nation, culturally ahead of us in a great many ways, and intrinsically kind and courteous. I learn this more and more, the longer I'm privileged to live amongst them. It could be something to do with their schooling. As mentioned before, all French children study philosophy. It's a great subject to enforce the old adage 'do as you would be done by.'

They have their problems, just like us, and I'm sad to read of a young man's arrest as the train from Paris to La Rochelle pulled in at Surgères, in possession of 3 kilos of cannabis. That's one helluva lot of powder! I'm told that since the TGV has routed through, crime has escalated. It's an unfortunate side effect of any town being blessed (?) with good travel communications, especially railways it would seem.

Les anglais et les français are beginning to grow more together in these parts. Clubs, and more formal associations, serving both are sprouting up all over the place, not least in

Matha. I sign up for advanced French lessons. We're a small class, just four of us, but it's fun. It's not the first time I've tried. When we arrived, back in 2002, Spouse and I joined the A.V.F. (Accueil des Villes Françaises, roughly meaning French towns offering a welcome to newcomers, both their own people and foreigners alike). It's an association with branches throughout France, and is a marvellous starting point for involvement in lots of different activities, not least learning the lingo. However, if you've taken French at school, you could find the lessons rather tedious. A bit like learning the ABC all over again!

This time round, I'm expected to know all the vast numbers of grammatical declensions and be able to produce them in written form, as well as spoken. It's challenging, but also very interesting. We start, as ever, introducing ourselves and then move on to family history. This surprises me, as much remains unspoken in these parts, not laid out on the table for all to see. The lady sitting next to me explains that her father was in the Résistance during the War, miraculously escaped capture by the Germans, and survived for two and a half years in the woods near Parthenay (in the Deux Sevres, one of Poitou Charentes' other Départements) engaged in Partisan activities until Liberation. Tragically, her brother died in France's War in Algeria, aged 20 and just before the Algerians gained their Independence from France in 1962.

I learn more and more about the Algerian War of Independence, and it seems that many of the young men from our own Commune of La Brousse were taken there to fight. Our immediate neighbour appears with bunches of tomatoes, bags of walnuts, duck and hen eggs, and enough vegetables to keep us supplied in soup all winter. He and Spouse get on like a house on fire, and become good friends.

He's happy to embrace any nationality under the sun, as long as they are not from the Mahgreb (North Africa). Old memories die hard, and his were enough to earn him a medal for outstanding bravery. We never find out what he did, and we dare not ask.

Some prejudices stay forever, too! I've been called to do a house not far from Matha, and am appalled when the elderly Brit refuses to sign the paperwork. He stands in front of me, arms folded, saying he won't. His wife tries to cajole him, a lost cause and one she's obviously tried several times. He's thoroughly obnoxious, shows no social graces, and informs me:

"I neither speak French, nor write French."

I ask him why he lives here:

"Because I can."

This is getting nowhere fast and it's looking like I've wasted an afternoon's work. I tell the racist git that I can't put the house on the market without his signature and not only his signature, but an Attestation d'Accord (a sentence, written in French, agreeing to give it to me to sell). This is not something we at the Agence have created. C'est le Loi (it's the Law). By this time, his wife (who happens to be very pleasant indeed) is pleading with him not to be so stupid. He finally relents, I pack my bag, and leave tout de suite.

It's not the first time I've come across him. We were at a party given by joint friends a few months earlier. I'd been chatting to a group of lovely French people from Cognac in one room, and Spouse had been talking to this very same unpleasant chap, who should have been stopped getting in at Calais, in another. Deciding it was time to socialise a bit more, and to talk to some of the anglais, I rejoined Spouse, just in time to hear him say:

"I'm going to stop you right there. Our son-in-law's black." I have fabulous selling clients in a little hamlet between St Jean and Saintes. She's French Algerian (there are many in this region) and harbours no hatred whatsoever, despite having had to leave her home as a young teenager, for a country she'd never even visited before. Her pride and joy is a poster sized photograph of Algiers before Independence gracing the living area upstairs. I love it, I love poster art. Every time I visit, she's cooking and the smells are unbelievably appetising. I wish, oh how I wish, they'd invite me for lunch! Her husband's from Brittany, a charming gentleman with blonde hair and blue eyes, a contrast to her own dark beauty. They're planning a move to the western outskirts of Paris, close to children and grandchildren, and the right side of the Capital for escaping to the glorious Breton beaches.

With high hopes of selling theirs, as opposed to somewhat unprofessional intentions of not caring about the house belonging to he who neither speaks nor writes French, I call it a day and head home to organise the list for a party we're hosting soon. Certain people who live near Matha will not be included in the guest list, not that I have any intentions of ever including them in anything! There are times when clients become friends, in several cases extremely valued ones, but this is not one of them.

Such outright xenophobia has no place in my life, but it's not long before an absolutely charming gentleman from

Wales comes and sits opposite my desk, evaporating the disdain I'm obviously still harbouring. He has a perfectly lovely town house for me to sell, here in St Jean d'Angely, complete with a newly installed oak kitchen, a beautiful walled garden, and a garage large enough for two cars. It's a good product, which should sell easily, enhanced by glorious antiques adorning the principal rooms. He's worked in France for many years, and is pretty much bi-lingue. I melt every time I hear the Welsh and the Italians sing, not that I have the nerve to request a rendering of 'Men of Harlech! Perhaps when I get to know him better ...

And where is he hoping to move to? Brittany! And what and where does he buy? A splendid fourteenth century house in pride of place in the middle of Mediaeval Moncontour, fascination in every stone, and depicted in the Church's stained glass window. It can't get much better than that.

As I work 'the patch' I come across more and more selling clients who wished they'd settled where they got off the Ferry, but we did exactly the same, fall for the usual 'we'll get as far south as we can easily drive in a day, and buy there.' And where's that exactly? Yep, Poitou Charentes!

37   Christmas in Expatria

The party passes enjoyably, in our 46.72 square metre living room (I'm an estate agent, don't forget!) which used to be stabling for several horses. Big isn't necessarily beautiful, as we find out all too soon, and huddle by the log burner at one end of it from November through to March. Unfortunately, all the original features had been stripped out before we bought The Old Smithy, not even leaving the cows' feeding troughs in what is now the enormous garage. There are thirty people enjoying home made small eats and lots of bon vin. They are mostly English but with our French friends from Alsace; an Anglo-German family; an Irishman; and our South American neighbour and her Scottish husband, it's quite an international gathering. The World goes round! So do the trays of sausage rolls Spouse has lovingly made in several batches, and stored in the freezer. Panic station:

"Get them back, they're not cooked!"

It's the lead up to Christmas again. Doesn't it come round quickly! We've been to the Carol Service in Saint Jean d'Angely this time, and followed it with an excellent meal in town, us and two other couples. The food's brilliant and the atmosphere matches it. Le Petit Gourmet is one of our favourites, and lives up to its name. A 'gourmet' is someone who's knowledgeable about food and appreciates its finesse. A 'gourmand,' on the other hand, is some who's greedy and is always eating. So beware of the difference!

Youngest son has been with us for a few days, and has played golf with Spouse in Cognac. I met them for lunch at the Club afterwards, and the meal was marvellous. They've obviously realised that roast lamb with tagliatelle and curry sauce is never to appear on the menu again! He's treated us to dinner at Le Scorlion, my very favourite top of the list restaurant in St Jean, and his visit has passed all too quickly. But that's the price we Expats pay for leaving our families behind in Blighty. Le Scorlion has an interesting owner chef, half Dutch, half Indian, but brought up in London. His food is second to none.

Our secretary, however, fails to convince her husband to try it out. She's married to a guy with a prestigious architectural firm in Saintes, and he has clients to entertain. She's invited along. She's very attractive, and oozes savoir faire. Actually Russian by birth, she was adopted as a child and became French. She reminds me of Lara in 'Doctor Zhivago.' Architect husband obviously falls into the category of not trusting 'British' chefs. They go elsewhere, despite her having tried Le Scorlion with me one lunch time and giving it the 'thumbs up.'

We're invited to friends in the little hamlet of Le Brieul Batard for Christmas lunch, on the day itself. Good friends from Villemarange do the driving. So glad they've been invited, too! It takes the pressure off talking too much. I get off to a good start by breaking a cut glass champagne flute, before even taking my first sip. Oh dear! The conversation springs into action and lunch is rather late coming, but it's good when it arrives. A little tension nearly spoils the event, in line with most Christmas Day meals, not only with subjects under discussion, but with the hostess (an excellent cook) forgetting to put the potatoes in to roast. No worries, she has one of those warming trolleys and nobody notices the time. Hostess and Spouse drink way too much, she giving me daggers of 'don't you dare spoil our fun' (for whom?) as she proceeds to refill his glass every time it gets half empty, doing exactly the same with her own. Christmas is my least favourite day of the year, in fact I hate it! Unless, of course, it's a packet of cheese and onion crisps and a glass of Guinness in Hay-on-Wye, or prawn sandwiches and a can of Guinness on the beach at Châtelaillon Plage.

It's all quiet on the housing front, has been all month, but the Big Boss has decided that we shall open the office on the 26th, Boxing Day! Guess who draws the short straws? Oh yes I do, but so does our office manager, deprived of extra days off with her young family. Neither she nor I are impressed. However, it comes as a breath of fresh air and beautifully bypasses the boredom of yet another dull day in December. We have clients, several of them job relocations from elsewhere in France. The French have Christmas sussed by not really celebrating it at all, and I hope that's the way it continues. Families eat together late on Christmas Eve, then treat the 25th as just another day, although most do take it as holiday. The restaurants don't put their prices up on the day itself, so we get into the habit of going out for lunch and enjoying the normality of what it becomes for us, except when we stupidly accept an invitation to spend it English style with friends, no matter how much we like them ordinarily. C'est vrai, ça ne marche pas (it's true, it doesn't work)!

We both a sell a house, me to a bank manager and his family moving from Angers, and my colleague sells to a professor and his wife moving from Paris. Better still, they are both my instructions, one in La Brousse and the other in Varaize. Oh the joy! Let me work at Christmas every year! We also take lunch together in the little crêperie along from the Agence, lively as ever and hugely good for office bonding.

The 27th has everyone back at work, and I treat myself to lunch alone at the Rendezvous de l'Horloge. As the name implies, this little favourite of mine nestles almost beneath the famous old clock in St Jean, the one which appears on post cards, along with the Abbey where Saint John's head resided for centuries before the Huguenots ransacked it! I have my usual fish soup, which comes with croutons, a little dip of something I never find out what it actually is, but it's delicious, and grated cheese. I follow it with mousse au chocolat noir and savour its rich flavour, and the moment of satisfied solitude in such a marvellous location.

It's been an expensive month, not least because my one contribution to the culinary celebrations of Christmas is the cake! I adore Christmas cake, and the more fruit and nuts, not forgetting cognac in it, the better. The French eat revoltingly sickly Bouches de Noêl instead, which are basically Swiss rolls covered in horrendous mounds of extremely yuchy, probably processed, cream. Commercially produced almond paste, marzipan as we know it, is a rarity in these parts. Forget it altogether, unless you're happy with little bricks of bright green and vivid red E coloured sweetness. And so I've bought genuine Provençale paste (80% almonds) from the Pâtisserie next to the Agence. It's divine! It's also forty two euros a kilo. By the way, Marie-Antoinette did not tell the peasants to eat cake. She told them to eat brioche, a half way product between cake and bread, with softer flour.

New Year hits with a vengeance and we awake daily to freezing fog. I find a hedgehog, frozen to death by the roadside, and bury it deep in a hedgerow. The portable ice rink in St Jean, popular with the local children, is prematurely taken away to be stored for the following year. We start to get calls to feed the market again. I drive cautiously through black iced country lanes and heavy fog in search of even more stone piles to sell to those of us foreigners under the illusion that South West France is warm the year round. Believe me, it's perishingly cold in winter. You'd be better off buying in Bournemouth!

Characters by the Roadside

38 Old Folks' Homes & Fosses

The nuns are after me again! Well, one is, but she's delightful and turns out to be an 'ex' penguin (in my days, they all wore black flowing gowns with white bibs). I'm called to her house in Villiers Couture, which she's ready to sell, no longer using it much as her maison secondaire. Many don't! It forms a pattern amongst the more affluent Brits. They think they want a holiday home in France, then realise there's more to ownership than turning up with nice clothes to unpack, nowhere to wear them, and biking it to the bakery for their morning baguette. The isolation of their rural retreats often fails to meet their dreams, the ferries get increasingly more expensive, Ryanair cuts flights, and very few of the local French actually want to get to know them at all. At first sight, they can either be met with moronic stares, or great shows of warmth and intrigue, but it gets hard trying to communicate with sign language. It all gets too tiring for many of them, and I get tired of being constantly asked for help. There has to be a balance and my manager's constant:

"Ce n'est pas ta responsabilité"

is a phrase I learn to appreciate, rather than knock. French agents rarely provide any kind of after sales service, not in the housing market, not in any kind of market. It's just not in their thought process so to do.

My ex nun happens to be Irish, and her humour jumps into action as soon as she opens the door to me. She has a couple of friends staying with her, and in no time at all we're sipping coffee and swapping stories. Her house is in stone, beautifully renovated, and sits in the middle of the village. It will sell well, but probably not 'till the summer. The villages are sad places in winter.

With nuns and convents truly in my thoughts, I detour to Loulay and to the nuns' run Maison de Retraite (Old Folks' Home) to drop off a pile of our Agency brochures and general publicity. It's possible some of the 'inmates' will still have properties to sell. Canvassing is something we are all obliged to do, and I'd rather target indoor possibilities than tread the streets in pouring rain and howling gales. We do that once a month, as a team, and it's pure hell! To my mind, the negligible amount of business it produces is not worth the effort. It'll take the whole Team to be off with flu, however, before the Big Boss says it's no longer obligé. The Maison de Retraite is calm and welcoming, also very spacious. Staff and Residents alike 'bonjour' me and it all seems rather fine.

This is not the first one I've been in. Amongst my previous clients in Cognac were one of my former Hereford colleagues and his wife. They've bought a highly sensible town house in Cognac itself, very wise so to do. I can see them using it often and for many years to come. It's lovely and will become even lovelier. It's within easy walking distance of everything in the Town Centre, the Theatre, the beautifully landscaped Park, and to a great choice of restaurants. Amongst these, of course, is the Domaine de Breuil, where we're invited to help ex colleague celebrate his sixtieth birthday in style, a lovely evening for us four old (adopted) Herefordians. I wish more of my clients would buy town houses, rather than semi dilapidated ruins to renovate, or already renovated huge stone piles they'll never be able to comfortably heat.

I was surprised to learn that the Legal Completion of the Sale was to be held in the Maison de Retraite in Cognac (not run by nuns). The Notaire, myself, and friend-clients all duly turned up to be met with the most appetising smells coming from the kitchen. First there, I had a wander round and it was all amazingly pleasant. The dining room was inviting, the tables grouped together attractively but not too closely, and many of them looking out over the grounds, not big, but with well tended flowerbeds. The Seller, a lovely elderly Frenchman, and his son arrived. Signatures given, job done! I shan't mind if I end up in an Old Folks' Home here en France. The Residents appear to be treated with a high level of respect, are taken out in mini buses for day trips, and some Homes work an exchange system which gives the Townies a chance to stay at the Seaside for a week or two, and vice versa. They don't seem to have the problems many of the U.K. establishments have, and generally appear to run smoothly and kindly. France is not ageist. The elderly are respected, not bullied; listened to, not silenced. U.K. take note!

Oh dear, back in the Office and there's a message for me to 'phone clients in Blighty and explain all about fosses to them, so here's the little I understand:

A fosse étanche is water tight, sealed in concrete, and has to be emptied.

A fosse septique (the most popular if enough land is available) comprises underground drainage pipes leading into a central reserve where the muck regenerates itself into pure water, thus technically shouldn't need emptying. The

Law, however, says it does every time a property changes hands.

A fosse toutes eaux does everything in the same place and in theory doesn't ever need emptying.

Tout à l'égout is mains drainage, which the whole of France is supposed to be linked to, but that seems to be turning into a 'pipe' dream, a politician's promise no doubt.

Basically, very few rural properties are as yet linked to mains drainage, even fairly large villages. Equally, the same applies to mains gas, hence the vast storage areas of bottled gas for sale at virtually every French petrol station.

Remember, this is a country where many rural homes still, in the twenty first century, don't possess any inside toilet facilities. The 'loo' is often a hole dug in the earth, with a wooden seat for the sophisticated, a bucket for the less fortunate. Granted, said equipment will be housed in a purpose built cubicle, and will have a makeshift door of some variety, but it's unlikely to have electricity, and will invariably stink. The men pee in the garden, and I don't ask what the women do! Our neighbours' grandson comes to our house to do his 'ca-ca,' and I'm not joking! (Eventually they install their own indoor facilities.)

Ah, there's another message on my desk. I've been fighting a battle to stay open at lunch time, making me the least popular person in the Agence. I'm used to that! And now there's 'une directive' from the Big Boss. We are to open from 09:00h to 13:00h and then we must close (I'm a law breaker!) We are to re-open at 14:00h and the door can close at 18:00h if we have no clients. That's exceedingly generous. In Cognac, the door stayed open until 19:00h. On Saturdays, though, we must close for two whole hours at midi. Obviously this is because he thinks the Town's Saturday market will be more attractive to house hunters than an 'open all hours' estate agency. Oh dear, I shall await the flack. Actually, all that happens is that those who want to carry on working the French way, that is to be closed whenever there are likely to be customers on the horizon, organise their appointments to fit in around country visits where there are likely to be cafés, or relatives! The secretary is pleased, and I am pleased. We are moving, very gradually, into the modern day. What's more to the point, we are now the only estate agency practice in Saint Jean d'Angely which doesn't close as the Grand Horlôge strikes noon.

39 Irish Invasion, Trip to Brittany

It's going well. The Market is buoyant again, and the last five months have seen eleven of my own instructions complete, but merely one of those has been to French clients. The Agence has only had thirteen sales in total, indicating that there are more British buyers coming through the door, than there are French at the moment. My selling colleagues are perfectly switched on Parisiennes, neither of them new to real estate. I've been expecting the local market to fall for a while now, and think it's started. The rest will follow suit, which will mean fewer Brits arriving, but for now it's busy. The French Government is on a mission to get people to build brand new, and that's where our greatest local competition is coming from. With a hundred and five mandats (legally binding agreements to sell houses on behalf of the clients mentioned therein) currently in my portfolio since I switched agencies from Cognac to Saint Jean d'Angely, that's an awful lot of responsibility to shoulder, and this time it IS 'ma responsabilité' to find them buyers.

This is a very different way of doing business than in Britain, where agencies are often satisfied with around thirty properties to sell at any one time, fifty if they're doing well, obviously not including the new housing developments they'll be acting for as agents for at the same time. We don't get those here in France. The system is very different, très compliqué.

The method here is for land to be released, only occasionally individually, but in what can best be described as fields, usually on the edge of villages, and pretty much always ex farm land. The land is then divided up into 'lots' hence the term 'lotissement' arises, translating as a housing estate in the making. Unlike in Britain, here in France the 'lots' are sold individually, and the buyers then build as, and pretty much what, they like. The final effect of this means a development of many different styles and sizes. Several building firms are springing up all over France, some of them even getting computer literate, although their websites are always sadly lacking in information.

Spouse and I decide to investigate, so off we go on a land hunt. Finding a field about to be released on the edge of the little town of Aigrefeuille d'Aunis, between Surgères and La Rochelle, off we go to a building company recently set up in Aytré, even nearer to our favourite city and harbour in France. We browse the 'show home,' just one example of his company's products, just one, this isn't Bloor or Bovis we're dealing with here. It doubles as his office, located on the High Street. A clever infill if ever there were one! We give him a budget of 250 000 euros, to include the land price of 82 000, and leave it with him to formulate a proposal for us to consider. Returning a couple of weeks later, he produces a plan for a stunningly lovely four bedroomed detached house, complete with 10m by 5m swimming pool in the garden. We are totally won over and day and night dream about it both to exhaustion and frustration. Shall we, shan't we? Not yet, buy maybe soon! The temptation of La Rochelle is strong.

Meanwhile, I have clients to attend to. The Irish are here big time these days, cashing in on sales the equivalent of a million sterling for a three bedroomed semi in Dublin, and almost as much in Holyrood (Belfast) although you get more for your money there, I'm told. It can't last long, but while it does, over to Poitou Charentes they come. They're buying beautiful homes of character, of which we have many on offer, and for a third of the price they'd cost in The Emerald Isle. Many retire here, and even more buy holiday homes, nice ones.

I show them a mini château, all for less than four hundred thousand euros. Strangely, they don't like it. He's an artist, and it's all about light! I had another one like him in Cognac. A Greek Australian, every room I took her into had the light in the wrong place for her yoga mat. Feng Shui is alive and well, not only in China, but here amongst my buying clients. I never had to take that into consideration in Hereford, although I could well have done. We catered for a good many Bohemian types buying on the Welsh Borders. There's even a Steiner School, and a seriously serious Buddhist Retreat Centre, not far from Hereford itself. I was asked once if I'd like to teach Italian at the Steiner establishment, duly spent a morning there, suitably impressed with the children making their own lunch, baking their own bread, but not at all taken in with being told I wouldn't be allowed to wear trousers, unless perhaps they were those funky flowy things. I don't do grunge! The angels did my head in, as well. They were all over the place, in the class rooms, on the walls of corridors, ummm, pas pour moi (not for me)!

I bid a cheerful farewell with the Irish, obviously not having anything I can sell them where the light will be right, and meet another Patrick. This time, a big bouncy dog called Paddy, rescued by my 106th selling clients. He's adorable. En route to meeting Paddy, I see a tractor holding up traffic in the middle of the country lane leading to Saint Pierre de Juillers. I'm delighted to be held up, not often getting the opportunity to see a deer of just a few months old crossing the road in front of the tractor. It makes a change from my last chasse season's encounter, when I saw a glorious pheasant killed on the road near Matha, just two cars in front of me. I stopped to see if it had survived, but it had not. Death had been mercifully quick and it was still beautiful, thankfully thrown into the kerb, not squashed. The chasse and its effects are now full on.

Megan's freaking out on a regular basis, refusing to venture even into the garden on Wednesday and Sunday mornings, sometimes all day on the Sabbath. The rota gives us one Saturday off work per month, and she dashes into the car to come with us to Brittany to stay with friends in Louargat, a small village near Guingamp, famous for its top performing football club. Also famous for its heroism during World War Two, when it was liberated by British Special Forces working with American Task Force A, the latter end of whose mission was to take the Breton Coast from St Malo to Brest. St Malo had already taken one helluva battering from the Air, and was all but totally destroyed by additional ground fighting and a few logistical hiccups, not least the water supply having supposedly and inadvertently been cut off by the Americans. It burned for several days, possibly longer, but most of its French population had already been driven out under German orders, an unusual 'gift' given the circumstances. Guingamp had among its people a huge number of 'Résistants,' and testimony to them, and to our own Special Forces, is given in its cathedral. The town lies in an area of outstanding natural beauty, less than half an hour to the superb headlands and bays of La Manche (English Channel).

It's a 'pont,' an unofficial three day weekend, exclusive to les français. We visit Paimpol, a bustling fishing port historically connected with Iceland, about as Deep Sea as one can positively imagine. In contrast, we have lunch down at Tréguier's barren looking waterside, and then visit its ancient, mediaeval, town up on the hill above. It's a beauty to behold, intrigue around every cobbled corner. Next stop Locquirec, afternoon tea beside the Sea. Very heaven, and Brittany continues to tempt us. But so does La Rochelle – quelle décision!

40 Twelth Century Monks in Anville

We passed through Morlaix only last week, when we were up in Brittany, so it's a bit of a coincidence that my next call is to put a town house in Matha on the market for people from that part of Finistère. It struck me as a rather sad and gloomy place, made dark by its famous viaduct right in the middle of Morlaix itself. I found it very over powering, like a monster holding the town to ransom beneath. But this is where my latest clients hope to return to, going back home. Perhaps the Bretons do that more than any other French. Certainly the number of houses owned by them, and up for sale with us, would bear testimony to that. Having seen a few of Brittany's pretty towns and villages, and its magnificent beaches, I can understand their desires to ditch inland France for such a truly amazing coastline. Breton Nationalism calls them back to the Homeland, too, just as it does the Welsh; the Cornish; the Catalans.

The house in the centre of Matha is a classic example of a maison de maître gone to semi ruin. The owners live elsewhere in town. They are pharmacists, whom I'm told repeatedly command amongst the highest salaries in France. With a whole lot of T.L.C. it will be stunning and a perfect place to bring up a family, or run a B n' B. It sells, but not by me. I do, however, know the people who buy it. It's he whose racism may have to take a bit of an about turn. Matha is not 'pure white.' Almost, but not quite!

Historical intrigue comes into my working day again, in the form of a twelfth century monastery in Anville, not far from Rouillac. I've had it on before, from Cognac, and have finally been given the go ahead to market it from St Jean. Strictly speaking, we don't venture that far into the wilds of the Charente. It's beyond the boundary with Charente Maritime, but we may just come across the odd American or two who can't resist its monastic charms. We have a few Australian and South African buyers on our lists, too, and they tend to buy into French antiquity. It's worth a try, and the owners are keen to sell before a job transfer to Belgium, where Monsieur is a boat builder and Madame is keen to join him. I'm repeatedly gobsmacked by the property's redundant beauty just waiting to be reinstated. Some of the work has been tackled, but a fair amount of it is still left to do. That's often the best time to sell. Many buyers shun totally renovated properties, preferring to put their own stamps on them. It'd make a fabulous setting for one of those mystery ghost parties. I'd even offer to dress up as one of the monks, or perhaps a visiting nun! I don't think it's been done in these parts yet. Now there's a thought.

'Ancient monastery provides perfect business opportunity for spookey residential weekends. Mediaeval square meals included.' There's the space to house several guests, and no-one will hear what they get up to in the depths of night. The walls are at least two feet thick and the doors so heavy, who needs locks on them! With two kitchens into the bargain, and that's what this piece of history is, it's ready to go commercial.

When the current owners bought it, they found several ancient coins, dating the premises to its presumed mediaeviality. From later centuries, they were faced with having to dispose of old medical ampoules, needles, dressings, and hundreds of containers still with drugs in them. They think it had been used as a military hospital of sorts during World War Two. Given the huge number of

German Troops in this area, this is a highly logical supposition to make.

I draw my own conclusions vis à vis why so many Alsaciens have made their homes here since the War. Given that their fathers' generation would have fought here, I imagine them returning to the even colder winters of Eastern France than we have here in the Charentes, and recounting tales of charming fields full of corn, cows, and vines for cognac. Perhaps some even bought, or maybe sequestered, land whilst whiling the time away between 'operations' and now their children's generation are profiting from their exploits. There must be an explanation, as there are many from Alsace now living in Poitou Charentes. The same applies to Brittany, where it was largely the Alsacien Regiments fighting, French against French. A quirk of modern history!

The opposite of this comes homes to me when I hear the tale of two French Prisoners Of War, held in Germany. They became friends and the country gentleman gave the city slicker (from Paris of course) a piece of land in his rural village, to celebrate their fraternité during incarceration and their liberté when it arrived for them. The two men grew into middle age, married, had families and have since grown old. The city slicker's son is now retired himself, and he and his wife are living very happily in the house his father had built as a maison secondaire, on the land given so generously by the country gentleman. I asked him why he liked it so much, why he had shunned an active retirement in Paris:

"My childhood was a happy one, helped by the kindness of my father's friend. I can think of no better place to live, no better way to say 'merci beaucoup'."

Having just had a 'holiday' ourselves, today is turning into a 'holy day.' My next appointment is at yet another former monastery, but this time back in Saint Jean d'Angely. Totally different from the one in Anville, this is only a century or so old, if that. I think I'm spun a bit of a yarn, and decide that although there may well indeed have been a monastery where the house now stands, there's certainly no evidence of it now. Ahh, but here's what the owners mean.

They lead me through a rather splendid stone arch in the garden, tell me it's twelfth century, and right next to it is the largest bay tree I have ever seen. I'm waiting for them to tell me it's also mediaeval, but it's a bay, not a yew! The path narrows as I'm lead up it, literally, and we arrive at a second little house at the bottom of the garden. It's delightful, a lot older than the main property, and it will make a good two bedroomed gîte or granny lodge. Back into the principal residence, it's mid nineteenth century, sensible, spacious, and slap bang in the centre of town. It sells well, at the asking price, by one and the same colleague who introduced it to the market, a double whammy for her, and another interesting one for me to write up in the meantime. It's a side of my job I love doing, that and advertising. I guess in another life I may have been a roaming reporter, a photographer perhaps, but here I am, an estate agent wandering amongst cornfields and vineyards to the villages of Poitou Charentes.

Church & Old Monastery in Anville

41 Angelica in Marais Poitevin

There's trouble at 'tmill and none of us can think why, but it's affecting morale and the net result is a lot of worrying and wondering. The manager's habit of not returning to the Agence before the daily close of play is beginning to grate on my colleagues' nerves. What's sauce for the goose is not sauce for the gander, and they want a bit of the liberté she's taking for granted. We can only assume she's having a liaison dangereuse. She's also not answering her 'phone, which our secretary finds even more frustrating. Maybe she sees herself as a general, leading from the rear! Let's hope discontent doesn't turn into mutiny.

It gets to me one day, so I take succour in treating myself to lunch away from the constant bickering. St Jean d'Angely has one enormous square, used for the open air market on Saturday, car parking the rest of the week, and three smaller ones. The one just round the corner from the Agence has several eating and drinking places spilling out on to the invitingly landscaped and paved areas in front of them, not least The Annexe. The meal is superb, and is just what I need after the morning's stress. I savour every delicious mouthful of the most beautifully flambéed gambas (the prawns are always good in France), Coquilles St Jacques (scallops) and langoustines, served with wild rice cooked with herbs, and a small medley of Mediterranean vegetables. I accompany this mini gourmet feast with a small pichet of very acceptable Medoc. The mousse au chocolat is just how I like it, smooth, rich and dark, not unlike a couple of those Californian heart throbs one comes across in films occasionally. With coffee, the bill's 22.40 euros pales into insignificance, given the relief it brings.

I spend the afternoon on the road. There are no clients around, and I suspect that's the reason for the discontent. The Big Boss has obviously had words with the manager, increased targets, put the pressure on. Perhaps he's also found that she's frequently not available when he expects her to be. She tells us she's prospecting. Oh yeah! I choose to believe her, thousands wouldn't (that's an old Liverpool saying). I'm not an innocent abroad, either. I sometimes pop in to friends' houses for an afternoon cuppa on my rounds. C'est necessaire! And so I drive round the villages in my secteur, looking for 'AV' boards, noting 'phone numbers down, taking photographs of hopefuls, and generally filling the hours before reporting back at closing time, as we do. Well, as some of us do!

It's to be a week of eating out, but that's fine by me. The next morning, the whole Team's treated to a breakfast meeting at the Hôtel de la Place, not my favourite eating place. It's very proper, except for the 'loo,' which is a dowdy cupboard under the stairs. The food's not too bad, sometimes good, but the aspidistra atmosphere hardly gives out happy vibes. But this is a freebie, and it's only coffee and croissants, courtesy of the chap we recommend to our selling clients on a regular basis to have their diagnostics done. C'est obligé.

Called the 'Diagnostic de Performance Energétique,' and commonly referred to as the D.P.E., it's the sellers responsibility to have this done at the initial stage of putting the house up for sale. As this is a legal requirement, we at the Agence are not able to market a property without a

D.P.E. in place, so it's a great source of business for the diagnosticians, who rely on estate agents for their leads. It covers energy consumption, gas emissions, electrical installations (nit picking to the extent of plugs and light switches), central heating, hot water heating, ventilation, doors and windows, roof insulation, swimming pools, and even risk assessment vis à vis natural disasters. One of the main causes for concern currently, is asbestos. Outlawed only as recently as 1997 in the construction industry, a good many French properties have asbestos roofs. I'm told that as long as the asbestos is not messed around with, this doesn't pose any problems. However, it becomes an increasing source of worry for both buyers and sellers, especially as everyone is now aware of the matter. At a sales completion I attended a while ago, the notaire handling the procedure informed the buyers to be careful, but to:

"Just remember! If you disturb the asbestos, you must wear masks and gloves. Then, bury it in the ground and nobody will know. Do not take it to the Tip."

Right then, in other words don't even think of a loft extension with windows!

Our breakfast host turns out to be from the same baker's family as the young Résistant murdered by the Germans in Varaize. He tells me this just as I'm about to take a bite out of a pain au raisin. It's another one of those poignant moments for me, but I'm appreciative of having the story verified, exactly as it was originally told to me. I'm not sure I want another croissant, just more café.

The end of the working week finds me in Niort. This becomes a regular event for me, visiting she who has now

273

become a friend, a close friend. Oh yes, it's the Dutch lady whom I sent to Italy to buy a house in the Lunigiana region of Tuscany. She who rang me to say she'd decided to move to France instead, to some non pronouncable place we'd never heard of, Poitou Charentes! She who is responsible for Spouse and I making the move ourselves.

Her town house in the centre of Niort is a semi derelict, three storeys high wreck, but she has great plans for it. The location is superb, but the amount of work it needs is far too much for a single lady to tackle alone. It's not small, either, but is like a tardis inside, as many of them are. I feel unsafe every time I visit, but bravely climb the stairs, several seriously dangerous, to the first floor living area she's cleverly created. The ground floor develops bit by bit into a sleeping zone, tucked into a recess of an enormous galleried room pre-dating Napoleon, which leads in turn to a pretty little stone walled courtyard. A makeshift kitchen begins to take shape amongst the rubble, and also a 'wet room,' becoming increasingly more in vogue. The top floor is currently the most inviting, if a bit difficult to reach. With the new roof installed above, it feels warmer than the rest of the place, and has good street views over the cobbles of Old Niort. I worry about her there on her own, but she has strength, both physically and of character.

Niort is way out of my territory. Located in the Département of Deux Sevres, one of the four which make up the Région de Poitou Charentes, property is considerably cheaper than it is in Charente, and Charente Maritime. The Vienne, the last of the four Départements but by no means the least in terms of importance, commands about the same prices as Deux Sevres. Its capital is the ancient city of Poitiers, made famous in Eleanor of Aquitaine's reign. Parts of the Great

Hall she entertained in still exist. It has a highly reputable university, is about the only multi-cultural city we come across in these parts, and of course Futuroscope (an ever growing theme park) nearby. I can't honestly say that I like Poitiers, though. Most of it is dull and even shabby, except for the main Square in the centre. A gloomy place, it does have one saving grace. Its airport, thanks to Ryanair!

I've just finished reading a book about how 'French Women Don't Get Fat,' which is a totally inappropriate statement, given that there seem to be as many drastically overweight women in France as there are anywhere else. Moreover, many of them of a certain age continue to have those 'short back and sides' haircuts which they love so much and which strike instant attention to fat necks! Only the rich and famous, the anorexic, and the 'wanna be' models, manage to maintain their slim forms, just like the World over. So, whilst waiting for houseguests to arrive earlier in the year, Spouse and I treated ourselves to lunch in the Airport's restaurant. They do a superb two course buffet, attracting the local Business Community as well as flyers and picker-uppers/dropper-downers.

With the book in mind, and its instructions to eat exactly as French women do, I braced myself for miniscule portions of all things healthy, easy to do with the 'mains,' but oh mon dieu, the desserts. Sitting at the next table to us were two exceptionally soignée (well dressed, well put together, those slim built successful types) and élégante women in their fifties or thereabouts. Up they got, away to the buffet, and back they came. Each one of them with no less than five portions of pudding. 'That's an easy act to follow, then' thought I. Not in with the remotest chance of five pieces of anything, I very smugly settled for precisely two of the multitudinous choices, quite sufficient merci beaucoup. Oh how good it was for the morale!

Back in Niort, the city is becoming more and more famous as a hub for many of the large insurance companies France has, several of them relocating to the vast commercial zones appearing on the périphérique. And of course, the likes of McDonald's, Burger King, D.I.Y. emporiums, children's toy stores, the usual stuff America's busy flooding the World with. The outer reaches of this ancient city must look like a fairground from the air, with its complicated system of roundabouts, and traffic lights galore. It's a challenge to navigate in rush hour, but I guess most cities are.

The ancient city itself is absolutely delightful, with its twelfth century castle keep complete with dungeons, standing proudly for all to see! The huge Saturday street market in the square below is a must visit experience. The River Sèvre flows through the middle of Niort, and there are lots of lovely walks along its banks. There are even Botanical Gardens, making it all a pleasant place to spend a day or two, combined with wandering through its attractive historical streets lined with specialist shops. If you need any angelica, this is the place to come. It's grown in the famous marshlands to the west of Niort, known as the Marais Poitevin, an area stretching almost to the Atlantic, finishing not far north of La Rochelle.

There are regions of marais in several parts of France, the word simply translating as 'marsh land' or 'swamp.' The Marais Poitevin Région of the Deux Sèvres has also been likened to Venice, except the water tends to be green, rather than dirty brown. (I adore Venice, but can't say the water's ever looked clean!) Here, the canals formed amongst the marshes give host to a magical scene of wildlife, boatlife, and charming stone cottages lining the banks. The little town of Coulon actually sits at the entrance to the Marais, but is close enough for the first stretch of water, the River Sèvre in fact, to pass through its centre and lead into the waterways. It has its fair share of gift shops, all around the angelica trade, but they're not overpowering in the slightest, and there are several places to stop for lunch before hiring a boat.

Further north again, but not far, is the Forét de Mervent, and its beautiful scenery is a dramatic change from the otherwise boring landscape around Fontenay-le-Comte, the nearest town of any size. On the edge of the Forest itself is Vouvant, a truly delightful little town which competes with our own St Jean d'Angely for property buying. Of course we go and suss it out one Sunday lunchtime, and soon realise why. A worthwhile, almost circular, trip from Niort is to head west into the Marais, north into the Forest, and east to Coulonges, another pleasant little town before heading due south and back to Niort, and back down into Charente Maritime, my favourite of the four départements in Poitou Charentes and the only one with a coastline. Of course I like it best!

42 Brits do Moonlit Flit

Another deal collapses, and although the sale isn't mine, it happens to concern one of my instructions. Here we go again! What's more, it's a house in our own commune of La Brousse, and we know the sellers very well indeed. This is the kind of embarrassment all estate agents dread, especially if it turns nasty.

The transaction's been sealed by our only occasionally in the office manager. Of course she just happened to be insitu the morning they arrived. On the surface, a pleasant enough couple, but oh how our opinions changed. Their behaviour was astonishing.

My desk is the one nearest the door, strategically placed below the 'English Spoken' sign, and in full view of the window. That's fine. I never forget to put my lipstick on, and give a McClean's smile at all who look in. (That was a 1960s' toothpaste advert.) And in they came. The woman deliberately avoided me to the point of rudeness, as I rose from my seat to say 'bonjour' or 'hello.'

"I want to speak to someone who speaks French." (She declared in English!)

"I do."

"No, I will only deal with someone who IS French."

(Her unpleasantness stopped me from announcing that my 25% share of Gallic blood may have qualified me. Anyone else was more than welcome to her.)

"That's fine, come this way and I'll introduce you to our office manager."

Her husband meekly followed, as embarrassed as hell as he tagged on behind.

And so they followed my colleague out of the door and into her car, to be driven to the little village of Villemarange (always makes me think of blanc mange) and to the house of maison secondaire owners from California and Blighty respectively. It didn't take long for the three of them to return to the Agence, all sporting smiles of satisfaction, Mrs English ignoring me, of course. The deal had been clinched. They'd signed on the dotted lines. A sale was in progress. Hands were shaken (not mine) and I was left to 'phone the owners in England with the good news, after they'd left the Agence. I have my uses!

The S.R.U. (the pulling out if you want to period) passed without a hitch, the lawyers were instructed, the D.P.E. properly in place of course, and everything was set for completion. And then the merde hit the fan. They'd been told in no uncertain terms how the sale would proceed. That if they wanted to terminate their side of the contract, it would have to be done before the end of the S.R.U. and sent to us, in writing, by registered mail. No other way would count, and if they didn't abide by this set of Government issued rules, they would continue to be liable to purchase the property, or recompense the sellers by ten per cent of the agreed purchase price, and also pay the full agency and legal fees. Mrs Clever Clogs insisted on having all this explained to them in French. Number One mistake, and not counted as a valid excuse during the aftermath.

The letter takes us all by surprise, not only in its illegality, but its form. It's a short note left in our letter box overnight and obviously after we'd closed, telling us that they are not going ahead with the purchase of the house. And who's left to contact them? Oh yes, it's me! They seem to have done a bunk, literally. Vanished into the vast plains of Poitou Charentes, or perhaps they've already taken a ferry back to Blighty. Wherever they are, they're impossible to track down and even Big Boss, by now fully informed and strutting and stressing like a fired up rooster who's lost his hens, can ill afford the services of French Interpol, or Europol as I think France comes under in such matters.

The manager, as in she who fixed the deal in the first place, wants to take legal action tout de suite. She knows what she's talking about. She has a Degree in Law from the University of Poitiers. She puts pressure on Big Boss. I'm behind them all the way. I want them to win. What these people have done is not allowed, not en France. Several meetings take place as the weeks pass by, but to my utmost surprise, les anglais get away with it. I'm disappointed, confused, it's supposed to be fail safe. In the greater scheme of things, it pales into insignificance. The house sells to better people after not too long a time, but that's not the point. Our contempt for les rogues takes a long time to dissipate.

What annoys the hell out of me is when I hear that they have returned to France and not only that, but they've bought elsewhere and that 'elsewhere' is rumoured to be La Brousse, in one of its other communes. That sucks! I guess it's a bit like parking fines and foreign number plates. 'Catch me if you can!'

I drive through the whole of La Brousse with a fine tooth comb, stopping at the Mairie in passing, determined to track them down, to expose them, to remind them of their commitments to the buyers they've let down especially. I fail! They've slipped through the net, and actually nobody hears of them, or if they do, they decide not to tell me. But it's a small country outpost and I'm pretty certain that, if they have indeed bought here, it won't be long before they're found out, and the system takes no pity on those who deliberately let others down. As it happens, the sellers finally close an other deal and move up to the Vendée and are very happy there, but that's not the point!

43 Expat Moans & Groans

I've handled three properties with home cinemas so far, two of them large enough to warrant sales of soda and popcorn, and far enough in the wilds of the countryside not to disturb the neighbours. The house I'm in this morning is kind of along the same lines, except this one is a tad upmarket, not in terms of the property itself, but with its own little theatre on the first floor. Whoever comes to watch a production here, however, will be well advised to wear at the very least a polar fleece, boots, and a woollie hat. They'll be about as comfortable as I remember being when I was treated to a production of King Lear at London's revamped Globe Theatre, except I'm relating to space now, not heat. We had balcony seats, for which those of us with slim enough legs (fortunately, that's me) were able to sit with them dangling through the balustrades over the Thespians below. As the afternoon performance progressed, a semi circle of legs could be seen turning deeper shades of sunburnt red (mine and our daughter's included)!

The Globe has been painstakingly recreated exactly as it would have been in Shakespeare's days, and 'pain' is the correct word to use when explaining its seating facilities. As a species, we have grown humungously over the last few hundred years, yet the benches (oh yes, benches) are about as close together as they'd have needed to have been back when anyone over 5 feet in height would have qualified for giant status. The first interval brought relief, but I'd forgotten just how many steps there were to climb down to get an ice cream. Getting back up again was ten times worse, not helped by some trying to be helpful usherette (sorry, I

know, more the language of matinées at the local 'flicks')
asked me if I were enjoying the performance:

"No, not at all ...."

as I poured out my tale of woe at scrunching legs through
railings because they wouldn't fit in front of the bench.
Spouse and daughter's 'significant other' must have been in
abject agony, but they weren't asked the question! It was a
lovely and kind birthday treat, and lunch beforehand was
exceedingly pleasurable, but the theatre itself? Naah, jamais
encore (never again). At least not until they do something
about the seating. I wonder how many more have
complained. We Brits tend to shut up and put up, and that's
why things which should be changed, rarely get changed, no
matter how much money people are being robbed of in the
meantime. I guess I'm just a Philistine! Comfort before
culture! These days, unlike in my youth, I'd actually rather
go for a walk on a deserted beach than sit and watch a bunch
of actors pretending to be those whom they are not!

Head in gear again, moments of reminiscing over, I'm in
one of those outstandingly pretty Charentaise stone rendered
large cottages, with the loveliest of light blue shutters.
They're totally rotten, but they do look gorgeous from a
distance. The solid oak front door is as difficult to open as it
is old to behold, but has functioned in all its splendour for
the last couple of centuries at least. Standing in three
thousand square metres of rich grassland, with daintily
landscaped flower beds at very kind to the eye intervals, it
all presents itself beautifully, despite being freezing cold
both outside and in. The current owners are of course
theatrical themselves, he the son of a travelling actor and his
wife from the days of the British Raj in India. They're

delightful, and it's just their maison secondaire, hence the lack of heating, but with its own stage and mini auditorium. Who am I to judge other people's priorities?

It's a pretty one to write up, and will appeal to all those thousands of dreamers back in Blighty, imagining themselves here in Poitou Charentes. When there's not much else to watch on television, our internet hits rise dramatically. So do the 'phone calls at the Agence the next morning, most of them a complete waste of time but it breaks the boredom of our own winter months, just as it does theirs. And those who do take the plunge and book in to see me here in Saint Jean d'Angely usually have fascinating tales to tell, in equal measures of happiness and sadness. I prefer the happy ones, of course, but listen to all.

The main reason for driving potential buyers around in my own car is (a) to get to destinations quickly and easily, and (b) to give them the opportunity to ask as many questions as come into their heads whilst I'm chauffeuring them. This usually happens the way it's intended to, focussing on property matters, but by no means always. It's as if I have 'agony aunt' tattooed on my forehead. I get clients escaping drug dealing sons and drug taking daughters, not that the two are always that way round. I listen to how one couple's house has been trashed, anything saleable taken to feed a heroin habit, and now their son's in gaol for dealing, about to be released, and they are physically afraid of his knock on the door. They've been through it too many times and are running away from the hurt and the constant worry. They only look at country properties, but isolation can bring its own problems, not least the lack of neighbours to call upon if necessity arises, or a quick arrival of the gendarmes!

I get second time rounders by the score, divorcées thinking a new country will help the new and next relationship. It seldom does. Often the most successful 'bien installé' (well settled) are the old hands at marriage, the 'able to cope with anything' brigade, merde included! I recognise the 'try againers' as soon as they set foot in the Agence. They have a completely different way of communicating with each other than those of us who've survived the distance, through thin and thick, that challenging sticky stuff, the merde alors. They always seem so incredibly nice to each other, these second timers. And as for the third and fourth timers, oh yes, I get a fair share of those as well. Personally, I wouldn't have the energy. Once is quite sufficient, merci. There's a lot to be said for not fighting over television programmes, or worse still, who's going to cross the garden in freezing temperatures to fetch in the logs.

Financial hardship drives many out of Britain, job losses, high mortgages, high costs of living and so on. Very few of my buying clients take on mortgages here in France, the majority trading up in space but down in value. It's possible to buy a mini mansion here for 200 000 euros, a first time buyer's price in many parts of the U.K. Retiring Service Personnel often buy in France (and Spain) not having previously owned property, cosseted by accommodation accompanying jobs. I get to refer to them as RSPs and have several. Police, Army, Royal Air Force and Royal Navy, and stacks of retired Clergy. These are put to work pretty much straight away in the newly developing parishes through Expatria.

'Give me a child until it's seven,' a Jesuit is thought to have said once upon a time. Certainly, it's not often the best idea to move a child to France if it's over seven. The children of high flying job moving Brits fare the best, dumped at the gates of the various International Schools in France's big cities, Paris, Lille, Bordeaux, Toulouse featuring mostly. The average young family moving to the depths of Poitou Charentes does not fall into that bracket, and their children are left to sink or swim. Many of them sink, almost at the first immersion. I'm told it's the same in Expat Limousin and Brittany. They often belong to parents who struggle to speak English correctly, let alone blessed with the tools needed to learn a foreign language. Many have never had a French lesson in their lives, find the nearest British/Irish pub (there are many) and will probably leave France still only able to say 'bonjour' and 'merci.'

Young children do well, respond to change, make friends fairly easily, and are the recipients of others wanting to get to know them. At that age, they are naturally inquisitive creatures, and the younger they are, the more likely they're inclined to inquire. But eight year olds upwards seem to struggle inordinately. Schools are run very differently in France. Free thinking is not encouraged, even though they study philosophy from almost the day they start. Learning is all very formal, even for the littlest ones, and walls are boringly under illustrated. Computers are rare in primary schools, and lunch is a long drawn out 'eat everything, or eat nothing' affair.

Admittedly, I've only been in three schools here but I've had a jolly good look round all of those and am totally disparaged. Parents aren't allowed to attend medicals. One of my buying mums is distraught over this. Toilets are without doors, just rows of short partitioning separating them, open for all who pass by to see. This leaves me understanding how French women can go for hours and not need to pee. They've been discouraged from doing so right from the start. The boys have outside urinals against playground walls, shock horror to girls from Blighty. Even those from France obviously learn to bottle it. I'm amazed there aren't more urinary tract infections in France, as this spills over into adulthood. Friends I increasingly make amongst the French come for meals and last for several hours without relieving themselves. I'm told it's considered ill mannered to ask to use the bathroom as "it may not have been prepared for you." Umm – they are very different. We are very different!

A school in Matha has over a dozen British youngsters at the moment, and it's causing big problems. They all stick together, learn very little, and some of them are turning into truants and delinquents. It's completely understandable. I have selling clients whose 14 year old son is rarely at school and has refused to go on an away trip unless his English friend goes too. He fails to accept his parents' logic that the raison d'être for booking him a place is precisely to improve his French, and to make friends amongst the locals. A typical outcome, they are moving back to England tout de suite. Guess who's buying their house? Another bunch of British hopefuls. And so the circle continues to rotate and with it will come a TV programme:

'Desperately Disenchanted Brits Return to Blighty.'

But not until we've sold a few more houses, please!

44 Motor Bikes & George Clooney

I'm back in one of my cinema selling houses, trying to negotiate a price reduction and failing with every explanation I attempt to offer. It's in Bagnizeau, one of the villages with a large Expat. population, so it should attract more. Like tends to follow like, even if subconsciously. There's many a one out there who thinks they want to fly solo, be the only anglais, and not actually realising that the same product appeals to them just as it has done to others before them, other Brits.

The house is a grand Charentaise with a prestigious driveway, gently curving as it arrives at the property itself. It looks traditional, but has glaringly white UPVC windows. Sacrilege! The Spanish wife has transformed the kitchen into one from the Costas, with objects galore filling every available space. From wine flagons to pottery plates, toy donkeys to matadors, strings of plastic onions, it's all here. The guy's a motor bike fanatic, the male equivalent of 'mutton dressed as lamb,' with his balding white hair tied into a silly little pony tail at the back. Not my type, but he's pleasant and proves to be amusing company. He takes me upstairs to try and justify yet again why the asking price has to remain at nearly half a million euros. It doesn't warrant anything near that type of money, which would buy a veritable cognac estate in the Premiér Cru, despite the cinema. It's the comfiest one of the three I've been dealing with, and has real cinema seats, a popcorn machine, an old fashioned bar area aka the 1950s/60s, and at 45 square metres has lots of space to invite the neighbours in for a film show or two.

I reminisce of my teenaged dates in the Odeon in Liverpool and the Essoldo in Birkenhead, probably both now bingo parlours, if the buildings have survived at all, watching 'The Ipcress File; Zulu; Doctor Zchivago; M.A.S.H.,' kissing and cuddling on the back row, as you do, as we did! Few of us married our 'first loves,' our cinema dates, unless we got 'shoved up the duff' and I managed to escape that trauma. Not all of my friends did, and several disappeared "to study nursing ... attend secretarial college in London," oh yeah! Where they really went was to homes for unmarried mothers, giving up their babes for adoption, and spending the rest of their lives with the often tragically enforced consequences of their loss, the deceipt, the heartache, and all largely so their professional middle class parents didn't have to suffer the embarrassment it would have caused them back then. That's what it was really all about! 'Philomena,' starring Judi Dench, is sure to be a box office hit, especially amongst my generation.

Another room of the same vast dimension lies at the back of the house, the arrière cuisine (back kitchen) but don't confuse these with the old terraced houses back in Blighty, where every house had one, as well as the front parlour. They are not the same! Les français often have two kitchens, even three in rural properties. There's the kitchen the World sees; the arrière cuisine where Madame fries and boils, bottles haricots, and steams various animal parts; and then there's the summer kitchen. This one's usually in a barn, or under a brick built shelter, and proudly boasts an inbuilt barbeque, a drinks' fridge, and a sink if the plumbing's been extended for the purpose of. There'll be seating for family and friends while they enjoy extended lunches at gingham clad tables by day, and starlit suppers by night. Tempting, romantic, the stuff of 'Escape to the Sun' dreams, but they are great creators of work and at times I feel I should adorn a little black skirt and frilly white apron!

We have what we call our own barbecue barn, which indeed it is, sporting the obligatory cooking area and chimney at one end, and lots of passion fruit flowers crawling down from the roof timbers. The side opposite the house is open, so we enjoy many a happy evening listening to the crickets, watching the stars and the bats as darkness intensifies, and chatting away 'till the small hours. The problem is, the happier everyone else gets, the more work falls upon me, all that ferrying stuff to and fro the house. I grow to resent it, and pull back on the hospitality lark. My commission does not run to domestic staff!

We've had sittings of forty plus for afternoon tea in the barn at one charity event, in rotas. A hundred and fifty altogether came that day, everyone of them able to enjoy an English 'Tea' complete with salmon and cucumber sandwiches, scones and Victoria sponges, all sitting comfortably and enjoying the August sun. Our largest barn had the jazz band playing and people dancing. I never would have thought in a million years that we'd have the wherewithal to host a garden party. Blimey, we've come a long way from our Edwardian town house in Hereford with its teeny back yard, sold for a lot more than we paid here in France! The view was good, though, watching the River Wye flow past the Cathedral opposite, and people playing tennis on the Bishop's Meadows behind. It was a great family house to have before the nest emptied.

Monsieur with the pony tail takes me to his garage opposite (that's something the punters will have doubts about right away) and shows me, not for the first time, his collection of motor bikes. Amongst the several, are two absolutely splendid Harleys in immaculate condition and gleaming from every angle. Next to them sits an antique Vespa, straight out of Italy, and still wasp like yellow.

I know which one I'd choose, speeding through the piazzas of Lucca, Siena, Roma, Milano, Como, preferably holding on to George Clooney (he has a house on Lago di Como) as we whizz through en route to a nice little trattoria up a cobbled backstreet. It'd have to be a tucked away place, perhaps in Bellagio or Menaggio, and certainly not in the piazza itself, or my driver may be stolen!

45 Dell Boy & Barbezieux

It's not often I'm in a night club. The last time was way back in the '60s, the Gaslight in Liverpool. Probably long closed down, but fun while it lasted, not that I used the gambling tables but the atmosphere was 'cool' in modern speak. This club's slightly different, not least in location. It was once une grande maison bourgeoise, and the original owners would turn in their graves if they could see what disastrous deeds have been done to it since. The walls are decorated in bright orange flock wallpaper, the chandeliers are ghastly, the furnishings are all plastic and purple, and hideous green screens divide the gambling and drinking areas, long since gone to ruin. No original features survive, and they would have been beautiful.

Barbezieux is just about at the southern most edge of my territory, and certainly not in my secteur, but we go far afield for the extraordinary. Dell Boy ('Only Fools and Horses' comedy series circa 1980s) would be in his element here. I'm not so sure about young brother Rodney, but guess he'd be frogmarched along. He'd be company for the real frogs, and I'm not talking the human natives here! Well, they call us the 'Roast Beefs' so I guess it's fair game reciprocating with 'Froggies.' Even a French politician (don't ask me which one) was rumoured to have said, when the Channel Tunnel was ready in France before we Brits had finished our end, and an Englishman enquired how that had possibly happened, replied:

"We did not ask the Froggies! We just did it." (I don't believe it!)

The pond is right in the middle of the ground floor of the club. Not a regular sized pond, this one is big, and contains various species of fish and frogs. I gawp in amazement, wondering how many drunkards have ended up in there when their chips have all been spent. A bit more digging, and it could become an indoor swimming pool. That'd be nice. I guess the pond may well have been used as an exotic bath at one time. Shades of Sid James and Frankie Howard amorising with a flotilla of scampily clad bimbos prancing round the edge come into my imagination, the lot of them eventually falling in, to emerge with lotus blossom and water lilies dangling from their beehive hairstyles. Sid's chuckling away in the background and Hattie Jacques is standing there, arms severely crossed. Of course there's another one in the harem, too. Barbara Windsor cooing and giggling, as only she still can. Carry on Clubbing, I can just see it! The kitchen is virtually non existent, but I guess old Dell Boy would find a way of cooking his mange tout ici. He'd have no problem buying them. There's a weekly market in Barbezieux, and young Rodney would soon be sent shopping:

"Au contraire, Rodders. Go and buy a baguette, Bro."

I can't imagine Raquel wanting to move into the apartment above the main club rooms. It's appalling, even by their standards. The décor is absolutely disgusting, typically gawdy French (they rarely do neutral) with some walls covered in what looks like dirty brown carpet, others in violent wallpaper in vivid purples, and paintwork fiery in orange and red. Even Al Capone would have drawn the line at having meetings up here, not that he ever left Chicago or New York. Every original feature has been stripped from every room of these vast premises, but with a bucket full of money, time and patience, it could all be reinstated into something rather ooo laa laa. The price? A mere 250 000 euros, give or take a little, and that buys a three storey mansion ripe for renovation. There's even an enormous walled garden at the rear, perfect for afternoon teas should it become gentifried. En route to Bordeaux, I can see coach loads of British tourists stopping for their 'Russian Earl Grey,' 'Ceylon,' or even 'English Breakfast,' before wandering through the market stalls to buy naff souvenirs of their time in Poitou Charentes.

Barbezieux St Hilaire, to give it the full name, lies in the southern part of the cognac producing area but in its Petit Champagne, as opposed to Segonzac's Premier Cru. The area's also famous for its agriculture, notably herds of hugely impressive Charolais and Limousin cattle. Some of these are proudly exhibited at the September Show, a bit like our own Royal Show in Warwickshire. The biggest difference, of course, is in the number of stands. At Stoneleigh, there are over a thousand. In Barbezieux, a mere one hundred and fifty or thereabouts. The Royal Welsh Show, at Builth Wells, beats the lot of them. We do things well on the Welsh Borderlands!

Just half an hour by car from Pons, take a look at the Pilgrims' roundabout on the approach to this old Roman town, strategically situated on the famous Route de St James de Compostella for overnight stops. It's worth doing a photographic tour of Pons' roundabouts until the Pilgrims come clearly into view on theirs, superb in their black statued presence. In the same general area is Jonzac, not to be confused with Jarnac. Jonzac has a very lovely château, worthy of an afternoon's detour.

The pleasure doesn't stop here, and it's not much further to Bordeaux itself, from where it's yet another easy drive to one of the most beautiful places in France, Saint Emilion. Apart from its exquisite wines, the picturesque town itself is worthy of an away break, long enough to take the little train through the vineyards and sample the produce. And whilst down in that region, Blaye and Bourg aren't far, either. Plus, of course, the Médoc Peninsula with Baron de Rothschild's 'pile' and others of similar ilk. I'm particularly fond of Margaux, the wine, not the girl, although I know a lovely one in Switzerland (not spelt the same way, though). There are many girls called Margaux in France.

All things considered, the South West of Poitou Charentes, where it borders Aquitaine, has a lot going for it. Great restaurants, too! It often seems that the further down we travel, the nearer the Sea we roam, the greater the culinary experience. Conversely, the Northern Coast of Brittany does rather well, too! But I guess I'm biased. Give me simply cooked shellfish or sea bass, preferably both, one after the other, and I'm anybody's. Of course, I'll need a glass or two of Chablis, or Sancerre, sans doubt! Give me an inland 'formule' and I'm on the next boat back to Blighty, escaping the awful offal fumes! Brrr, skin bubbled brown tripe, balls of throat innards (oh how they love their gésiers), calf's head (oh yes they do, and they gleefully call it tête de veau), frog's legs (cuisses de grenouilles), rabbit's liver (foie de lapin), and even worse (if that's at all possible) calf's foot (pied de veau). And that's not all. The French are very brave about what they eat, not squeamish about blood either, whether it be served up as boudins noir or boudins blanc (black or white puddings).

For me, it's a constant challenge, just as it was when we lived in Hong Kong and came face to face with jelly fish served with great glee, webs of ducks feet swimming in brine, chicken cooked in mud, the face given to the person of honour or the youngest at the banquet, eyes staring. That was my first meal, I was the youngster, and itdidn't get any better! An Anglo-Chinese friend from those early days (like myself, a Liverpudlian by birth) still reminds me that I carried a 'Mars Bar' in my bag that night, which I hungrily consumed in the secrecy of the taxi en route home! And banquets in Beirut? Forget it, I'm saying nothing, except 'chaq'un son gout,' each to their own taste and bravery!

I take the long drive back from Barbezieux to the Agence, the car on cruise control so that I can equally concentrate on the glorious scenery. It envelops me from every direction, far reaching horizons of sunflowers ahead, cows and corn either side, and vineyards in the rear mirror. I have clients to pop in and see in Pons, which means a little stopover in Saintes afterwards is perfectly justifiable. After another 'please-reduce-your-price' time wasting hour passes, I'm in the English Shop in the shadow of Saintes' Roman Ruins, stocking up on Baked Beans and Bisto Gravy, HP Sauce, some Chinese and Indian spices, and a few paperbacks to read before bedtime. Oh the joy! Coffee flavoured Walnut Whips and Fry's Peppermint Creams. Divine providence is shining down upon me today. They even have Bendicks' Victoria Mints, my all time favourite treat, but not with the Palace of Westminster on the box anymore. Tantalising white mint encased in luscious black chocolate; the picture may have gone, the name slightly changed, but they remain as delicious as they ever were. Bring'em on!

Pons' Pilgrims en route to St James de Compostella

46 Cultural Differences Encore

I know, I'm a bit critical at times, a bit hard on some aspects of French cuisine, but hopefully I'm equally full of praise for its culinary ecstasy when it happens. I remind myself periodically of the hardship the French have suffered, compared to us, their 'cousins' over the Channel. Our Industrial Revolution came many years before theirs did, making us wealthier sooner. Our road and rail networks preceded theirs, allowing us to distribute a wider range of goods and services, including food, sooner. We are an island race, they are not. We have not been occupied in modern times, they have and not once, but several times within recent history. Yes, rationing was still in place when I was a young child, but I belong to the post 1939-45 War's 'Baby Boomer' generation.

Although I well remember going on the bus from Crosby through Bootle (where the bugs wear clogs) to Liverpool in the 1950s, and passing through war ravaged slums en route, I cannot remember shortages of any food products at all influencing my own childhood. I was even an 'Ovaltiney' complete with badge and certificate of membership! I realise I was amongst the lucky ones, and obviously that poverty did exist big time in Liverpool, still does, but there was food available, and that's the only point I'm trying to make here. In France, it was not. We have no concept of how hard it was for them, and still often is. There seems an even bigger division between those who are rich, and those who are not, here in France than in the U.K. That will increasingly change, though, as young bankers and hedge funders flitter and flounder wealth around with abandon, increasing poverty levels not seen for decades in London.

Perhaps the fact that we ate tongue (yuch), corned beef rissoles, and spam (horrible pink stuff) was evidence indeed of food poverty, but it could equally have been because my mother was half French and she actually liked such things. Also, I guess it was all good for us. Since living in France, I've certainly identified lots of peasant food I was brought up on, no doubt influenced by the French side of my heritage. But we still had lovely drinks at bedtime (Ovaltine), fresh orange juice, a spoonful of malt before school, and sweets once a week. We often had fish n' chips on the Fridays we visited my grandmother in Crosby, the French one, who hated cooking. I always volunteered to queue for them. It was a time when children were safe to do such things. They've often been credited for Britain's success in wartime, good nourishing food for the masses, introduced of course by Jewish Immigrant into the East End of London even before the First World War. Succulent cod, chips, and mushy peas, not forgetting the pickled onions for the grown-ups!

Here in France, especially in rural areas, life was very different and traditions die hard. For that reason, I do understand why 'formules' are still based on the little that was available throughout many people's lives, and that remains the same even today in the poorer areas of 'the Hexagon' France is sometimes called. The gap between those who have, and those who have not, has a huge influence on what restauranteurs choose to put on their daily menu boards. Lunch at Saint Martin de Ré will average fifty euros per head. Lunch in any one of the thousands of rural small town restaurants will come out at ten, maybe twelve, and will be a treat for many. Even I admit to sometimes being lucky!

In my working day, I come across villages with outdoor communal bread ovens and my colleagues can still remember the time when they were the only source of cooking for most of the rural population, even during some of their own childhoods. I'm talking 1950s and '60s here! Villagers would scratch their initials into the bottom of casserole pots, and take their stews to the bread oven for cooking after the bread making had finished. Nowadays, the bread is baked in copious quantities in impressive bakeries, and the baguettes distributed throughout the countryside. Those long tall bags in the souvenir shops are precisely for putting baguettes inside. Go through any rural village mid morning, and every gate will have a baguette bag suspended from it. Most people do have their own cooking facilities nowadays, even if only a small gas ring or two (I'm not joking here) but they still find it challenging sometimes to actually use their kitchens. Hence, the concept of the arrière cuisine, of course.

This can have its dangers. I get a call one morning to say that a house I've put on the market for a family in Ballans, has gone on fire and will have to be withdrawn from sale. It's a newish bungalow for want of a better description, although they don't call single storied modern boxes that in France. Everything is a house, except when it's an appartment. Madame had been cooking chips and left the chip pan on, on top of the old stove in the garage. There's a super duper one in the kitchen but that's just for show. Leastwise, there was! The damage is extensive and they're having to vacate the premises. It's not the first time this happens during my time as an estate agent here, and it won't be the last. My thoughts turn to a fabulous house in Jarnac, with a kitchen suitable for an advert in 'Country Living.' It's never used. Madame cooks in the garage. We are in the 21st

century but they are still living in the 19th! It all slots
perfectly into place and I accept more, rather than criticise.
When the punters ask:

"Why?" I reply:

"Because they are French," a statement of fact, not of
nastiness!

That doesn't stop me wanting to tell builders to put wash
hand basins in 'loos,' and to give them windows to evacuate
the smells! It doesn't stop me asking selling clients to make
their beds before going to work. I take clients into houses
where they have neither sheets nor duvet covers, and I find
this particularly hard to cope with, mais c'est la France.
More than a few leave unwashed dishes in the sink, clothes
drying on 'maidens' in living rooms, or in heaps on the
floor, toilets left uncleaned and with the lids up for all to see
what lurks below the water line. I give up trying to change
them. One owner curtly, and in all seriousness, responds:

"Do not take your clients upstairs, Madame!"

"But Madame, you want to sell your house!"

Au contraire, I go into veritable mini palaces, spotlessly
clean and inviting, clutter free and ripe for selling. I guess
it's like the restaurant issue, an ever widening gap between
where I like to lunch and where I dread to! As Forrest
Gump's mum says (what a great film):

"It is as it is, and it ain't no isser."

Vive la France!

301

47 Lingo, Ladders & Lamplights

I continue to struggle with the lingo at times, which is actually rather ridiculous, given the statistics. I've read (can't remember where) that the English language has around half a million words, German has approximately one hundred and eighty thousand, and French a mere one hundred thousand or thereabouts. Despite this apparent incredible lack of available vocabulary, I struggle to find sufficient words for a good many situations which meet me head on, and am constantly picked upon for using certain things incorrectly. Fortunately my colleagues in St Jean d'Angely are considerably kinder to me than the ones in Cognac were. Clients can be a bit tricky at times, too, especially those born and raised in rural Poitou Charentes. Dialects and me don't seem to go together very well at all, to the point of my not being able to realise that they are even speaking French! 'Double Dutch' translates into "speaking like a Spanish cow," and had I not been made of stronger stuff, no doubt I myself would be mooing by now!

Today's clients are going to struggle big time where they're going next. Neither of them speaks French, after owning their property here for a fair few years. She's Welsh, but from its English speaking south eastern part. Had she had Welsh lessons as a child, perhaps her brain would have been trained to click into other languages. He's possibly from The Midlands of England and I imagine secondary modern educated, great for learning how to hold a spanner, but not great for reciting 'amo, amas, amat ...' Perhaps he does in bed. Naah, doesn't look the type!

Oh yes, they are joining the brave band of warriors heading for The Balkans, Bulgaria to be precise. They tell me they can buy a mini mansion for fifteen thousand pounds and that the infrastructure is just fine. I do hope they're right. What they have now, is a tumbling down ruin of a smallish house, so unfit to live in as yet that they doss in a caravan and wash in an overgrown paddling pool. It does, however, come with one enormous barn. It's in a very pleasant hamlet, has gorgeous views, a bit too close to Beauvais for my own personal liking, but that has nothing to do with it, especially since I've taken on board the bravery of some its occupants during the War. I generously value it around 50 000 euros bottom line, fees on top, to be paid by the buyer, as is the norm here. After lots of disappointment from her, and a little bit of aggression from him (I'm used to that) and my lungs reeling from the effects of chain smoking in front of me, I'm desperate to escape from the situation. Passive smoking in a caravan is not funny! I say I'll take it on at anything up to 80 000 for starters. I'm only giving it that much because of the barn, ripe for development and which could become a stunning family home. The dilapidated house could be turned into a gîte, and there's enough land for a pool.

In my attempts to scarper, I foolishly agree to market it at over a hundred thousand euros, and that's one helluva lot for a building plot, even though it's one with a barn and a ruin. I shall face the music when I return to the Agence, that's for sure, and I doubt that it'll get listed for the next Caravane. However, they've agreed to let me put a board up, always great for advertising. I just happen to carry spares, so do the deed there and then. Oh yes, I travel complete with tool box, 'A Vendre/A été Vendu' signs, and torch.

Signs can be extremely puzzling at times. I used to think 'à été vendu' meant the house was just for sale in summer, until I revised my verbs and discovered it actually means 'it's sold.' The first one's easy: 'à vendre' = for sale. A really confusing one had me totally perplexed one day when I was driving to Ruffec for a sales' completion. Lunch time was looming near, when there I saw it, and oh how pleased I was: 'Votre pub est ici.' Great, a pub. That'll do me nicely. Search as I did, I never found it. Of course not. It translates as 'put your publicity here.' I don't think any of them quite stick in my mind as much as the first one I saw in Italy. 'Fai da tè.' Why on earth would anyone put a huge poster, just on leaving the autostrada from Milan to Como, telling their significant other to 'make the tea?' On a par with the old 'Your dinner's in the dog' one near Sainsbury's in Hereford a few years ago, this making the tea advert was right up there with it. Out came the dictionary, and the verb drills, and oh how stupido of me. It means D.I.Y. and was obviously referring to the Italian equivalent of B and Q. 'Fai' comes from the verb 'fare,' to make or do, and 'tè' is one of the many pronouns for 'you.' Now there's a language with lots of words, Italiano!

I've bought my ever so powerful torch in the little old town of Burie, conveniently placed for Cognac, Saintes and Matha, at the Quincaillerie. That's a word which took me a very long time to pronounce correctly. Most of the small towns here still have an Ironmonger's, but they'll no doubt start to disappear soon. The big boys are moving in, and setting up on the commercial estates springing up around every medium sized town upwards. We have Monsieur Bricolage in St Jean d'Angely, in Cognac, in Saintes; and Weldom are creeping up behind them. The larger cities have la crème de la crème, in Leroy Merlin. La Rochelle has a spectacular one, which becomes the focus of many a conversation we Brits have when we're not actually traipsing its hallowed aisles. The torch is a must have item. In England it used to be the safety alarm. I still have mine, standard issue when female estate agents became occasionally endangered. I never had to use it, but was grateful for having it with me when I came face to face with a Rottweiller at the other side of a serving hatch one day!

Here in France, I find myself in dark and derelict properties as a matter of everyday life. It's not a pleasant part of the job, and I learn to be selective. But we are a women only agence, the 'Charlie's Angels' of real estate, as one of our sellers affectionately dubs us. Hence it's the old 'someone has to do it' game. Each in their own secteur! They're a far cry from the new homes I sold for the big developers in England: Bryant, Bovis, Bloor, Persimmon, Virgin! Safety alarm, torch, and a hard white hat with its Virgin logo artistically scrawled across in red. I have them all!

Staircases are another danger zone. Several of the properties here do not possess them, and these can be anything from former cognac distilleries to family homes, sometimes both in the same place. I draw the line at visiting these with buying clients until some form of safety barrier is erected to save them from the sheer drop below, sometimes in excess of twenty feet. I have an English couple selling up, returning to Blighty with their teenaged children. The landing is a potential death threat, but they do create a semi wall for me, be it from dodgy plasterboard. At least it looks safe! I am not insured for such accidents in the making, so thank them profusely and set to work to sell it. Measuring the house was a nightmare, and one I can do without repeating. All part of a day in the life of an Estate Agent in Rural France!

Parish Garden Party at the Old Smithy

48 Biryani, Books & Baked Beans

St Jean d'Angely not only has an enormous outdoor market every Saturday, stetching out from the impressive main square down the cobbled lanes, but also an indoor one every Wednesday and Saturday morning. The town becomes a mecca for locals and les anglais alike, and we now have three market stalls run by Brits. Two of them are outside, but the main one is in the old Market Hall itself. It sells everything an Expat missing 'home' yearns for. We can buy baked beans, chutneys, marmalade, gravy granules, jellies, blocks of Cadbury's chocolate, all the favourite breakfast cereals not available in France (although the selection in the supermarkets improves by the month almost) and virtually everything else a typically British kitchen store cupboard houses. It's run by a lovely young couple, expecting their first child and hoping to settle here. Time will tell on that one! They also offer a delivery service to and fro Blighty, a 'Man With A Van' kind of thing. These are springing up throughout France, and seem to be doing a roaring trade, cheaper than Pickfords by far!

Take a walk around the perimeter of this ancient Market Hall, and you'll find Poppy's Curry Stall, run by an Anglo-Indian couple. Their take-away curries are excellent, and the Brits flock to buy them with almost as much enthusiasm as they do the fish n' chip, and pizza vans which tour the villages around Matha.

Round the other side of square is the book shop, selling volumes of English language paperbacks in various states of tattiness and pristine condition. The chap running this stall annoys me intensely one day. En route back to the Agence, I stop at his selection and choose one I fancy reading. The price? Two euros! I don't have any small change on me, so promise to return with it tout de suite. He's having none of it. He knows exactly where I work, that my office is less than two minutes away from his book barrow, and yet he refuses to trust me. With two euros owing! Forget it. He can get stuffed!

Round the corner from the market place, Sarah and Jessica have just opened a café, down the cobbles from the Grand Hôrloge. Sarah is often on the road buying more antique tea sets and small items of silver, which add to the café's charm and are all available for sale, leaving daughter Jessica capably in charge. On market days, of course, both of them are to be found serving tea in bone china cups, and home made cakes. Les femmes françaises soon aquaint themselves with this little bit of luxury, and I pop in perhaps more frequently than I should, but it's great for networking. Every opportunity to leave a few business cards usually brings rewards.

I make a point of buying something from the grocery stall every morning it's open (except my one Saturday per month's day off). I listen, I chat, and more often than not gain new clients. It's half the battle won. That and staying open at lunch time!

Greetings cards are pretty awful, très naff, in France, and not only scarce, but vastly overpriced. A lady who lives in Saint Savinien just happens to design and make her own, is English, and is extremely talented. They are a truly professional product, produced from her own water colours of the Charente Maritime, and which she sells in Sarah's café. This becomes a great grapevine for me and I soon learn that the artist wants to sell her house. Sarah sends her to me. I get the deal. It's what it's all about, so do I feel guilty playing hookey and taking tea outside the office? Mais non, pas du tout! Saint Savinien's not in my secteur, but when it comes to cementing deals amongst British sellers, I have an excellent working arrangement with my colleagues, especially when the clients don't speak French. We go as a friendly twosome. I do the talking and all the translating; she does the measuring, takes the photographs, and signs off the official paperwork. We are a team, ça marche!

Saint Savinien is very beautiful, and sits on the crossroads leading to Rochefort, Saintes, Marennes, and Saint Jean d'Angely (the closest). The River Charente flows widely here and it's a boat lover's paradise. The little town itself is très charmante and attracts many tourists in the summer. A Swedish owned restaurant adds to its appeal, with jazz evenings as well as excellent cuisine. There are many such small towns here in Poitou Charentes, but this is one of my favourites. It's retained its local culture, yet at the same time has become rather cosmopolitan in flavour, thanks mainly to the Swedes' commercial venture. France welcomes foreigners openly, often with kindness and egalité rather than curiosity, although that happens the further inland one travels.

Spouse and I find ourselves in Marennes one Sunday lunchtime, not knowing what to expect but having read that it's a great place to eat shellfish straight from the Sea. Fishermen's shacks line the Estuary and serve their catch to those of us lucky enough to discover them. We sit at the very last one and Megan settles beside us, totally unperturbed by the huge black and white cat sitting on the slipway, eating giant sized prawns. She's used to this. She's got her own shellfish eating cat at home, Gemima. The food keeps coming, seven platters, one after the other, with huîtres (oysters), moules (mussels), coques (cockles), coquilles St Jacques (scallops), crevettes (large prawns), crabes, and langoustines (crayfish). It's divine, and costs us precisely fifty five euros, in total, that's for both of us, and includes a large pichet of vin rosé. The home made mayonnaise is delicious, and the baguettes are just right, not too crusty, and nice and light. The setting is like something out of a film, and we can't believe how utterly amazing and beautiful it all is. It's beauty in a rugged kind of way, basic yet powerfully uplifting, nature at its best. Rick Stein should come here! Perhaps he already has? I know he has a penchant for La Belle France.

We carry on to Brouage after lunch. Certain towns lay claims to certain people. I'm thinking Amiens and Saint Jean d'Angely both claiming the head of Saint John the Baptist. Brouage, and Saint Malo up in Brittany, both reckon that their man founded Canada, Samuel de Champlain and Jacques Cartier respectively. Personally, I associate Cartier with the watches I could never in a million years afford to own, not that I would want to. Well, maybe, just the little diamond studded one which stared out at me from a window in the Mandarin Hong Kong's shopping mall all those years ago. But I don't do opulence, so it wouldn't have been my style! I prefer the discrete and understated look, myself. But let's not get disrespectful here. Jacques Cartier did sail to Canada in 1534, and did explore the whole of the Saint Lawrence Seaway and most of Newfoundland. It was from him that Canada got its name. It means 'village' in Huron, the language the native people of the same name used, and chose it for the Country it became.

He went on to make two more trips to The New World from Saint Malo, up in Brittany, under the auspices of King François the First (1515-1547) he whose fame is based in Cognac.

I don't think I'd have liked Cartier, though. He didn't care much for the Native Tribes, nor for the native wildlife. Few explorers did. The group of islands in the region now called Les Iles aux Oiseaux (the Islands of Birds), were considered fair play for a day's shooting practice when he allowed his crew to kill over a thousand birds, causing one species to become extinct (the Great Auks). He must have known what was going on, but I guess his generation didn't understand the meaning of conservation. I'm glad to say that Les Isles aux Oiseaux are now a Canadian Government Bird Sanctuary.

Back to Brouage and Champlain, servant of King Henri the Fourth (1589-1610) and also a Protestant, in line with a high percentage of folk in these parts back then, of course. Champlain was born in Brouage, but actually sailed to Canada from Honfleur, up in Normandy (and very lovely). From there, he discovered Quebec. I guess date wise, Cartier wins, but Brouage is still hugely proud of its famous son, and has a museum devoted solely to Champlain and Canada. It took another half century for Brouage to be fortified, considered necessary after the Siege of La Rochelle in 1627/28. This was all our fault, as it was our good old Duke of Buckingham and his men who decided to take possession of the Ile de Ré, and storm the fortress at St Martin de Ré in the process. The French defeated us. Some historians label this defeat as the most important battle of the Thirty Years War (1618-48).

It was yet another war in which religion played an enormous part, with Protestant strongholds decimated throughout France. Louis XIII (1610-1643) Catholic son of Protestant Henri, of course had already captured our own Saint Jean d'Angely and reclaimed it for his loyal 'Holy Roman' subjects. Being so close to La Rochelle and Ile de Ré, and Louis XIV's reign in full swing (1643-1715), the architect cum engineer Vauban, perhaps the most famous France has ever seen, was instructed by the King to turn Brouage into a fortress. Born poor, and orphaned young, he later became the Marquis Sébastien le Prestre de Vauban, and was responsible for many of France's bastide towns and cities. Brouage is a fine example of his work and remains pretty much intact to this day.

We walk its walls, admire the open Sea beyond, stop and have a cuppa outside a souvenir shop selling baskets and post cards, and take too quick a peep in the Canadian Museum. En route back to Rochefort, we drive through winding lanes which take us through salt marshes lined with grazing sheep, and one field of cows which would probably prefer to be kept further inland. I just hope the ground's not too soggy for them. I note the similarities between this part of Coastal Poitou Charentes and the Coast where Brittany and Normandy meet. Both have salt marsh fed sheep, both have fortress cities built by Vauban (Brouages and St Malo), and both have famous explorers who left their shores for Canada and The New World. Both also serve up huge varieties of sea food par excellence!

49 Grabbed In A Kiss

I'm back in Cressé, the village of the disastrous meal expensively sold to us by the drunken owner, and a bar full of 'Fag Ash Lills' who wouldn't have been out of place in 'Benidorm.' I have a job finding the house I'm to put on the market, and when I eventually emerge from the car and head for the tall iron gates, they are suddenly opened for me. That's fine, but what happens next is most definitely not! I have never met this man in my life, and he pounces on me enthusiastically and proceeds to 'do the bises,' as we say here. I kiss very few people, and certainly not strangers, so this takes me aback and I fall short of winging him one with my brief case. Realising I'm not impressed, he steps away and mutters something along the lines that everyone kisses in France. He's wrong, they do not. I tell him that not even, especially not, les français do the bises on first meetings. This is an urban myth put out by les misguided anglais. Handshakes are the order of the day, especially when business is about to be done. I compose myself, accept his apology, and we shake hands.

We go inside the house, where his wife greets me and instinctively offers her hand. I take it. She offers me coffee. I drink it. Happily! He joins us, and I sit and listen to their reasons for moving to France, and their reasons for now wanting to move again. However, they plan to move elsewhere in France, not back to Blighty. They are retired farmers and are keen to move to the scenic hills of the Limousin. They arrived here in the aftermath of the last 'Foot and Mouth' crisis, the one which Tony Blair got so totally, and heartlessly, wrong. It's a sad story and my mind flies back to Herefordshire during that period. I got close to many people affected by the disease, first hand, working

313

alongside farmers, not by simply reading papers and watching television news' broadcasts.

The property is semi-detached, and the adjoining house is shabby and not at all attractive, which is going to be the first hurdle. However, it comes with a large garden and its own gîte, up and ready to accept holiday makers. It's spacious, but she'll have to clear the humungous amount of clutter they obviously didn't feel up to relieving themselves of before their move to France. Few people do. I see it all! The tea sets my parents' generation would have got as wedding presents circa the 1940s, the prints of England in times gone by, the ornaments filling every nook and cranny. The annual school photos of grandchildren growing up without grandparents, now self exiled in France. Few Expat houses belonging to people of a certain age differ. (Mine does. I don't do clutter!)

 The purposefully hung on to disarray in the house I'm currently in continues on the first floor, embracing the French habit of laying stupid little rugs all over slippy wooden floors. The French themselves are the worst. They love to put them at the tops of staircases. Often dish cloths (I joke not) they are lethal. I shudder to think how many folk have slipped on them and fallen head over heels down the stairs, often without handrails to break their fall, I might add. I start measuring up the first bedroom I come across, and the next thing I know is that I'm clinging on for dear life to a dressing table positioned next to the window. It's a matter of that, or falling right through the window itself. Shards of glass always seem to be miraculously unharmful in James Bond films, but I don't risk my chances. Oh yes, I've slipped on a perishing little mat, can't even call it a rug. In falling, I bend a finger back badly, but not badly enough to seek medical intervention. Phew!

I'm not especially calm in this place, have got over the double cheek kissing from a stranger, only to be flat on the floor in he and his wife's guest bedroom. I utter not a sound. It would hardly be professional. I shake myself, straighten the clothes I'm wearing, check in the mirror that I look presentable, apply a bit more lipstick (it does wonders for the morale) and head back downstairs:

"Please remove ALL those rugs from ALL those wooden floors upstairs, tout de suite. I am not insured for clients' accidents, and I don't think you will be."

They listen, and I make a point of noting on their file that the place is a tad dangerous, but then so are a good many of the properties we place for sale. The only difference this time round, is that this one is English owned. They are, however, lovely people and they've experienced dreadful times as farmers back in Blighty. I can empathise with them, and leave on a warm and friendly note. It won't be an easy property to sell, but many of them are not, and there is indeed a buyer for every house!

Lunchtime is looming, I'm near Néré, so I head for my favourite little bistrot. Suitably refreshed and relaxed, I head off to Loiré sur Nie after lunch. It's vaguely en route back to Saint Jean d'Angely from Néré, give or take a few country twists and turns. I have a delightful cottage I've been instructed to sell, right in the heart of the little hamlet and beautifully and sensibly presented. Oh boy, does it give off sad vibes, though. It's one of those days. First the fall in Cressé, and now yet another couple set on moving to the

Limousin, but for different reasons. When I arrive, Madame gives me the low down. Their son is at agricultural college in the Creuse. He's only seventeen (oh the joys of being seventeen again, the freedom, the discovery, the satisfaction, but obviously not en France) 'Those Were The Days My Friend,' and oh yes, so they were! The boy comes home every weekend. It takes him seven hours! Heaven help his future wife! Of course it goes without saying that said boy is an only child, much worshipped and adored, especially when an 'only' is the male of the species. And then, she tells all. It's not only about the boy, but her husband has cancer and travels to Bordeaux three times a week. That's a tall order, and by moving to the Limousin he'll have a specialist cancer unit on their doorstep. I learn of an Expat marooned there, who's cured of an extremely rare type of cancer in an amazing state of the art oncology unit, like in the middle of nowhere! To appreciate the Limousin, it's first of all necessary to have travelled to the wildest reaches of Wales, or the Scottish Highlands.

To have medical facilities of such a high level, outside Paris, is truly phenomenal. France does well with its health statistics and it's why many of us appreciate being here. We feel cared for, catered for, and never made to feel a nuisance. Once in 'the system,' once bien installé en France, one's official nationality takes second place to the level of care one receives. I applaud their ability to embrace us all on an equal footing, once we ourselves have made the effort to integrate, which is what acceptance is all about.

I feel I'm 'getting there,' and am even considering applying for French Nationality. I pick up the forms from the Mairie, inwardly digest them, and then balk at the prospect of eighteen months' (at least) bureaucracy to fight my way through, and prepare for a written test, an oral test, and only then being given their sign of approval. Mind you, I'd get the chance to start all over again, even with a new name on offer for all applicants. Now there's an exciting thought. Who shall I be? Naah, perhaps I'll just stay as me!

I have the most amazing, totally splendiferous, house to sell right in the heart of Matha. It's stunning, absolutely beautifully equipped as an upmarket 'Bed n' Breakfast,' and run by a delightful chap living on his own from Blighty, and his occasionally visiting girlfriend. They'd both like her to be here more often, but business is quiet in Poitou Charentes in winter, so needs must.

With a grand entrance hall, wood panelled in solid oak, three reception rooms and a catering styled kitchen on the ground floor, five en suite bedrooms with luxury taken to a level most French hotels would envy, and an additional six rooms on the second floor, ripe for restoration, this is an incredible purchase for the mere sum of 445 000 euros, including agency fees. I can see the walled garden serving afternoon teas to elderly tourists fed up with seeing yet another vineyard, and wouldn't mind volunteering making scones and carrot cakes for the purpose of! Actually, that's a silly idea, no time! In my next life, my retirement life, maybe.

Matha has a thriving outdoor market every Friday, and an indoor one open on Tuesday, Friday and Saturday mornings. It's a great little town, and this house is crying out for a new owner. I find one, a couple searching for the very thing, but only he's here. Yet another lone house hunter, wife back in Blighty. He'll bring her out once he's put his short list together. He loves it, and takes copious amounts of photographs, emails them to his 'other half,' and we arrange a second viewing. All's going well, the owner's very excited, and I'm calmly optimistic.

Such optimism is a dangerous thing in Real Estate. He views not just once more, but twice more. We're in with a chance. And then, oh no, c'est la merde encore. He announces that he's driving east to the Limousin. I'm not happy. I wait a week before I hear from him again, to be told that he's decided upon there, and not here. It's not a good idea to berate the competition, so I play it mildly.

The weather in the Limousin is that of extremes. The Région comprises three Départements, Haute-Vienne, Creuse, and Corrèze, all of them outstandingly lovely. It's a land of lakes and mountains, forests and enchanting mediaeval towns and villages. Straight out of a fairy book, but oh so hot in summer and oh so cold in winter. Huh, I've told the wrong person. He's not only from Scotland, but from Sutherland, just about the most northerly outpost in The British Isles. The winter of the Corrèze will be like water off a duck's back, and the heat of its summer will have them bathing in the lakes and thinking they've arrived in Paradise, watching the ducklings cavorting towards them as they float by. I ask what his wife thinks of all this, to be told that she's leaving the decision to him. Of course! Don't they all? Actually, no! But enough to scupper a deal every now and then. The task of telling my hopeful seller in Matha the bad news falls upon my shoulders, of course. All in a day's work.

Perhaps I should go and explore the Limousin as it's fast becoming our main competition, taking a much stronger hold than it did when I first started work in Cognac. Back then, it was 'Dordogneshire' which took the lead, but that's all 'Britted' out now. More English than England, especially its cricket teams. However, all is not lost, as ever more and more people from the Dordogne are finding the winters way too bad for their arthritis. We have a new breed of buying clients, and they come in two factions. There are those from Dordogne, escaping the constant mists and wet weather, and there are those from Spain.

My next clients feel the need to escape the cranes they give up counting at twenty seven as they see the new blocks of high rise flats going up all around them. They've been living on the Spanish Mediterranean for over ten years, and it's not only the cranes which finalise their decision, but the ketchup. Emerging from a restaurant one night, they are met with what they can only imagine to be blood in the gutter. It's not. It's tomato ketchup, becoming a regular sight as revellers pour out of the pubs and clubs to the 'chippies.'

Other clients leave Expat Spain when their hearts fail them, and I'm not talking romance here, but medical matters. I'm told the heat is too intense for them once they reach a certain age, and with few being able to afford to escape FROM the sun in the summer months, they are left with no choice but to sell up and move north, to France. They are becoming a great source of business. Sellers from here sometimes head FOR Spain, of course, but they are in a minority. Most of the trade moves north, to us here in Poitou Charentes, and beyond, some even reaching the rural outposts of Finistére, Brittany's least populated region, which must come as a huge shock after the glitz of the Costas. Finistére literally translates as 'the end of the earth,' and I wonder how they'll cope in such isolation, outstandingly beautiful though much of it is. At least they'll be near the ferry ports if it becomes a mere half way house before the eventual return to Blighty.

I finish the day with my thoughts dashing from the rural and isolated beauty of Limousin, to the sun soaked beaches of the Costa del Sol and the Costa Brava. Lush green fields and gently undulating valleys, extensive lakes, contented cows and free range pigs versus fish n'chippies, high rise flats and badly behaved Brits on hen and stag nights. I know which one I'd choose, but it's not a choice I have to make. Phew!

(Apols to family and friends we know who've chosen Spain over France. It can't all be bad!)

Typical Charentaise 'studio,' Villiers Couture

50 Matha, Israel & Palestine

There's a lot of activity in Matha, and mouths are muttering as to how much the Town's taxes will rise to pay for the restoration of the Salle des Fêtes. We've been to a comic opera there, 'comic' because of the hilarious behaviour of the clientele, not the 'opera' itself, which was absolute rubbish. It all made for a very amusing evening, especially as we'd told visiting adult children and their guests that they should dress for the occasion. They, and we, needn't have bothered! We adjourned to Pinnochio's afterwards for a meal, and the conversation was as priceless as the performance had been. We gained 'brownie points' for being the only anglais there, all dressed up and seriously out of place. It remains a night to remember!

There's a rumour afoot that the Mayor has plans to invite a delegation to Matha to discuss his Twinning Proposal, hence the need for the Hall to look its level best. The outside is being done first and as I drive past, I am suitably impressed. I'm told that he's allowing an expenditure of over forty thousand euros for the smartening up, no structural work, just painting and decorating. Perhaps new 'loos,' perhaps a bit of work to the stage. I'm not sure how successful his idea will be, given that he's hoping to Twin with not one town, but two. The problem is, one is in Israel and the other is in Palestine. One can but wish him bon courage! He'll need buckets full of it.

I seal the deal on another sale in one of my northern most outposts, in one of the Communes of Villiers Couture. It's a very lovely maison de maître, set behind high gates, with a walled garden adjoining open countryside, and additional land perhaps suitable for a pony or two. A young British family are buying it. The current owners are in Paris, and are not being very communicative, not that there's anything unusual in that. It happens all the time. I spend hours sending emails back and forth, never to be replied to, ditto leaving messages on their ansafone, and in the end have to ask the Notaire to get involved. Fortunately in France, the notarial fees are fixed, so they can't screw the public, unlike their counterparts in the U.K. are accredited with doing. 'Phone calls are not individually itemised and charged to clients, letters don't carry payment premiums, and they are available even on Friday afternoons! I have the greatest respect for French Notaires.

Whilst 'up north,' I prepare another beautiful property for the market and this one is truly stunning. It's way out of territory for my colleagues, but I'm always happy to bring buying clients up here. I love driving, ambling through the glorious countryside of Poitou Charentes between appointments, the more widespread, the better. Prices are lower the nearer to the Border with Deux Sevres one travels, higher the closer one gets to La Rochelle. The garden could be classified as a small park, superbly landscaped, and the whole acre's enclosed by majestic stone walling. It's not easy to find, and I'm not surprised to discover that the current owners are a retired Army chap and his wife, reluctantly returning to Blighty once a sale's agreed. In such a secluded location, for the first time ever I wouldn't have minded having 'satnav' but my love of maps excludes the temptation to succumb to such a thing. I worry that there'll be a whole generation growing up who won't be able to read them, just as there'll be a wave of youngsters ill equipped to actually write using their hands. I stand by the side of the swimming pool, and listen. There's no other sound to be heard, but birdsong. It's divine. At moments like this, it's a struggle to set mind in gear and get busy with camera and clipboard. I search for my electronic measuring device (my one 'soph' to joining the twenty first century) and head back inside. A pot of tea awaits me, and even traditionally served scones. The jam is so good, it must be from home grown strawberries. How civilised a job I have!

I just about have time to detour back to the Agence via one of Matha's outlying villages. I need to get the owners of a rather lovely, but ridiculously over priced property, to lower their expectations and approve a reduction. The guy's a retired French Police Inspector, brimming with Gallic self confidence, and not in the slightest bit interested in being sensible. His wife is never at home, and of course I need both signatures. It's not going to happen, so I listen to his tales of when he attended the U.K. Police Force's Staff College in Warwickshire. He's actually a nice bloke, and the house is lovely, very spacious and well presented. Unfortunately, its location is not particularly upmarket, the village it's in has no facilities and has definitely seen better days, and he's wanting a hundred thousand more for it than the infinitely superior product I've just left behind. And this one's not even detached, pour l'amour de Dieu!

The following morning starts on as much of a low as the previous afternoon with the Gallic 'Copper.' I have a sale agreed on a house just a few doors from ours in Esset. In all the years I work in real estate in these parts, I only get to sell two which are subject to mortgages being granted. All the rest are cash deals, and go through relatively smoothly from start to finish. This one is different. It's subject to one of the leading British Building Societies granting its funding, and they are being unbelievably awkward.

I'm to meet their young man from an office absolutely nowhere near here, not even in the same Région de France. In fact, it turns out that he's come all the way from the North, Lille to be precise. Like why? They have a Branch in Bordeaux! He's very charming, obviously well brought up, and gifted with that 'je ne sais quoi' of les hommes français. He's young enough to be my son, but I shan't hold that against him. What I shall, or at least those who send him here, is his complete lack of local knowledge, and the sheer amateurish approach he takes to his job in hand. The bloke's useless! He decides against investigating the outbuildings, as he's obviously concerned that he'll look très ébouriffé (dishevelled) on the train back to the sophisticated Nord de France. The same obviously applies to why he won't go up in the loft. However, he does deign to measure up the house itself, taking care not to attract any cobwebs.

With typically limited lateral thinking (the French don't often appear to shine in that department), and obviously not much vision of how great this house could become, his Report is a disaster, and results in potential buyers sending their own man over from the U.K. It's all doom and gloom, as this man's not much better than the last one, creating all sorts of phenomenally over the top sums needed, should his clients proceed with their purchase.

They don't. The sale collapses. I have to go and see the owners, a delightful couple well into their eighties, who live close by. He's already had one heart attack and I don't want to be responsible of news bad enough to cause another. His wife is reduced to tears in front of me, but he bears it stoically. I feel truly awful, and certainly like une femme dans la merde. The potential buyers get off with presumably just having to pay the surveyors' fees. It's been built into the Sales Agreement that the deal is 'subject to mortgage being granted,' thus saving them from any compensatory charges to pay. I think of the old folk wanting to tidy up their assets, perhaps genuinely needing the money tout de suite. I never have been able to divorce myself from people's emotions in what is usually their most important transaction in life. Probably why I've not made us rich! In theory, we work for the buyers in France, because they pay the fees, but that doesn't mean we can't empathise with the sellers. As far as I'm aware, the mortgage may or may not actually be granted in this case, and it throws all sorts of questions my way vis à vis the legal hoops and loop holes of when is a mortgage offer a mortgage offer, and whether the continuation of the sale depends on the granting of one, the mere offer of one, or its acceptance. For future reference, I need to get to grips. In England, I never had to, wasn't allowed to. Oh what a can of worms I'm left to sort!

I have nowhere to go but back to my desk in Saint Jean d'Angely to drum up other clients, and I shan't be trying to sell it to anyone else needing financial help secured against property back in Blighty. Another lesson learnt, the hard way! Just like it's a huge risk to have buying clients who instruct solicitors in the U.K. What do they do? Screw things up usually, not least in time taken between offer and completion. Because of the way French Property Law acts, it is also an absolutely unnecessary waste of money, but try telling that to some of the anglais, even those whose solicitors north of the Channel have gone on holiday when the notaires south of the Channel have everything all done and dusted and ready to sign. Often not trusting the French notaires, the buying clients refuse to sign anything until the lengthy Christmas and New Year holidays in particular are over, bringing their lawyers back to the scene which they have created, only to cause delays and a lot of unnecessary expense.

As it happens, the old folks' house sells again pretty quickly, and this time to a young local family, finance all sorted, and builders already instructed to transform it to its former glory. This is achieved in relatively little time, and it looks stunning. I admire it whenever I pass by, and can't help thinking what a great opportunity the others have turned down. Also how much commission I've lost in the process! 'Twas not I who did the deal second time round. Shucks! Mais c'est la vie. We win some, we lose some!

I'm not exactly thrilled the next time I get a call from Nord Pays-de-Calais. It's a man from Lille again. Oh no! What's more, he's a bank manager. This is too traumatic to even consider, but I brave the meeting and he and his wife have a very small window of opportunity to purchase a house here. It has to be near St Jean, so perhaps they'll be interested in the one that's just gone pear shaped. I give it a try, but fail instantly. They don't want old. The Bank moves him every three years and whatever they buy, has to be an easy sell. No worries. With quite a portfolio building itself up locally, I take them to a modern one quietly situated in Blanzac, sufficiently back from the main road to Matha, but feeling as if it's actually in the country. Stretching a point, it is. They like it, they really like it. All it needs is a lot of wallpaper stripper and a few cans of paint. They'll probably choose to install a new kitchen, too. It belongs to a local business couple, who've given me two of their properties to sell, so to clinch this deal will be good for them, good for the Agence, and good for me.

Back to the office, lots of smiles all round. But not before vast numbers of extra photos are taken, and a walk around the immediate area (all part of the service). The paperwork's all signed, and no mortgage is required, just a small loan (obviously at preferential bank employees' rates). Hands are happily shaken, and there's time for a quick coffee together. At least something's going right!

Typical village scene near Matha

51 Time Wasting Stealth in Gibourne

The London terrorist bus incident back in 2005 has left a lady in one of our neighbouring villages with no choice but to return to England. Her daughter was thrown from the top deck, and is still traumatised and in need of her mum. C'est normale. 'Mum' finds my name through the 'grapevine,' and asks if I'll go and have a cup of tea with her. It's one of those situations where an 'agony aunt' ear may lead to an instruction to sell the property, so I accept gracefully, not realising I have met her before, in England! I get the impression that she doesn't really want to leave France, not just yet.

Over tea, we discover that we both moved here from Herefordshire, and know some of the same people. It gets even more coincidental when she informs me she was one of my clients in Hereford. I don't remember her, but she does me. It happens! Her house here is delightful, semi detached but not intrusively so. It's in immaculate condition, oozing with well preserved character, perfect and welcoming in every way. Like many Charentaise houses which look large from the outside, it's not actually got many rooms inside, but those it has are spacious, plus there's a small gîte the other side of the courtyard, beautifully presented. With a quarter of an acre of prettily landscaped garden, complete with a delightfully designed in ground swimming pool, it's a highly marketable commodity. Until she tells me what she wants for it, three hundred and twenty five thousand euros. I suggest that she needs to lower her thoughts and to start with a '2' at the beginning. She says she'll think about it and let me know. It's Saturday afternoon, a lovely sunny day, so I leave her to her thoughts and think 'oops, there goes another one.'

I don't hear from her again for a while, and then my mobile 'phone bleeps a call from her. She's ready, and she lets me do it at just a few euros under the three hundred thousand mark. (A '2' is psychologically preferable to the punters than a '3!') I'm back measuring up this time, taking endless photographs, and getting her to sign the paperwork. We're launched.

A referral agent I work with in the U.K. sends me a charming couple from Ireland. We're getting a fair smattering of Irish buyers at the moment, from North and South. After a day's viewing in the same general area, looking at the much bigger properties their wish list demands, I stop the car outside this latest addition to my portfolio:

"Naah, it's going to be too small,"

comes the joint chant from beside and behind me. They're going in with one of their sets of parents and are looking for something which will accommodate both branches of the family. Despite my trying to sell it to them via its own ready made gîte, ideal for Granny and Grandpa, the protestations remain the same. We drive on.

I've learnt enough by now not to make a note of my having stopped outside and making the suggestion. It's firmly logged against their names, and on file back at the Agence. They disappear and I never hear from them again. But I hear OF them. Oh yes, 'Mum' desperate to return to England rings to tell me:

"I've sold my house."

"Wonderful, but to whom, and through which agent?"

"Through the Referral Agents in England who sent them to you."

I'm getting suspicious, and a little bit livid by this stage. I investigate, to discover that our very own chain of Agencies in Surgères has someone working for them who took it upon herself to invade St Jean d'Angely's territory and do a little bit of property pinching. And all because she had nothing of her own to show them when the U.K. lady rang to ask if she had!

"But I showed it to them first. You knew they were my clients. I even told you I'd stopped outside with them, hoping to be able to knock on your door."

She's relied on me so darned much, and now this happens! Why didn't she think to tell them they had to deal with she who put the idea into their heads? So then, naivety doesn't always leave us and at times we fail, this time yours truly! It's going to cost me, and put my faith in human nature to the test again:

"Yes, they told me, but said the Surgères lady took them out as well, and they asked her if she could contact the Owner of the house you stopped outside in Gibourne and arrange a viewing. They thought it'd save you the trouble."

"And rob me of my commission! AND it was through me that the Agence in Surgères was able to link up with her in the first place. So much for loyalty."

I feel duly stabbed in the back and am not a happy bunny, not at all. And it gets worse! Some of us have more audacity than others:

"Hi, I'm wondering if you could come round and help me with all the paperwork. I'd be really grateful if you could. I don't speak enough French. Can you come to the Completion with me, as well?"

I'm staggered, and remind the Owner that she hasn't sold through me, and that she should have had the decency to tell Surgères Office that they were already clients of Saint Jean d'Angely, and that any such viewing should be made through yours truly:

"No, there's no way I can do that. It would be highly unethical of me to get involved. It's not my sale."

She's the one who's not a happy bunny now, and I do feel sorry for her, but it's beyond my control. I wish her well, and never hear from her again. Another one down the tubes. This time, I'm actually very disappointed. She's a nice lady, just hasn't played the game right, perhaps didn't know the rules! I try and think kindly of her. However, I take a little bit of sour glee when she tells me what she got for it:

"Two hundred and fifty thousand euros."

Like a great many, I could have got her that the first day she gave it to me to sell. Greed rarely pays dividends!
The market is definitely tumbling, sellers are getting desperate and buyers are getting more astute at bargaining. I foresee a downward spiral and it's not far round the corner. Perhaps it's time to think about selling our own house. It

was, after all, always going to be a five year project and we've already exceeded the limit. It's ready for the market, and it makes sense to maximise investment whilst we still have a window of opportunity. The trouble is, where to go, and what to buy when we go there?

I take a few minutes out and have a chat with my main competitor in St Jean. I have no intentions of selling it, or even pricing it, myself. Never a good idea! He reluctantly agrees to take a look, informing me that we:

"Live in the sticks."

I can't disagree. La Brousse does translate as 'the Sticks' after all. He arrives, stands at the gates, arms crossed:

"It's actually rather nice."

"So what did you think I lived in?"

"But it's La Brousse ... alright, I'll do it, but you'll not sell to the Brits. You've modernised it a bit too much. I see the Scandinavians or the Dutch buying it, perhaps Parisiens."

Like why should we care who buys it?!

It's Monday morning. He wouldn't have come if it had been an any otherwise busy day, and nor would I have been here to introduce him to Spouse. Tuesday follows and we have our first viewing. It's a gloriously sunny day and the five of us sit outside in our massive garden and enjoy coffee together. The countryside is at its best, although the sunflower heads have already turned black. The vines are still full of grapes, the vendange just around the corner.

Some of the maize has been harvested, but there's enough left to colour the landscape. It is indeed all rather nice, and as we sip coffee with these prospective purchasers, we look at each other, both contemplating giving all we have created, up. But we do! By Friday we've agreed a sale, and my competitor is absolutely right. They are not English. Their roots are Welsh and Norwegian respectively. His 70th birthday is coming up and he's on a mission to buy in France before turning the corner.

The next couple of weeks are filled with puzzlement and excitement in equal measures. We refuse to do anything until the S.R.U. is passed and the purchase is secure. If it falls, then so be it. We'll have 10% of the agreed selling price to look forward to. With nothing to lose, except time to find the next abode, we trawl the internet at every available moment, leastwise I do. Decision taken, 'The Sticks' quickly lose the attraction once fallen for and we create a check list. Wherever we go next has to be in a market town, with views over interesting countryside, and the house has to be new, or nearly new. I add my own. It has to be near the Sea! I don't care which Sea. It can be the Atlantic, the English Channel, or even the Mediterranean, just so long as I can spend the retirement about to hit me on a sandy beach with my dog beside me. It's not much to ask! However, bugged on a daily basis by he who's agreed the sale on our behalf, I annoy him intensely by refusing to do any house hunting:

"You know darned well that the sale's in with a high chance of collapsing."

"This one isn't going to do that. Go and find another house!"

And so we set off on the long drive northwards ...

52 Au'revoir et à bientôt !

We ditch the original idea of moving to la belle La Rochelle, not quite ready to live in an apartment at this stage of our lives, which is all we'd be able to afford after living in 'The Sticks' for such a long time. There'd be no point in living 'near' La Rochelle, but not 'in' it, and we don't like suburbs. Aigrefeuille has lost its previous appeal as it really is too far inland, although it does have its own lake. Naah, it's dead in winter and we've have enough of that malarkey!

Pornic is a very lovely little coastal town in the Pays de la Loire and close to the start of the Loire Valley. It's also not far from Nantes, so fantastic a city that it's constantly voted the best place to live in The Hexagon. We've already stayed in a lovely hotel in Pornic for a couple of nights, eaten copious amounts of splendid sea food, walked along its lovely headland, gazed at the yachts in the harbour, and taken ourselves into the city centre of Nantes in less than half an hour's drive. It's on the list! I'm getting head in gear for the next move, but Ryanair doesn't fly into Nantes, the TGV serves Saint Nazaire, also not far from Pornic, but that's an expensive form of transport back to Blighty, and it's still a very long drive up to the nearest ferry port on the English Channel. It falls short of our requirements logistically, so we move our search more northerly.

Our priorities have changed since 2002. The times they are a changin', the times are bringing us grandchildren, creating a new tribe, and we want to have easier access to them, better travel links to the U.K. Back to the drawing board!
Moving up the Atlantic Coast, I research Vannes, famous for its mediaeval centre; the charming little town of Auray, put

on the map by Benjamin Franklin; and Lorient, the wintering home of many Transatlantic yachts, including Ellen MacArthur's at one time. The same stringent travel back to England inconveniences apply, though, so there's little point in keeping my research in Morbihan, the Département they are a part of. It's an outstandingly beautiful area, but we have to dismiss it as this time round it has to meet a whole new bunch of criteria. Never mind, we'll be able to drive down and explore it fully when we are settled in where my research lands us next.

We settle, theoretically, on the Côtes d'Armor, the northernmost part of Brittany and just as gorgeous as its southern cousin. We've already stayed with long known friends from Herefordshire and now living in a traditional Breton house they've renovated beautifully. Standing in its own grounds, it comes complete with its own wood, a stream, and a couple of little cottages, one of them straight out of 'Hansel and Gretel.' Black Mountain scenery recreated! They're between Louargat and Ménez Bré, one of Brittany's most famous monoliths, with far reaching views if the old legs would do the climb. We're tempted to join them somewhere closeby. But it's not the place for us.

It's isolated, the nearest town of Guingamp oozes history but also has lots of rather sad looking dark buildings. A lot of Inland Breton towns (Pontivy's one of them, although there's a great Chinese Restaurant there, l'Auberge de Chine in Rue du Fil) remind me of those in Scotland, visited annually for over twenty years, with their dull stone and aura of hardship. Even in Edinburgh I feel sad when I look up at its four or more storey high grey buildings climbing into skies which rain down on them way too much for my liking. It rains a lot in Scotland. It rains a lot in Rural Brittany, too, the further inland one goes. It's all too dark and dreary for much of the year, and much of it still belongs to a bygone age.

I'm after bright and cheerful coastal architecture, rather than historic, this time round. We'll do that when we visit Mediaeval Dinan! After the shutter-closed towns and villages of the Charentes, where time continues to stand still and strangers are still stared at, its time is up! Inland Brittany, scenically beautiful as it truly is, would bring us the same utterly, drearily, dead centres of time podded populations, few of them interested in breaking free, and widening their horizons.

It's been a great experience, a highly valued one, but I never did fancy the 'Good Life,' although have got dangerously close to living it in 'The Sticks' of La Brousse. I shall miss the cornflowers and the wild poppies, the far horizons over the vineyards, and the friends we've made, but they'll move in time, at least the Brits amongst them will. Expatria is a transient place for most of those who try it.

I want light, lots and lots of light, streaming across the Sea and turning into star filled skies at night. I want to walk along the beach with Megan, and see her wallowing in the waves like a polar bear, and chasing kites along the sand. I want to watch the amphibian fishing fleets leave the shores for the oyster beds and the moules we'll enjoy as they return to their makeshift coastal cafés of summer, and serve them up fresh from the Sea. Most of all, we both want good communications. This is a logistical move, a half way house between the 'now' and the inevitable 'then,' when time may see even us back in Blighty, but not yet please!

Life in France is good, very good, and we have much to be thankful for, to remember, to laugh about. From thinking of my uncles in Yoga, to Aquarobics in Saint Jean d'Angely, and to prawn sandwiches and Guinness at Chatellaillon Plage. From the ghastly 'formules' I've been forced to take on Team Tuesdays, to the outstanding cuisine of the superb restaurants we've had the undeniable pleasure of eating in together as a couple, and with family and friends. From learning how to survive in a foreign workplace, to actually embracing and enjoying it. To losing several British friends we've made en route (they've taken boats back to Blighty) to winning a fair few French ones.

Their patience with us is hugely appreciated, and together with their amitié (friendship), is highly valued. From the stress of initially coming to terms with the incessant bureaucracy we've had to struggle through at times, to the kindness we've been shown by the professionals, especially the medical ones we've had treat us. They earn a fraction of their counterparts in the U.K. but the service they provide is par excellence. We are enormously grateful to them all, well, to most of them! (Don't ask me about the dermatalogue in Dinan!)

It's been fun writing this, highly enjoyable, but another chapter is about to begin, perhaps leading to another book. Next time, if there is to be one, it will be set from our new home near the ancient sea port of St Malo, founded by Maclow back in the sixth century. He was a Welsh monk, in case you're wondering ...

Au'revoir et peut-être à bientôt !

And to all who made this journey possible, you remain an integral part of it. Merci beaucoup !

Lightning Source UK Ltd.
Milton Keynes UK
UKOW02f0056241015

261240UK00001B/177/P